Business

Ethics, Failures, Scams, Frauds, Punishments

Ram K Narayan

notionpress.com

INDIA • SINGAPORE • MALAYSIA

ISBN 979-8-89133-693-3

Index

Note from the Author

Dear Reader,

Economic crime and fraud continue to be a significant challenge for companies. The frequency with which the economic crimes are reported in the media from their sources such as Courts, Law Enforcers, Regulators etc., prompted the writer to write this book to re-emphasize the following:

- ✓ Frauds are caused only because of human greed and their poor upbringings.
- ✓ No one single person, entity or body can be held responsible for fraud when corporates fail.
- ✓ Fraud is deliberate and exploitive in a number of ways. It requires a concerted effort at numerous levels to be vigilant and ask appropriate questions in order to properly unpack red flags before they are disregarded.
- ✓ Fraud does not always result in corporate failure, nor do corporate failures occur only as a result of fraud. However, in some of the biggest corporate failures across the globe, fraud was involved.
- ✓ A major factor leading to corporate frauds is ineffective governance despite more regulations.

- ✓ The extent of punishments imposed on the Culprits by the Courts, Law enforcing Agencies and the Laws have failed to deter frauds.

The book has been divided into thirteen Chapters covering aspects of Business Ethics, Leadership Qualities; Human Traits; Teachings and Practice of Business Ethics in ancient times including learnings from Indian texts and Scriptures; Corruptions and their kinds; Some instances of classes of people involved; Cyber Frauds; Major Scams; Corporate Frauds in India; Global Frauds and Failures; Punishments for Frauds under some Acts; Failed Start-ups in India; Failed Global Start-up Companies; Unique case wherein lenders abused their position in manner akin to Fraud against own interests.

This is the fourth book of the Author who had published earlier three books viz., Management of Risks under the Companies Act, 2013 {Sep. 2020}; Corporate Governance in India-Challenges {June 2021} and The Reservoir of Central Acts passed by Parliament for all {June 2022}.

The author is grateful for the sources of information that is available in the Court Orders; Websites; Relevant Acts and Regulations; Research information available on public domain.

The author extends his gratitude to the reviewer of this book.

Shri.Shailesh Haribhakti is a renowned Chartered, Cost Accountant, and a Certified Internal Auditor, Financial Planner, and Fraud Examiner, with over five decades of experience. Mr Haribhakti is the Chairman of Shailesh Haribhakti & Associates Chartered Accountants, and the Vice Chairman of GOvEVA Consulting Pvt Ltd. He has been conferred with the Global Competent Boards Designation (GCBD) by Competent Boards Inc, Canada. Presented with the honorary PhD title of "Doctor of Letters" by ITM University. He has been awarded the 'Vivekananda Sustainability Award – 2022' by Vivekananda Youth Connect Foundation. A proponent of a clean and green environment, he is credited to have successfully established the concept of 'Innovate to Zero' and technology enabling CSR/ESG/Sustainability. In recent times, some prominent Boards and Board Committees led by him have been recognised with coveted awards, which speak of his penchant for excellence in the areas of corporate governance and sustainability.

The author expresses his gratitude to the team members of the publisher of this book viz., Notion Press, for all the support and guidance extended during the process of publication.

The author hopes that the book will be of value to the community of Directors, Corporate Professionals and Students of management and commerce.

Sincerely.

Ram K Narayan

October 5, 2023

Reviews of the Book

SHAILESH HARIBHAKTI 42 Free Press House, 215,
Nariman Point, Mumbai 400021

To,

The Reader,

Ramakrishnan's latest book on 'Business ethics, failures, frauds and punishments' is a valuable resource for many professionals. Chartered Accountant, Company Secretaries, Forensic specialists and others involved in crime prevention and punishment including police and the justice system.

In an easy to read and cross reference manner, the book clarifies many concepts, definitions, procedures, techniques and policies that can make our Society more harmonious.

I will personally have a copy ready at hand! Congratulations for an inspired and painstaking business relevant book!

May many benefit from reading it!

Regards & Best Wishes

Shailesh Haribhakti

Date: 21st September 2023

Mumbai

Chapter I

Business Ethics

A. Definition

What is Business Ethics?

The word ethics is derived from the Greek word 'ethos', which means character. Ethics is a branch of philosophy concerned with human character and conduct. It is the discipline dealing with 'what is good and bad' and with moral duty and obligation. Ethics is the embodiment of moral values, which describes what, is 'right' and what is 'wrong' in human behavior and what 'ought to be'.

Ethics is a "consideration and application of frameworks, values and principles for developing moral awareness and guiding behavior and action. Ethics implies good character and morality and refers to generally accepted human character and behavior considered as a desirable by society.

Business ethics means the behavior of a businessman while conducting a business, by observing morality in his business activities.

Business ethics is the prescribed code of conduct for businesses. It is a set of guidelines for dealing with various procedures ethically. The discipline comprises corporate responsibility, loyalty, fairness, respect, trustworthiness, restrictions of insider trading, rules for related party dealings and disclosures, guarding secrecy, business sustainability, customer dealings, bribery and corruption, brand protection, human resources behavior etc.

B. Principles of Business Ethics

Following are the underlying principles of business ethics, the lack of which often cause the downfall of otherwise intelligent, talented people and the businesses they represent.

Leadership: Leadership is the capacity of a company's management to set and achieve challenging goals, take fast and decisive action when needed, outperform the competition, and inspire others to perform at the highest level they can. Leadership provides direction for a company and its workers. Leadership involves showing workers how to effectively perform their responsibilities and regularly supervising the completion of their tasks. Leadership is also about setting a positive example for staff to follow, by being fascinated about the work, being motivated to learn new things, and helping out as needed in both individual and team activities. The challenge before real leaders is to adopt and ensure that the others do adopt the ethical standards laid down by the company to achieve the goals.

- **Accountability** - Holding persons responsible for their actions. Commitment to practice ethical values and ensuring others to follow.

- **Integrity** - Adhering to a set of moral standards at all times. Others notice when a leader works with integrity, which leads to respect and confidence in his decisions. Strong integrity can influence one's honesty and obedience to rules and regulations.
- **Respect for others** - Everyone deserves dignity, privacy, equality, opportunity, compassion, and empathy.

Honesty: Honesty requires a commitment to telling the truth, regardless of the consequences. It encourages trust and bonding among colleagues and between a business and the public. Employees want to work for honest leaders, business owners want honest employees and clients want to do business with honest partners. This means sharing favorable and unfavorable news with the same candor and directness, leading to a reputation of reliability.

Respect for laws: If there is a legal grey area, leaders should err on the side of legality rather than exploiting a gap.

Responsibility: Promote ownership within an organization, allow employees to be responsible for their work, and be accountable with necessary authority. Being responsible in the workplace means taking ownership of one's tasks. Responsibility includes thinking about how one's actions can affect those around him/her and making choices that consider other people. Employers and employees depend on responsible workers to make the best decisions without requiring constant supervision. Being responsible demonstrates maturity, capability and discipline.

Transparency: Without divulging trade secrets, companies should ensure information about their financials, price changes, hiring and firing practices, career growth development opportunities etc., to those interested in the success of business.

Compassion: Employees, the community surrounding a business, business partners, and customers should all be treated with concern for their well-being. People often want to work in an environment where they feel valued and cared for and do business with companies that display compassion towards consumers and the community.

Fairness: Everyone should have the same opportunities and be treated the same. Fairness also means avoiding preferential treatment and encouraging everyone to share their thoughts and ideas. A fair workplace promotes inclusion and equity in-house as well as for clients and customers. Fairness in the workplace creates a unified environment where employees feel comfortable, which increases involvement.

Loyalty: Remaining faithful to employer, coworkers and customers to demonstrate one's commitment. One can develop lasting partnerships and a firm foundation for future success when the person proves his alliance and honor commitments.

- **Creation of ethical practices** - Business must develop a defined code of ethics for their business practices and share this with all employees. Th code of conduct/ ethics must include *inter alia* guiding principles, reporting procedures, and training programs to enforce ethical behaviour.

- **Implementation of Good Business Ethics** - Once conduct is defined and programmes implemented, continuous communication with employees becomes vital. Leaders should constantly encourage employees to report concern behaviour—additionally, there should be assurances that whistle-blowers/ anonymous reporters will not face adversarial actions.

- **Environmental concern** - In a world where resources are limited, ecosystems have been damaged by past practices, and the climate is changing, it is of utmost importance to be aware of and concerned about the environmental impacts a business has. All employees should be encouraged to discover and report solutions for practices that can add to damages already done.

- **Compliance** - Companies must ensure all practices of the company adhere to the applicable laws, rules and regulations framed by the Government and the Code of Ethics of the Company.

- **Trustworthiness** - Trustworthy workers keep their word to customers, colleagues and employers. Honouring commitments proves that others can be counted, making the person a trusted employee and coworker. Trustworthiness also involves being dependable and meeting one's obligations.

C. Leadership

Essential Qualities of Good Leader

1. They communicate clearly.
2. They are passionate about their work.
3. They do not care to go after personal popularity
4. They keep their minds open and are receptive to new ideas.
5. They ensure that the employees have the necessary resources to do their job efficiently.
6. They believe in delegation of responsibility and authority but retain accountability.
7. They are good motivators when the employees perform well or they fail to perform as expected of them.
8. They treat others respectfully as they would want to be treated.
9. They lead by example
10. They value mutually beneficial relationships, and actively seeks them out.
11. They never stop learning

Some of the things good leaders generally do not do?

1. They do not fear to lead.
2. They do not change the vision
3. They do not devalue relationships with co-workers
4. They not only motivate their coworkers, but also embrace their dissenting opinions
5. They do not think about work-life balance. Their first priority is always work; it's what they live for.
6. They do not break commitments.
7. They think big. They are bold. They look for challenges.
8. They never stop asking questions.
9. They believe that anything can be achieved with the right attitude, with the right persons in the team.
10. They are not dictators.
11. They do not let their fear stop them from taking safeguarded risks
12. They do not shy away from change. They inspire and enable others to face challenges and learn new things.
13. They do not repeat the mistakes.

Chapter II

Human Traits

Businesses are managed by individuals for and on behalf of the Entity. In respect of corporate entities, the person(s) charged with the responsibility of running the Company, act under the guidance, superintendence and control of collective body of individuals called the board of directors.

No two individuals are alike and the same person does not conduct himself in the same manner always. The reason being people have different family upbringings, educational backgrounds and are inculcated from childhood with different values, different ethos, different aspirations, different faiths, beliefs and so on.

A. Traits according to Scriptures

Two kinds of traits, namely, Divine and Demonical, according to the Scriptures are nature to human beings. Little elaboration of these traits is as hereunder:

Divine Traits

(i) Fearlessness {*for doing right things*}

(ii) Purity of heart;

(iii) Steadfastness *{very devoted, loyal to person or belief or cause}*;

(iv) yoga *{harmony between mind and body}*;

(v) almsgiving;

(vi) control of the five Senses *{touch, smell, sight, taste and hearing}*;

(vii) Yagna *{worshipping the Supreme}*;

(viii) Austerity;

(ix) Straight-forwardness;

(x) Noninjury;

(xi) Truth;

(xii) Absence of anger;

(xiii) Renunciation;

(xiv) Serenity *{absence from mental stress or anxiety}*;

(xv) Absence of calumny *{false and defamatory}*;

(xvi) Compassion to beings;

(xvii) Un-covetousness *{generosity. bigheartedness, kindness, liberality}*;

(xviii) modesty;

(xix) Absence of fickleness;

(xx) Vigour;

(xxi) Forgiveness;

(xxii) Fortitude *{strength of mind to encounter danger or bear pain or adversity with courage}*;

(xxiii) Purity of mind *{naturally pure and is free from unnatural impulses which hinder onward march}*;

(xxiv) Absence of hatred;

(xxv) Absence of egoistic pride.

Demonical Traits or negative emotions

(i) Ostentation {excessive display of vain and unnecessary show for attracting attention or admiration or envy-pretentiousness};

(ii) Arrogance or Ego *{attitude of superiority manifested in an overbearing manner or in presumptuous claims or assumptions}*;

(iii) Self-conceit *{exaggerated opinion of one's own qualities or abilities-vanity or inflated pride in oneself}*;

(iv) Anger;

(v) Harshness *{brusque, hard, unfeeling, unkind, brutal, acrimonious, ill-tempered}*;

(vi) Ignorance *{lack of knowledge, understanding or education}*

While it is common to come across people with Demonic traits, it would be rather rare to meet a person with even many of the divine virtues. The reason being in the modern fast changing world - with the demolition of joint family system of living and rampant competition in every walk of life, elders in families fail to teach good value system to the young ones in their formative years. Hence, people grow up to possess less of the divine virtues. That perhaps is major reason for the domination of corruption, failures, scandals and crimes in the business world right across the globe.

One can see the evidence of the existence in abundance of all undesirable traits through the conducts of politicians, businessmen, government servants, private sector persons, persons in educational institutions, professional body members including unfortunately judiciary as well. Driven by personal greed people do indulge and compete with each other in embracing negative traits without remorse for individual realisations in this materialistic world.

One can see pages after pages of write ups on corporate governance and codes of ethics in every annual report of companies. But experience have evidenced that these are only on paper to comply with the statutory requirements and generally seldom practised. The statutory requirements cover areas such as maintenance of Books of Account; Accounting Policies; Secretarial Standards; Shareholders' rights; Duties and Obligations of Key Managerial Personnel; Role of Independent Directors; Ethics of Auditors including their appointments, tenure, powers, duties etc.

B. Re-cap of Indian History

The history of India is traced from the human activities dating back to the 75,000 years. However, the main beginning of the ancient Indian history is marked by the Indus Valley Civilization, during the period of BC 3300 BC to 1300 BC being as India's first civilization.

*The ancient period in the Indian history has broadly been categorized as:

- Pre-historic Period {Stone Age; Bronze Age; Iron Age}- 2.5 million BC to 600 BC.
- Classical Era {600 BC to AD 476}
- The Middle Ages {AD 476 to AD 1450}
- Early Modern Era {AD 1450 to AD 1760}
- Modern Era {AD 1760 to Present}

*{Your Dictionary}**

Following are the different sub-divisions of India's early historic period:

Vedic period: {1500 BC to 500 BC}

This historical period gained its name from the sacred text of Hindus, the Vedas. Vedic Civilization marked the foundation of Hindu religion and its association with Indian culture.

The Rig-Vedic period witnessed the social as well as agricultural development of the Aryan society.

It was during this early historical time that the Ramayana and the Mahabharata, the two great Sanskrit epics came into existence.

Greek and Persian conquests: Cyrus, the Persian King of the Achaemenid Empire conquered the country in 530 BC and ruled for two centuries,

Period of Maurya Empire: {322 BC to 185 BC}. The Maurya Empire is regarded as the first main kingdom in the ancient history of India – both geographically as well as politically powerful. The empire flourished most during the 37 years' rule of Ashoka the Great from 268 BC to 232 BC

The Golden Age in the ancient history of India included the rule of dynasties viz.,

Satavahana Empire {50 BC to 250 AD}; Kushan Empire: The period witnessed a rise in the country's foreign trade, art and culture.

Gupta Dynasty {Golden Age 300 AD to 800 AD}: Being one of the largest empires in the world, who had military and political strength.

Medieval India (AD 700 – AD 1857) - Covering Slave Dynasty; Khilji Dynasty; Tuglak Dynasty; Sayyid Dynasty; Lodi Dynasty; Mughals {AD 1528 to AD 1857}

British India {AD 1857 to 1947}

C. Where India stands today?

According to review of the World Bank, India is one of the fastest growing economies of the world and is poised to continue on this path.

Indian economy has been ranked as the fifth largest global Economy in terms of GDP next to USA, China, Japan and Germany.

The growth of the past two decades has also led to India making remarkable progress in reducing extreme poverty. Between 2011 and 2019, the country is estimated to have halved the share of the population living in extreme poverty - below $2.15 per person per day.

India has the distinction of becoming only the fourth country in the world after China, USA and Russia to send a landing module (Chandrayan 3) to land on the moon's surface successfully duly witnessed by millions of people on earth. In fact, through ISRO, India has the distinction of being the first nation to land near the Moon's South Pole on August 23, 2023. In September 2023, ISRO launched the first solar observatory mission-Aditya-L1 and in the process joined Europe, USA, Japan and China who have launched such missions.

Now Some Global Comparisons where India is lagging

(a) **Global Sustainable Competitiveness Index** published by SolAbility, a Consultancy firm, that measures the potential of nations to sustain or increase wealth in a resource constrained, globalised world, based on five broad parameters namely, -

Intellectual Capital & Innovation, Economic Sustainability; Governance Efficiency; Natural Capital;

Resource Efficiency & Intensity and Social Capital, had ranked India in 2022 to 120th. Position out of 180 countries with a score of 39.3 while Sweden was ranked as number 1 with a score of 60.7. The Global average Sustainable Competitiveness score in 2022 was 43.1.

Theoretically some of the challenges of ranking low in the GSCI are said to be:

- Reduced potential to achieve sustainable development and green growth in the short and mid-term future.
- Increased vulnerability to resource scarcity, environmental degradation, social unrest or economic instability.
- Lower attractiveness for foreign investment, trade or tourism due to poor performance, status, risks or opportunities.
- Higher obstacles to innovation, productivity or competitiveness in the global markets due to low intellectual capital, resource efficiency or governance efficiency

(b) **Global Corruption Perceptions Index**

The ranking has been at the same level as it was in 2021 viz., 85 out of 180 countries with a 40% score. Denmark is ranked at No. 1 with a score of 90%.

The low ranking is sadly due to the poor ethical standards right across the system, be it, business, government or politicians in general. The successive Governments have been combating with deep concerns this malice but with little success!

Yet India is the place for Business Opportunities and Growth

India is one of the fastest growing countries in the world, it is also going through a period of unprecedented economic liberation, granting overseas investors more access to its vast and varied market than ever. A large, young population and a strong export sector await expanding businesses, with a potential consumer base that far outstrips most other nations in the developed and developing world.

Political stability and broad consensus on reforms is also a big pull for expanding companies, and the well-developed banking system and vibrant capital market highlight the maturity of its financial system. But doing business in India can still be a challenging endeavour.

**India takes the Global Stage in 2023 - G20 Presidency

India assumed the Presidency of the G20 in 2023. This is an organization rooted in the concept of international governance and the need for cooperation to address global economic challenges. India's presidency of the G20 is seen as an important platform for advancing its interests and for promoting the country's profile on the global stage.

India, being the only major global economy slated to have 6+% GDP growth figures in the years ahead, outplaced Britain in 2022 to become the fifth largest economy in nominal GDP terms *{one way to measure how well the economy is doing. It differs from real GDP in that the first one does not include the changes in economy in prices due to inflation in nominal GDP terms}*.

The G20 Presidency gives India a unique opportunity to strengthen its role in the world economic order. With the theme of 'Vasudhaiva Kutumbakam,' India is steering an ambitious, people-centric agenda to address global challenges and facilitate sustainable economic development.

Through a range of activities and events, India is able to demonstrate its commitment to multilateral cooperation and building bridges between different countries and regions. Being a great power is a function of capabilities, interests, and recognition. Economic and military power, nuclear and space capabilities, a defining role in global affairs and systems, normative weight, and a critical mass of diplomatic, cultural, intellectual, R&D, and technological resources, high-impact foreign policy management, and external projection of hard and soft power are prerequisites too.

India has been active in G20 meetings and has taken a leadership role in several areas, such as promoting inclusive growth, increasing investment in infrastructure, and strengthening financial regulation. India has also used its membership in the G20 to advocate for developing countries' interests and promote economic cooperation and integration between developed and developing countries.

The World Bank has warned of a possible global recession in its latest forecast, cutting down global growth estimates for 2023 and 2024, owing to factors like the geopolitical scenario, persistently high inflation, and higher interest rates. However, India remains a promising figure in the current scenario. The multilateral bank reiterates that India is undeniably a global powerhouse and that the Indian presidency of G20 will unleash its potential, pay heed to insights and feedback from members, and contribute to the international community.

The G20 Presidency gives India a unique opportunity to strengthen its role in the world economic order and become a global soft power. As India sets an ambitious, people-centric agenda to address global challenges and facilitate sustainable economic development, it is expected to contribute to the international community and build bridges between different countries and regions.

***{Invest India Feb 2023}*

Chapter III

Teachings and Practice of Business Ethics in Ancient Times

A. Ancient Indian Management Wisdom

It is an undeniable fact that "Ethics" remains low in the priority list of managements in general. This is explained by the fact of the far too many business failures, scams and bankruptcies keep surfacing despite the organizations coming with innovative management, best practices and stricter government regulations. Surely, such happenings are matters of serious concern.

Today's system suffers from low ethical leadership as compared to the essence of teachings of ancient Indian scriptures. Many businessmen who vigorously swear by the holy books or Gods or donating vast amounts to religious institutions are known to be practicing corrupt means to amass wealth for themselves and for their future generations.

On the contrary, ancient wisdom gave prime importance to values and qualities like humanity, pride, non-violence, tolerance, simplicity, self-control, absence of ego, non-attachment etc.

Indian wisdom can be applied effectively in any managerial area as it amply addresses the management related issues. However, the contribution of western management philosophies and theories cannot be ignored but integration of both will be helpful in achieving effective results.

B. Essence of Vedas in Modern Management

The Vedas mainly focused on the path of action viz., Righteousness, Public good, Innovation, Efficiency and Learning.

Vedas consist of ancient value systems that emphasize on 1) truth, 2) Austere 3) Sense control, 4) Peace of mind, 5) Righteousness, 6) Charity, 7) Mercy and 8) Renunciation.

It is the belief that every individual has a divine power for self-development and if an individual brings about his or her self-development then automatically it will benefit him, the organization and the society.

According to Indian vedic beliefs - truthfulness, kindness, calmness, and harmlessness are the four parts of **dharma.**

The Indian concept of **Gunas** namely, sattwa, rajas and tamas are very relevant in people's organizational behavior. For instance, **sattwa** represents purity, poise, transparency, clarity etc.; **rajas** is characterized by craze for fame, passion, pride, display of power, etc. and **tamas** is characterized by anger, greed, ignorance, discrimination, etc.

People possess more than one guna at the same time though in varying combinations, and also with the predominance of one over other. Every manager must manage himself first, before he can even try to manage anybody else. **Self-analysis** through introspection is essential to know and discover oneself. Self-analysis and **self-criticism** help to locate areas of friction and disharmony. Only when one has **self-knowledge,** can he undertake to manage himself. Introspection involves self-examination of one's own thoughts, feelings, emotions, sensations and passions, as well as one's dreams and desires, goal and ambitions, strengths and weaknesses.

Dharma in Indian philosophy means 'duty' and is almost synonymous with integrity and rightness. Dharma stands for all those ideals, philosophies, purposes, influences, teachings and experiences that shape our character.

Each organization in Indian ethos is a living entity and must practice own dharma and character for India to become a true global power/leader in every front.

Indian culture which embraces ancient philosophical viewpoints is nothing but a collection of human values. These values assume special significance for corporates in every sphere of activity. Such values include sincerity, commitment, responsibility non-possession, moral conduct, curiosity to learn, efficiency, innovation, impartiality, fairness and so on.

Performing one's duty is fundamental concept of work ethics. One should fulfil one's commitment and be accountable for results. He should be dedicated to hard work. He should protect the interest of the organization he works for.

C. Morals, Ethics and Values: Indian Context

While it is important for a business to have morals and ethics, it is equally important for the people at work also to have morals and ethics.

1. Definitions

Morals

They are the principles concerning distinction between right and wrong or good and bad.

Ethics

Ethics are standards of behavior that guide in making moral judgements.

Values

Values include morals and religious beliefs or deeply held personal convictions that influence how one acts in business or in personal life. As far as the business is concerned it would mean putting the needs of customers, employees and clients before anything else.

2. **Importance of good morals and ethics in Business**

   Companies are required to be concerned with how their actions affect the lives of people and what they can do to improve their reputation. The more they invest in ethics, the more money they cans save on problems caused by unethical practices such as poor - quality lawsuits, high employees' turnover, prosecution and penalties for offences etc.

3. **Business Ethics and Reputation**

   Business ethics is designed to bring long lasting reputation for the Company. High investment in ethics brings higher profitability enabling the Company to invest even more into ethics.

4. **Business Ethics drives employee behaviour**

   Good business is built on the foundation of ethics, integrity and honesty. Treat employees well, promote team working and reward them for good job performed. Motivate employees to consider that they belong to the Company in all respects.

5. **Learning**

   Business needs to adapt itself to changing times by changing their practices as may become necessary.

Pursuit for profit cannot be the sole consideration for business. Profit comes from created value.

6. **Business Ethics and Bottom-Line**

   Business conducted in ethical manner will have positive effect on the bottom-line. Ethics is more than a moral issue.

7. **Ethical Behavior and Challenge**

   Being ethical is not always easy. It can cause trouble with customers, other businesses and even other employees.

8. **Create and maintain a Company-wide Ethics Policy**

   While approving the Ethics Policy, the Board of Directors must ensure that such a policy aligns with the Company's values

9. **Reporting of unethical Practices**

   Prompt actions must be initiated to protect the interests of the Company when any unethical practice followed by any one is reported.

10. **Training and education on Ethics**

    Every Company should have an Ethics Policy to deal with situations where unethical practices against employees or agents crop up or reported. More important is to ensure that every employee understands the policy and explained the pitfalls arising out of detection of unethical practices.

D. Learnings from Vedas and Indian Epics

Indian Civilization had deeply ingrained ethos from Vedas and Epics containing rich moral values in governance.

The Rulers, persons of great character, eminence etc., from the time immemorial had practiced and demonstrated the following attributes for their subjects to follow over thousands of centuries:

- **Honesty**, faithfulness, intelligence, well versed secular and sacred law, willingness to offer advice, bold, free of jealousies towards each other and allied to the Company's goal. It includes ethics, integrity, character, trustworthiness, truthfulness, morality, rightness, high consistency between word and deed etc

- **Vision** - the ability to chalk out a future in legalistic way and steer towards attaining the goals with reasonable risks after ensuring proper and adequate risk mitigating and management thereof.

  The leader must have control over his 'mind' to be able to express a balanced view and take far reaching positive decisions. He should develop himself the skill to see ahead of time and spot early opportunities. He should possess the willingness and ability to invest and reap benefits out of such opportunities for internal and external stakeholders.

- **Right intentions** without prejudice to the positive consequences arising out of Performance, he should avoid greediness, earn and keep what is just and give up that which belonged may belong to someone else. The temptation to step over rights of others is the cause of corruption in business and politics.

  Corrupt persons create unequal distribution of wealth and opportunities not only for themselves but for future generations as well, thus the poor becomes poorer and the rich becomes richer.

- **Balanced decision making** - The leader should indulge in well-balanced decision making-spiritually, mentally, emotionally and physically.

- **Right Image** - The leader must have a clean image, an unblemished character to command respect and not demand it; he must be a self-made person.

- **Actions** triggered only by duty.

  Perform duty honestly. A CEO/promoter must practice the principle of 'trusteeship' which essentially means that he is merely a trustee of the organizational wealth, his role is to create wealth for stakeholders; not for himself, he's just a custodian and should not be corrupted by power.

- **Non-contravention** of the standards of efficiency to avoid ills. But work without fear or favour', or with neutrality. Be just; impartial and active with action.

- **Self-learning** continuous acquisition of knowledge and skills. Set High Benchmarks for Performance and strive for improvements by self-assessments.

  The universal law of Cause & Effect relationship is certain. The person must constantly drive towards increasing his good qualities and reducing the bad ones by 'Minimizing maximum weaknesses and maximizing minimum strengths for one's personal and professional growth.

- **Self-confidence** - Should also be able to convince others of the rightness of goals and decisions.

- **Patience** and control emotions. Imbibe the trait of not being provoked into meaningless fight and arguments.

- **Self-control and restrain in speech** - Ensure honesty has enduring value as it is not a virtue that would remain consistent and the temptation to make easy gains through corrupt means can override the trait of honesty any time.

- **Vigilance** and Transparency

- **Ability to differentiate between right and wrong and good and bad** - Have insights and foresight, to perceive underlying dynamics of matters to forecast the results.

- **Fairness in dealing with Grievances** - Encourage honest persons to perform duties; do not unjustly maintain silence, do not threaten, defame and abuse the complainants or arbitrarily dismiss responses;

- **Share Knowledge** - Do not hide your limited 'sphere of competence' by being selfish. It is important to foster the culture of 'knowledge sharing' within teams; cross-teams and cross departments barring confidential matters.

- **Respect equality among people** - Contribution from all quarters is equally important irrespective of their individual position or experience in the organisational hierarchy. The common factor amongst the leaders and their followers is the common organisational vision, mission and interest.

- **Rewarding informants** on details about wrong-doing to strive towards corruption free company. People practising wrong deeds will meet their destiny.

E. Essence of Bhagavad-Gita in Modern Management

The Bhagavad-Gita teaches us the importance of work and how it should be executed and self-management.

Managerial effectiveness can be gained in three ways: mind-management, management of duties and the principles of self-management

(a) One should work with commitment by practicing detachment which can be gained through self-control by conquering the desires.

(b) Work culture in an organization is ensured when everyone perform without any conflict for the betterment of his or her own as well as of others.

(c) One can manage oneself if he raises his spirits to overcome his weakness and open the door of opportunities awaiting him.

F. The Business & Management lessons from the Bhagavad Gita

1. Be clear about ones' goals and stay focused on them regardless of the obstacles that may arise.

2. Abstain from staying attached to the results of actions as often it would be impossible to control the outcome of ones' efforts. All one can do is to put forth the best effort and trust that the Universe will take care of the rest.

3. Be prepared to make sacrifices for the greater good. Business leaders often have to make either fight against adversaries and make sacrifices for the greater good of their companies as long-term goals are more important than the short-term.

4. Be fearless in the face of obstacles and challenges while implementation of actions.

5. Surrender to the divine and let go of your ego as one will realize that there is a higher power at work and that we're not in control of everything.

6. Identify, Recognize and Accept Equality in Life.

7. Anger is a weakness that affects people's judgment and causes them to make bad decisions.

8. Change is inevitable. Do not feel guilty and worry about things that have already happened and things that might happen. This makes us unable to enjoy life in the present. We also lose focus on our goals.

9. Control of ones' desires is necessary. Otherwise, desires may take control of ones' life. Getting caught up in the desire will only cause harm.

10. Control of mind through meditation is essential to achieve Inner Peace.

11. It is important to cultivate the trait of detachment from material possessions and their outcomes. One came into this world with nothing but they take things from this earth but they have to depart with nothing when the time comes.

12. Man is what he/she believes in. With positive beliefs, good things happen. If one thinks he/she can be happy even when things go wrong, he will be happy. But if they let revenge take over their mind even when things are going well, then you will have negative thoughts.

13. One must realize that success and failure are two aspects of life. When these two aspects become a part of our professional lives, they start to influence our mental health. One has to try to maintain equanimity in life between the two.

14. The discipline of speaking effectively and the discipline of staying calm under pressure are essential for effective leadership.

15. Leaders need to be able to stay calm under pressure so that they can think clearly and make good decisions even when things are tough.

16. Be generous. One should perform acts of sacrifice, charity, and penance to keep oneself pure.

17. Leaders should always share their knowledge and be approachable. They should never seem distant. They should be good teachers to their followers and good friends who help them move forward.

18. It is important to prioritize tasks what is important. We need to set boundaries for ourselves and stay clear in our heads about what needs to be done first.

G. Most relevant lessons applicable to leaders of for modern Business

Leadership is a powerful enabler that can leverage an organization to great heights, fame and a credible position among the stakeholders. On the other hand, if the quality of leadership is bad, the same organization will experience a downward slide leading to its eventual destruction.

Lessons to be followed by modern Business

1. **Develop a Code of Ethics**: Develop a code of ethics for the business that outlines the principles of ethical behavior that all employees are expected to follow.

2. **Lead by Example:** As a business leader, it is his responsibility to lead by example and demonstrate ethical behavior in all aspects of the business. This would mean that the leader has to develop a high degree of equanimity and an understanding of the principle of mutual dependence.

   Leaders derive their credibility, respect and power from their unwavering commitment to walking the talk. This is because, if the leaders say something and do something else, the followers will not take the leader very seriously. Rather, they will do a similar thing as their leader and nothing else.

   Unfortunately, many leaders believe that they have the freedom to take decisions the way they think is right and have the authority to execute things.

   There are also leaders, though fewer in numbers, who believe strongly in nourishing leadership talent around by creating space and agenda for others. They derive their joy by becoming irrelevant in many day-to-day matters pertaining to running the institution.

3. **Make Ethical Decisions:** When making business decisions, the impact of ones' decisions on all stakeholders must be considered and decisions that are fair and just are made.

4. **Foster a Culture of Ethics:** Foster a culture of ethics in the business by promoting ethical behavior and rewarding employees who demonstrate ethical behavior.

5. **Training of Employees:** Provide training to employees on the principles of ethical behavior and the code of ethics for your business.

6. **Monitor and Enforce Ethical Behavior:** Monitor the behavior of the employees and enforce the code of ethics for them.

7. **Develop a sense of equanimity:**

   The world is full of dualities, it will blow hot and cold and we will experience joy and happiness as well as some unpleasant moments. These are the realities of life and they will come and go. If we do not learn to endure them and go through this life as a roller coaster ride, we will never be able to exhibit leadership traits.

   Developing a sense of equanimity enables an individual to master the art of handling the world around us by handling ourselves while engaging in the thick of activities.

8. Principle of Mutual Dependence:

Today's era is characterized by dominance of individuality as a value of life.

Joint families have given way for nuclear families.

Children are constantly taught the virtue of one's own hard work leading to excellence in their studies and other pursuits in life.

The spirit questioning everything (as opposed to the spirit of inquiry) and seeking one's own understanding of the issue is another aspect promoted today.

The idea that begins as individuality gets transformed into selfishness. This has taken away the culture of sharing.

The way we approach life will be dominated by "what is in it for me?" in order to achieve ultimate prosperity and success in whatever we do we need to honor the principle of mutual dependence.

9. Inspirational Leadership:

Leadership is at its best only when it becomes inspirational. Inspirational leadership has several attributes such as-

- Outgrow own vision from the narrow perspective of "what is in it for me?" to an opportunity to make a difference to the people and the place that they associate with

- Not afraid of anyone and not generating any sense of fear in others
- An ability to dramatically transform people and entities that comes to their contact in a sustained fashion.
- Leave behind an impact that guides a large number of people and organizations for a long time to come.

People endowed with modern education, scientific knowledge and wherewithal to perform need to imbibe spirituality to make a winning combination of an inspirational leader.

Chapter IV

Corruption

A. Definition

Corruption is a form of dishonesty or a criminal offence which is undertaken by a person or an organization which is entrusted in a position of authority, in order to acquire illicit benefits or abuse power for one's personal gain. Corruption may involve many activities which include bribery, influence peddling and the embezzlement and it may also involve practices which are legal in many countries.

Corruption is a malice, which is eating into the very ethos of our society and taking a toll on the economy.

Political corruption occurs when an office-holder or other governmental employee acts in an official capacity for personal gain.

Corruption and crime are endemic sociological occurrences which appear with regular frequency in virtually all countries on a global scale in varying degrees and proportions.

{Wikipedia}

B. Types of Corruption

Petty corruption occurs at a smaller scale and takes place at the implementation end of public services when public officials meet the public. Example: registration offices, police stations, state licensing boards, and many other private and government sectors.

Grand corruption is defined as corruption occurring at the highest levels of government in a way that requires significant subversion of the political, legal and economic systems. Such corruption is commonly found in countries with authoritarian or dictatorial governments but also in those without adequate policing of corruption.

Systemic corruption (or **endemic corruption**) is corruption which is primarily due to the weaknesses of an organization or process. It can be contrasted with individual officials or agents who act corruptly within the system.

Factors which encourage systemic corruption include conflicting incentives, discretionary powers; monopolistic powers; lack of transparency; low pay; and a culture of impunity. Specific acts of corruption include "bribery, extortion, and embezzlement" in a system where "corruption becomes the rule rather than the exception.

{Wikipedia}

C. Causes of Corruption

Greed of money, desires.

Higher levels of market and political monopolization.

Higher levels of bureaucracy and inefficient administrative structures.

High levels of in-group favoritism.

Gender inequality.

Poverty.

Low levels of education.

Lack of commitment to society.

Extravagant family.

Unemployment.

Ineffective monitoring of corruption policies.

Fearlessness against corruption.

D. Analysis of Corruption

(a) **Public Sector** Public corruption includes corruption of the political process and of government agencies such as tax departments and the police, as well as corruption in processes of allocating public funds for contracts, grants, and hiring.

(b) **Judicial corruption** refers to the corruption-related misconduct of judges, through the receiving or giving of bribes, the improper sentencing of convicted criminals, bias in the hearing and judgement of arguments and other forms of misconduct. Judicial corruption can also be conducted by prosecutors and defense attorneys. An example of prosecutorial misconduct, occurs when a politician or a prosecutor open investigations and file charges against an opposing politician.

Corruption in judiciary may also involve the government using its judicial arm to oppress opposition parties.

(c) **Military corruption** refers to the abuse of power by members in the armed forces, in order for career advancement or for personal gain by a soldier or soldiers.

Another example of military corruption, is a military officer or officers using the power of their positions to commit activities that are illegal, such as skimming logistical supplies such as food, medicine, fuel, body armor or weapons to sell on the local black market. There have also been instances of military officials, providing equipment and combat support to criminal syndicates, private military companies and terrorist groups.

(d) **Natural resources** Corruption includes industrial corruption, consisting of large bribes, as well as petty corruption such as a poacher paying off to ignore poaching. Any valued natural resource can be affected by corruption, including water for irrigation, land for livestock grazing, forests for hunting and logging, and fisheries.

(e) **Police corruption** is a specific form of police misconduct designed to obtain financial benefits, personal gain, career advancement for a police officer or officers in exchange for not pursuing or selectively pursuing an investigation or arrest or aspects of the "thin blue line" itself where force members collude in lies to protect their precincts, unions and/or other law enforcement members from accountability. One common form of police corruption is soliciting or accepting bribes in exchange for not reporting organized drug or prostitution rings or other illegal activities. When civilians become witnesses to police brutality, officers are often known to respond by harassing and intimidating the witnesses as retribution for reporting the misconduct.

Another example is police officers flouting the police code of conduct in order to secure convictions of suspects—for example, through the use of surveillance abuse, false confessions, police perjury and/or falsified evidence. Police officers have also been known to sell forms of contraband that were taken during seizers (such as confiscated drugs, stolen property or weapons). Corruption and misconduct can also be done by prison officers, such as the smuggling of contraband (such as drugs or electronics) into jails and prisons for inmates or the abuse of prisoners. Another form of misconduct is probation officers taking bribes in exchange for allowing paroles to violate the terms of their probation or abusing their paroles.

(f) **Private sector** corruption occurs when any institution, entity or person that is not controlled by the public sector company, household and institution that is not controlled by the public sector engages in corrupt acts. Private sector corruption may overlap with public sector corruption, for example when a private entity operates in conjunction with corrupt government officials, or where the government involves itself in activity normally performed by private entities.

(g) **Legal corruption** facilitated by lawyers is a well-known form of judicial misconduct. Such abuse is called Attorney misconduct. Attorney misconduct can be either conducted by individuals acting on their own accord or by entire law firms. A well-known example of such corruption are mob lawyers.

Mob lawyers are attorneys who seek to protect the leaders of criminal enterprises as well as their criminal organizations, with the use of unethical and/or illegal conduct such as making false or misleading statements, hiding evidence from prosecutors, failing to disclose all relevant facts about the case, or even giving clients advice on how to commit crimes in ways that would make prosecution more difficult for any investigating authorities.

(h) **Corporate crimes** In criminology refers to crimes committed either by a corporation (i.e., a business entity having a separate legal personality from the natural persons that manage its activities), or by individuals acting on behalf of a corporation or other business entity.

(i) **Corruption in education** in the form of admissions to schools and universities is traditionally considered one of the most corrupt areas of the education sector. The cost of corruption is that it impedes sustainable economic growth. Corruption includes bribes to bypass bureaucratic procedures and bribing faculty for a grade.

(j) **Healthcare Corruption** Corruption, the abuse of entrusted power for private gain. Corruption in health care poses a significant danger to the public welfare. Corruption occurs within the private and public health sectors and may appear as theft, embezzlement, nepotism, bribery up till extortion, or as undue influence. and occurs anywhere within the sector, be it in service provision, purchasing, construction and hiring.

Transparency International has described the six most common ways of service corruption as follows:

absenteeism, informal payments from patients, embezzlement, inflating services also the costs of services, favouritism and manipulation of data (billing for goods and services that were never sent or done)

(k) **Professional Corruption out of greed** Example: Despite provisions of Section 144 of the Companies Act, 2013 viz., the auditor shall not render certain services, many auditors render prohibited multiple services to same company or group by setting up different firms under same control by using combination of alphabets and even having same business addresses. How will such unscrupulous auditors, having lost their independence, report on the wrong doings by their Clients?

E. Methods of Bribery

Bribery involves the improper use of gifts and favors in exchange for personal gain. This is also known as kickbacks. It is a common form of corruption.

The types of favors given are diverse and may include money, gifts, real estate, promotions, sexual favors, employee benefits, entertainment, employment and political benefits. The personal gain that is given can be anything from actively giving preferential treatment to having an indiscretion or crime overlooked.

Bribery can sometimes make officials more susceptible to blackmail or to extortion.

Embezzlement, theft and fraud - involve someone with access to funds or assets illegally taking control of them.

Fraud involves using deception to convince the owner of funds or assets to give them up to an unauthorized party.

Examples include the misdirection of company funds into "shadow companies" (and then into the pockets of corrupt employees), the skimming of foreign aid money, scams, electoral fraud and other corrupt activity.

Graft is a form political corruption - which is defined as the unscrupulous use of a politician's authority for personal gain. Political graft occurs when funds intended for public projects are intentionally misdirected in order to maximize the benefits to private interests. The political act of graft is when funds intended for public projects are intentionally misdirected to maximize the benefits to private interests of the corrupt individuals.

Extortion and blackmail - Extortion is the practice of obtaining benefit through coercion. Making unfounded threats in order to obtain an unfair business advantage is also a form of extortion.

While bribery is the use of positive inducements for corrupt aims, extortion and blackmail center around the use of threats. This can be the threat of physical violence or false imprisonment as well as exposure of an individual's secrets or prior crimes.

This includes such behavior as an influential person threatening to go to the media if they do not receive speedy medical treatment (at the expense of other patients), threatening a public official with exposure of their secrets if they do not vote in a particular manner, or demanding money in exchange for continued secrecy. Another example can be a police officer being threatened with the loss of job by their superiors, if they continued with investigating a high-ranking official.

Influence peddling - is the illegal practice of using one's influence in government or connections with persons in authority to obtain favors or preferential treatment, usually in return for payment.

Networking - Both business and personal can be an effective way for job-seekers to gain a competitive edge over others in the job-market. The idea is to cultivate personal relationships with prospective employers, recruiters and others, in the hope that these personal relationships will influence future hiring decisions. This form of networking has been described as an attempt to corrupt formal hiring processes, where all candidates are given an equal opportunity to demonstrate their merits to selectors. The networker is accused of seeking non-meritocratic advantage over other candidates; advantage that is based on personal fondness rather than on any objective appraisal of which candidate is most qualified for the position.

Abuse of discretion - refers to the misuse of one's powers and decision-making facilities.

Favouritism, nepotism and clientelism - involve the favouring of not the perpetrator of corruption but someone related to them, such as a friend, family member or member of an association. Examples would include hiring or promoting a family member or staff member to a role they are not qualified for regardless of merit.

F. Standing of India on Corruption Index

Corruption in India is an issue which continues to affects the economy of the country.

1. **Corruption Perception Index**

   In Transparency International's 2022 Corruption Perceptions Index, India **scored 40** and thereby occupied **85th rank among the 180 countries** in the Index. The best score of 90 was awarded to the first ranked Denmark.

   Various factors contribute to corruption, including officials siphoning money from government social welfare schemes such as the Mahatma Gandhi National Rural Employment Guarantee Act and the National Rural Health Mission. Other areas of corruption in the past included India's trucking industry which is forced to pay billions of rupees in bribes annually to numerous regulatory and police stops on interstate highways.

   The media has widely published allegations of corrupt Indian citizens stashing millions of rupees in Swiss banks. In July 2021, India's Central Board of Direct Taxes (CBDT) replied to Right To Information (RTI) requests stating undeclared assets of Rs 20,078 crore identified by them in India and abroad following the investigation till June 2021.

The causes of corruption in India, *inter alia,* are said to include excessive regulations, complicated tax and licensing systems, numerous government departments with opaque bureaucracy and discretionary powers, monopoly of government-controlled institutions on certain goods and services delivery, and the lack of transparent laws and processes.

There are significant variations in the level of corruption and in the government's efforts to reduce corruption across India.

2. Politicians

Indian politicians generally lack good education, hail from poor families, sizeable number even have criminal backing.

Their capacity to amass wealth disproportionate to known sources of income seldom comes into scrutiny particularly if he/she is from the Ruling Party.

In fact, politicians of the opposition camps who have orders issued on them for investigation by investigating agencies like CBI, E D, EOW etc., are seen to cross-over to the Ruling party to keep the investigations against them closed or suspended indefinitely.

The investigating agencies generally do not go after corrupt union ministers.

Many of the regional politicians indulge in land grabbing and real estate scams perpetrated with the aid of bureaucrats.

It is a known fact that some Mafia bosses even serve(d) as ministers.

India's political elite have little regard for the country's justice system as they manipulate and corrupt the system.

India does not have a separate legislation dedicated to political scams.

The *amicus curiae* appointed by the Supreme Court in the matter relating to criminal cases against MPs/ MLAs has pointed out that as of July 2022, 44%of Lok Sabha members and 31% of Rajya Sabha members have criminal cases pending against them.

The Supreme Court has been monitoring expeditious disposal of criminal cases against MPs and MLAs since 2016. In his 17th report dated 14.11.2022, the Amicus had pointed out that 5,097 cases are pending against MPs/MLAs out of which more than 40% i.e., 2,122 cases are pending for more than 5 years.

As per report of the Association for Democratic Rights, 236 out of 542 Lok Sabha members (44%), 71 out of 226 Rajya Sabha members (31%) and 1723 of 3991

State Legislators (43%) have criminal cases against them as of July 2022.

The report further states as under:

The ADR report analyzed the election affidavits of 763 sitting MPs out of 776 seats in the Lok Sabha and Rajya Sabha.

- Out of the 763 sitting MPs analyzed, 306 (40%) sitting MPs have declared criminal cases against them and 194 (25%) sitting MPs have declared serious criminal cases including cases related to murder, attempt to murder, kidnapping, crimes against women, etc., it said.
- When it comes to criminal cases, about 139 (36 per cent) out of 385 MPs from BJP, 43 (53%) out of 81 MPs from Congress, 14 (39%) out of 36 MPs from TMC, 5 (83%) out of 6 MPs from RJD, 6 (75%) out of 8 MPs from CPI(M), 3 (27%) out of 11 MPs from AAP, 13 (42%) out of 31 MPs from YSRCP and 3 (38%) out of 8 MPs from NCP have declared such cases against themselves.
- As for serious criminal cases, about 98 (25%) out of 385 MPs from BJP, 26 (32%) out of 81 MPs from Congress, 7 (19%) out of 36 MPs from TMC, 3 (50%) out of 6 MPs from RJD, 2 (25%) out of 8 MPs from CPI(M), 1 (9%) out of 11 MPs from AAP, 11 (35%) out of 31 MPs from YSRCP and 2 (25%) out of 8 MPs from NCP are facing such cases.

- Eleven sitting MPs have declared cases related to murder (IPC -302), 32 sitting MPs have declared cases of attempt to murder (IPC -307), while 21 sitting MPs have declared cases related to crimes against women. Out of these 21 MPs, four MPs have declared cases related to rape (IPC -376).

- The average worth of assets of each MP from both the houses is Rs 38.33 crore. In comparison, legislators who have declared criminal cases against them have average assets amounting to Rs 50.03 crore.

- In terms of parties of billionaire MPs, fourteen MPs from the BJP, seven each from the Bharat Rashtra Samithi and YSR Congress Party, six from the Congress, three from the Aam Aadmi Party, two from the Shiromani Akali Dal and one from the Trinamool Congress have declared assets worth more than Rs 100 crore.

Many of the biggest scandals since 2005 have involved high level government officials, including Cabinet Ministers and Chief Ministers. Some of them are: the Coalgate Scam, 2010 Commonwealth Games scam (₹70,000 crore), the Adarsh Housing Society scam, the Coal Mining Scam (₹1.86 lakh crore), the Mining Scandal in Karnataka and the Cash for Vote scams, Fodder Scam, 2G Spectrum Scam, Housing Loan Scam (2010), Kerala Solar Panel Scam (2013), DLF Land Grab

Case (2013), Narada Scam Case (2014), cash for Vote Scam (2015).

3. **Failure of Lok Pal**

Ineffectiveness of country's top anti-corruption authority Lokpal has only caused Lokpal officials to squander huge public money without any accountability. As a result, the corrupt bureaucrats and politicians keep committing acts of corruption with impunity. While investigations and prosecutions of individual cases take place, lax enforcement is affected due to shortage of trained police officers, and overburdened and under-resourced court system resulting in lower number of convictions, the report said.

4. **Bureaucracy - Bribery**

Bureaucracy and bribery have become intertwined in India, resulting in a vicious cycle of corruption. Despite numerous attempts to address this issue, corruption continues to have a debilitating effect on India's economy and society. The Indian bureaucracy suffers from indecision and risk aversion, resulting in an inordinate focus on routine tasks, coordination failure, process overload, poor perception, motivational issues and a deterioration in the service quality of delivery.

5. **Land and property**

In cities and villages of India, groups of municipal and other government officials, elected politicians, judicial officers, real estate developers, and law enforcement officials, acquire, develop and sell land in illegal ways. Apart from this, slum-dwellers who are allotted houses under several housing schemes such as Pradhan Mantri Gramin Awaas Yojana, Rajiv Awas Yojna, Pradhan Mantri Awas Yojna, etc., rent out these houses to others, to earn money due to severe unemployment and lack of a steady source of income.

Corruption is proved to be rampant in the following areas also:

- Tendering processes and awarding various Government funded contracts
- Public Distribution programs and social spending contracts.
- Hospitals and health care in Government Hospitals
- Tax Departments
- Black Money generating illegal activities

6. **Battling India's malaise of Corruption** *{CVC's site on address to India CEO Forum}*

It is worthwhile to note the concerns of Central Vigilance Commission of India (CVC) in minimizing the corruption in the Country and what the Private sector companies as "Supplier" of corruption may do in this respect.

A report on bribery in India published statistics of Trace International states that:

- 91% of the bribes were demanded by govt. officials.
- 77% of the bribes demanded were for avoiding harm rather than to gain any advantage.
- Of these 51% were for timely delivery of services to which the individual was already entitled.

7. Role of Private Sector in Fighting Corruption

The private sector which forms the "supply side", which actually pays the bribes, primarily for overcoming their shortcomings in terms of - poor quality of their product/service, high price of their product or to create a market for their goods which otherwise are not in demand. Thus, they pay bribe to stay in competition despite these handicaps or to avoid true and fair competition.

Corruption is the anti-thesis of a free, fair, competitive and efficient market, as it distorts the objectivity, transparency and fair play in the market. It may therefore be argued that business entities are obliged to maintain integrity in order to maintain the efficiency and sanctity of the market. It would be self - destructive to distort the very market on which they are dependent for their existence.

Therefore, the theory X of corruption economics advocates that given an opportunity and if the fears of the private sector are allayed, they will at all cost stand up against corruption. It is this thinking that has given rise to instruments like Code of Conduct and Integrity Pact through which we try to involve the private sector in fighting corruption.

International efforts have equally focused on tackling the "supply side" of corruption and most of the countries have either formulated their own Foreign Corrupt Practices Act or are signatories to Anti-Bribery Conventions. Therefore, international pressure is building up on countries to formulate laws and take action against the private business in their countries who attempt to bribe foreign governments to obtain contracts. This is aimed at achieving fair play and competitiveness in international business. International economic and financial organizations are strongly pursuing this. As Indian companies are becoming globally competitive, we may sooner or later have to address these concerns.

G. Anti-corruption initiatives of the Government

(a) Right to Information Act, 2005

An Act to provide for setting out the practical regime of right to information for citizens to secure access to information under the control of public authorities, in order to promote transparency and accountability in the working of every public authority, the constitution of a Central Information Commission and State

Information Commissions and for matters connected therewith or incidental thereto.

Democracy requires an informed citizenry and transparency of information which are vital to its functioning and also to contain corruption and to hold Governments or their instrumentalities accountable to the governed.

Revelation of information in actual practice is likely to conflict with other public interests including efficient operations of the Governments, optimum use of limited fiscal resources and the preservation of confidentiality of sensitive information.

(b) Right to Public Services laws

Right to Public Services legislation in India comprises statutory laws which guarantee time bound delivery of services for various public services rendered by the Government to citizen and provides mechanism for punishing the errant public servant who is deficient in providing the service stipulated under the statute.

Right to Service legislation are meant to reduce corruption among the government officials and to increase transparency and public accountability.

Madhya Pradesh became the first state in India to enact Right to Service Act on 18 August 2010 and Bihar was the second to enact this bill on 25 July 2011. Several other states like Bihar, Delhi, Punjab, Rajasthan,

Himachal Pradesh, Kerala, Uttarakhand, Haryana, Uttar Pradesh, Odisha, Jharkhand Maharashtra and West Bengal have introduced similar legislation for effectuating the right to service to the citizen.

(c) Indian Penal Code, 1860

(d) Income Tax Act, 1961

(e) The Prevention of Corruption Act, 1988

This is an Act of the to combat corruption in government agencies and public sector businesses in India

(f) The Benami Transactions (Prohibition) Act, 1988, name changed to **Prohibition of Benami Property Transactions Act, 1988**

This Act of Parliament is to prohibit certain types of financial transactions. The act defines a 'benami' transaction as any transaction in which property is transferred to one person for consideration paid by another person. Such transactions were a feature of the Indian economy, usually relating to the purchase of property (real estate), and were thought to contribute to the Indian black money problem. The act bans all benami transactions and gives the government the right to recover property held benami without paying any compensation.

(g) Prevention of Money Laundering Act, 2002 {PMLA}

This is an Act to prevent money-laundering and to provide for confiscation of property derived from money-laundering. The Act and Rules notified there under impose obligation on banking companies, financial institutions and intermediaries to verify identity of clients, maintain records and furnish information in prescribed form to Financial Intelligence Unit - India (FIU-IND).

(h) The Lokpal and Lokayuktas Act, 2013

The Act commonly known as **The Lokpal Act**, is an anti-corruption Act of the Parliament which seeks to provide for the establishment of the institution of Lokpal to inquire into allegations of corruption against certain important public functionaries including the Prime Minister, cabinet ministers, members of parliament, Group A officials of the Central Government and for matters connecting them.

(i) Whistle Blowers Protection Act, 2011

This is an Act of the Parliament which provides a mechanism to investigate alleged corruption and misuse of power by public servants and also protect anyone who exposes alleged wrongdoing in government bodies, projects and offices. The wrongdoing might be in the form of fraud, corruption or mismanagement. The Act also ensures punishment for false or frivolous complaints.

(j) The Black Money (Undisclosed Foreign Income and Assets) and Imposition of Tax Bill, 2015

This is an Act aiming to curb black money, or undisclosed foreign assets and income and imposes tax and penalty on such income.

(k) Formation of Anti-corruption police and courts such as-

The Directorate General of Income Tax Investigation,

- Central Vigilance Commission and
- Central Bureau of Investigation
- Civic anti-corruption organizations such as-
  - Bharat Swabhiman Trust,
  - India Against Corruption movement
  - Jaago Re! One Billion Votes
  - The Lok Satta Movement,
  - Right to Recall Party
  - Electoral reforms

Following are the findings of India Corruption Survey, 2019 by Transparency International:

- 51% citizens of the country had paid bribes.
- The Prevention of Corruption (Amendment) Act 2018 which was hailed as a force that would deter the

Government employees from indulging in bribery has starting to show some effects, as is evident from the numbers from this year's survey.

- Awareness about existing state hotlines/helplines to report corruption is still a big issue as 61% citizens in this year's survey said they were unaware of any such hotline in their state.
- Although CCTVs are a slight deterrent, bribery still continues in Government offices despite major computerization. Agents continue to thrive and cash is still the preferred way to pay bribes.
- Property registration and land issues is a top area of corruption
- Citizens say there has been no reduction in instances of bribery by police in the last 12 months.
- Majority said they paid bribes due to coercion or inefficiencies prevailing in Government offices

The Government of India is finding it a daunting task to eradicate the deep-rooted corruption from the Society to make the Country Corruption-free.

Corruption occurs not just in India but everywhere in the world, especially in places where the risk of getting caught is low and the rewards are high. It is also a question of personal integrity and dignity. It is unethical to hoard money and gain an advantage by wrong-doings. It results in social inequality, widens the gap between the rich and the poor, makes the administration slow and makes the country shameful in the eyes of the world. What starts as greed and selfishness turns into corruption.

H. Factors leading to Corruption

1. **Lack of effective management and organisation:** results in failure to control corruption at various levels especially in Public Sector set-ups. Corruption starts at Inefficient and inappropriate appointments to the managerial posts, The abuse of unworthy empowerment of such undeserving employees without appropriate controls and fears leads to spread of rampant corruption.

2. **Lack of good moral human values:** Good virtues and values are integral part of a human being. Such values naturally get ingrained in a person depending upon the environment in which he is brought up, education levels of himself and family members, moral values taught in formative years of life etc. Any such qualities lacking in a person leads him often into corrupt and dishonest actions for self-enrichment without fearless and no efforts.

3. **Lack of Leadership by Example**: Those leaders with poor moral standards do not curb their own personal tendencies to adopt and practice corrupt practices. The peers and subordinates also, as a result, encouraged without fear or guilt to indulge in corrupt practices for self-enrichment as if it is a matter of right.

4. **Lack of fear of Accountability:** Rules and regulations on Corruption are, it may be experienced, widely publicized in Companies as a matter of tick of the box exercise. Yet the management is perceived to be turning blind eye on the compliance aspects by defaulting employees. Certain sectors of industries such as Building industry are known to be openly indulging in corruption of high magnitude to satisfy the needs of the administrators as well. The Government machinery has been a mute spectator and thereby an accomplice to the corrupt practices.

5. **Lack of control and vigilance:** Despite the enactment of Prevention and Corruption Act, the levels of corruption have not come down much. Corruption continues to breed corruption due to the tolerance of people, lack of outcry by the public against the corruption, and unwillingness of the powers and mighty to take strong actions on offenders for their own reasons.

6. **Elections:** Elections is the biggest offender. During election times in the whole country every political party indulges in rampant and open corrupt practices including distribution of cash and in kind without any fear and serious checks. The poor and illiterate public are the victims of such influence.

(I) Some of the Effects of Corruption

(i) Havoc in Society and economy.

(ii) Hampers development of the nation

(iii) Breeds unequal opportunities by increase of rate of unemployment, increase in hunger, and poverty, revenue loss to the Government, amassing of black money, abuse of power and position etc.

(iv) Erosion of moral and ethical values.

Chapter V

Some Corruption Cases Involving Politicians

Political Scams

There are many deep rooted political scams involving politicians belonging to Parliament and Legislatures. Only some of them are illustrated hereunder:

1. **Coal allocation scam or Coalgate Scam (2012)**

   The scam came into public knowledge in 2012 after the CAG levied allegations against the UPA government for allocation of coal blocks to public and private enterprises. Out of the total 216 coal blocks allocated between 1993-2010, 194 coal blocks were sold to these public and private enterprises for captive use. The CAG report observed inefficient and possibly illegal allocation of coal blocks. It estimated loss to the exchequer to the tune of ₹10.7 lakh crore but it later toned this amount down to ₹1.86 lakh crore in the final report.

   The CAG questioned over arbitrary administrative decisions while allocating the coal blocks and not following the particular procedure of the competitive bidding.

After BJP filed a complaint with the Central Vigilance Commission (CVC). The CVC directed CBI to probe the matter for corruption. At least a dozen companies were named in the FIR that resulted in a criminal investigation. Accusations ranged from malicious means for securing allocation, overstating net worth, non-disclosure of prior allocation and hoarding rather than the development of allocated resources. Industrialists like Naveen Jindal and Kumar Mangalam Birla have also found their name in FIRs in the Coal Scam, though Birla's name was dropped in 2014.

The CVC ordered a CBI enquiry into the allegations following complaints by BJP MPs. A PIL moved in the Supreme Court sought cancellation of all the 194 coal block allotments. The court, monitoring the CBI probe into the coal scam, asked the agency not to disclose probe details to the government.

In April 2013, the Standing Committee on Coal and Steel in its report tabled in Parliament said that allocation of coal blocks between 1993 and 2008 was done in an unauthorized manner. It also said that allotment of mines where production has not started should be cancelled.

In a landmark judgement on 25 August 2014, the Supreme Court declared illegal all allocation of coal blocks between 1993 and 2010 and cancelled the allocation of nearly 200 coal blocks.

In August 2022 the CBI sought maximum punishment from a Delhi court for former Coal Secretary H C Gupta and former joint Secretary in the Ministry of Coal (MoC) for irregularities in the allocation of a coal block in Maharashtra.

The special CBI court also observed that three union coal ministry officials, were guilty and made "dishonest misrepresentation of facts to the then Prime Minister Manmohan Singh while recommending the allocation of a coal block in Madhya Pradesh to Kamal Sponge Steel and Power Limited (KSSPL).

2. Vyapam scam

The Vyapam scam revolves around the Madhya Pradesh Professional Examination Board (MPPBP), a government agency in charge of administering 13 different admission exams in the state, commonly recognized as 'Vyapam.' These entrance exams are conducted for government job recruitment and admittance to educational institutions throughout the state. Politicians, high government officials, businessmen, and others in Madhya Pradesh were involved in the admissions and recruitment scam. It included employing imposters to give exams regularly, taking advantage of exam hall seating, and providing corrupt officials with forged answer sheets.

Many of those responsible for exposing these horrendous revelations — whistleblowers and journalists (43) have died in a series of mysterious events. Around 77 lakh people are suspected of paying bribes to get into colleges and acquire government employment.

The sheer scale of the scam came to light in 2013, when the Indore police arrested 20 people who had come to impersonate candidates for PMT 2009. The interrogation of these people led to the arrest of Jagdish Sagar, the leader of an organized racket involved in the scam. The state government established a Special Task Force (STF) on 26 August 2013.

Subsequent interrogations and arrests uncovered the involvement of several politicians, bureaucrats, MPPEB officials, racket leaders, middlemen, candidates and their parents in the scam. By June 2015, more than 2000 people had been arrested in connection with the scam. These included the state's ex-education minister Laxmikant Sharma and over a hundred other politicians. In July 2015, the Supreme Court of India issued an order to transfer the case to the country's premier investigating agency, the Central Bureau of Investigation (CBI).

Many senior personnel including Justice Bhushan who heads the Special Investigative team and Indian doctors including Anand Rai (the whistle blower in this case) are of the opinion that the Vyapam scam was functional since the 1990s when they themselves took their medical exam They also believe that similar "systems" of proxies giving medical exams are operational in other states of India as well.

In May 2023, the special CBI court, in Indore convicted two accused under IPC sections 120B, 419, 420, 467, 468, 471, 201 and section 3/4 of the Affiliated Examination Act, 1937 and convicted three other accused who acted as middleman under IPC sections 120B, 419, 420, 467, 468, 471 and 201 in the case related to 2013 admission scam to imprisonment of maximum of five years along with a fine of Two thousand rupees. Two accused were acquitted in the matter.

3. Adarsh Housing Society scam

The Adarsh Housing Society Scandal was a significant political scandal that surfaced in 2010. The issue included the Adarsh Housing Society's development of an apartment complex in Mumbai for the families of servicemen who had perished in the 1999 Kargil War.

The scam was unearthed in November 2010 which forced the then Chief Minister of Maharashtra, Ashok Chavan, to resign.

In 2011, a report of the Comptroller and Auditor General of India said, "The episode of Adarsh Co-operative Housing Society reveals how a group of select officials, placed in key posts, could subvert rules and regulations in order to grab prime government land – a public property – for personal benefit."

In January 2011, the Maharashtra government set up a two-member judicial commission to inquire into the matter. After deposing 182 witnesses over 2 years, the commission submitted its final report in April 2013 to the Maharashtra government. The report highlighted 25 illegal allotments, including 22 purchases made by proxy. The report also indicted four former chief ministers of Maharashtra: Ashok Chavan, Vilasrao Deshmukh, Sushilkumar Shinde and Shivajirao Nilangekar Patil, 2 former urban development ministers and 12 top bureaucrats for various illegal acts.

The Central Bureau of Investigation (CBI), the Income Tax Department and the Enforcement Directorate (ED) have been investigating allegations that three former chief ministers of Maharashtra were involved in the scam.

The Bombay High Court ordered the building to be demolished in 2016, stating that it was built unlawfully. The society took their case to the Supreme Court, which issued a stay on the demolition in 2018.

The Indian army has seized the building after directives from the Supreme Court.

The Adarsh housing society scandal exposed serious flaws in India's system of governance. The fact that influential people could use their power and connections to get illegal benefits highlights the need for reform.

In addition, the slow pace of investigation and prosecution, in this case, shows how difficult it can be to bring those responsible for corruption to justice.

4. **Choppergate scam (2013) | Rs 3600 Crore |**

The Chopper deal involved money paid to middlemen and Indian officials in 2006 and 2007 in order to purchase helicopters for high-level politicians.

According to CBI, this amounted to Rs 2.5 billion transferred through bank accounts in the UK and UAE. Several Indian Congress politicians and military officials were accused of accepting bribes from AgustaWestland in order to win the Rs 3600 crores Indian contract for the supply of 12 AgustaWestland AW101 helicopters. The helicopters are intended to perform VVIP duties for the President of India and other important state officials.

In February 2023, the Supreme Court denied bail to Christian Michel James, an alleged middleman in the AgustaWestland chopper scam cases, who is being probed by both the Central Bureau of Investigation and the Enforcement Directorate.

5. **Bofors scandal (1980-1990) | Rs 64 crores**

Bofors scandal was one of India's major weapons-contract political scandal that occurred in the 1980's and 1990's. This scandal was attributed to the Congress party accusing the then Indian prime minister, Rajiv Gandhi, and several other Indian and Swedish government officials of receiving major kickbacks from Bofors AB — a Swedish arms manufacturer.

It was alleged that Bofors had paid Rs. 640 million in the form of kickbacks to the Indian politicians and important defense officials to win a bid to supply India's 155 mm field howitzer, a short gun for firing shells on high trajectories at low velocities.

The scale of the scandal was so huge that it led to the defeat of the congress party in the 1989 general elections.

The Delhi High court in 2004 quashed all charges of payoffs against former PM Rajiv Gandhi and others.

6. **2G Spectrum scam | ₹1.76 trillion |**

Politicians and government officials under the UPA coalition government were named in this scam. This scam surfaced when CAG revealed that the government, in 2008, had undercharged mobile telephone companies for frequency allocation license that used to create 2G spectrum subscriptions for cell phones. According to the CAG of India "the difference between the money collected and that mandated to be collected was Rs 1.76 trillion.

In February 2012, the Supreme Court declared the allotment of spectrum as "unconstitutional and arbitrary" and cancelled the 122 licenses issued in 2008 under A. Raja, then Minister of Communications and IT.

On 21 December 2017, the special court in New Delhi acquitted all accused including prime accused A Raja and DMK chief M Karunanidhi's daughter M Kanimozhi as the CBI could not find any evidence against the accused in those seven years.

However, on March 19-20, 2018, the Enforcement Directorate and CBI respectively filed appeals against this verdict in the Delhi High Court.

The Delhi High Court in April 2022 rejected appeals against the dismissal of petitions challenging the legality of CBI's appeal against the trial court verdict in the 2G scam case saying that there was no merit in the pleas before it.

7. **Commonwealth Games scandal | Rs. 70,000 crores**

In 2010, New Delhi witnessed the Commonwealth Games (CWG) scam, one of the major Indian scams involving pilferage of Rs. 70,000 crores. It is estimated that out of Rs.70,000 crore spent on the Games, only half of the said amount was spent on Indian sportspersons.

The CVC, involved in probing corruption in various Commonwealth Games-related projects, found discrepancies in tenders – like payment to non-existent parties, will-full delays in execution of contracts, over-inflated price and bungling in purchase of equipment through tendering – and misappropriation of funds.

Reports of CVC revealed that Suresh Kalmadi, the Chairman of the Organising committee of the Games, offered a contract of Rs 141 crore to Swiss Timings for its timing equipment which was unnecessarily high by Rs 95 crore. The CVC then asked the CBI to probe certain aspects of the games' organisation.

On 25 April 2011, CBI arrested Kalmadi. In addition to Kalmadi, the CBI named two companies and eight persons including former Secretary General Lalit Bhanot and former Director General VK Verma as accused. On 26 April 2011 he was sacked from the post of president of the Indian Olympic Association.

Kalmadi's membership of the Indian National Congress Party was suspended after being arrested and charged with corruption. On 26 April 2011 he was sacked from the post of president of the Indian Olympic Association. On 1 July 2013 he lost the election for the post of president of the Asian Athletics Association, a post which he had held for 13 consecutive years.

Suresh Kalmadi was in jail for 10 months and the court asked him to pay a surety amount of ₹500,000 in 2012. He was allowed by a Delhi court on 13 July 2012 to go to London for 2012 Olympics. He was, however, restrained on 25 July 2012 by the Delhi High court from participating in the opening ceremony of the London Olympics, saying his participation can cause "embarrassment" to the nation.

He claimed to be suffering from dementia during course of investigation while in Tihar jail Medical tests were not conclusive to be able to prove his claim.

8. Kargil coffin scandal

George Fernandes who passed away on 29 January 2019 was implicated in the corruption case called 'Coffin Gate' exposed by a sting operation by Tehelka, a news portal. In the war with Pakistan, in 1999 India had emerged victorious.

The then government had ordered to bring the bodies of martyred soldiers in a flag-draped aluminum casket and had signed a deal with US-based Buritrol and Baizarces, a company based in America that rendered funeral services.

The Comptroller and Auditor General of India's report reported several flaws in the procurement of the caskets, which were said to be of very low quality and highly-priced. The NDA government had purchased 500 caskets worth $2500 each which was presumed to be thirteen times the original amount.

A charge sheet was filed by the CBI) in a CBI court in Delhi and a case was registered against Fernandes, for alleged abuse of official position for personal gains and several others. This scandal was met with the widespread protests from other political parties such as Congress, which led to Fernandes resignation as defense minister during the course of the investigation.

However, the CBI in its investigation could not prove Fernandes' involvement and the special CBI court eventually gave him a clean chit in 2013. The special court could not find any evidence against other accused and discharged them.

9. **Hawala scam - USD 18 Million | Key accused: Jain brothers**

Also called the Jain Diaries case was an Indian political and financial scandal involving payments allegedly sent by politicians (black money) through four hawala brokers, namely the Jain brothers.

In 1991, an arrest linked to militants in Kashmir led to a raid on hawala brokers, revealing evidence of large-scale payments to national politicians. Those accused included L. K. Advani, V. C. Shukla, P. Shiv Shankar, Sharad Yadav, Balram Jakhar, and Madan Lal Khurana.

The entire list contained politicians from the BJP, Congress and independent MLAs and MPs, with amounts varying between Rs. 50,000 to Rs. 7.5 crore. Many were acquitted in 1997 and 1998, partly because the hawala records (including diaries) were judged in court to be inadequate as the main evidence.

10. Karnataka mining scandal | Rs. 16,085 crores | Key accused: Karunakara Reddy and Janardhana Reddy

The Bellary mining scandal which shook Karnataka and went to become a national scandal involved the mining baron Reddy brothers from Karnataka, who were ministers in Karnataka. The Bellary mining scandal also led to the resignation of the former chief minister of Karnataka BS Yeddyurappa and later he was faced with the eventuality of a BJP government collapse. He is alleged to have caused a loss of about Rs. 16,085 crores to the Karnataka state government by giving illegal extension in the mining leases.

The increasing iron-ore prices across the globe driven by huge Chinese demand brought a lot of focus to the iron ore rich Bellary region of Karnataka. This iron ore is alleged to have been illegally mined after paying a minuscule royalty to the government. The major irregularities involve mines in Bellary, including those of Obulapuram Mining Company owned by the Reddy brothers.

Through investigation it became clear that Reddy brothers had paid huge amounts of money to bag contracts to the Obulapuram mining company. Lokayukta in its report during the period of 2006 to 2010 had stated that nearly 12.57 crore of tonnes of iron ore were exported from Bellary.

Lokayukta also uncovered major violations and systemic corruptions in mining in Bellary, including in the allowed geography, encroachment of forest land, massive underpayment of state mining royalties relative to the market price of iron ore and systematic starvation of government mining entities.

Granting him bail in 2015 - he was arrested in September 2011 - the Supreme Court had ordered him not to visit Ballari, In August 2021, the Supreme Court granted some more relief to him by relaxing his bail conditions, the court allowed him to stay in his hometown of Ballari, a little over 300 kilometres north of state capital Bengaluru.

"Trial has not even started in the case and the petitioner has not violated bail conditions so far. Hence, he is permitted to go to Ballari...Meanwhile, the trial court may expedite the trial in the case," said a two-judge bench of Justices Vineet Saran and Dinesh Maheshwari.

G Janardhan Reddy, who is being prosecuted by the CBI for involvement in illegal mining in Ballari region of the state, was arrested by the Bengaluru Police's Central Crime Branch (CCB) unit for allegedly receiving funds from a finance firm accused of swindling hundreds of investors through Ponzi schemes.

11. Chandrababu Naidu Produced Before ACB Court In Vijayawada Day After His Arrest in an alleged Skill Development Corporation scam

The former Andhra Pradesh CM was arrested in connection with the alleged Skill Development Corporation scam after a pre-dawn police operation at early hours on September 9, 2023 by the CID from a marriage hall outside which his caravan was parked. He was produced before the Anti-Corruption Bureau (ACB) court in Vijayawada the following day after his medical check-up. Later he taken back to the SIT office. Following his arrest, several TDP leaders were placed under house arrest.

Naidu was arrested under relevant IPC sections, including Sections 120B (criminal conspiracy), 420 (cheating and dishonestly inducing delivery of property), and 465 (forgery). In addition, AP CID has also invoked the Prevention of Corruption Act against him.

The Andhra Pradesh Skill Development Corporation was established in 2016 to focus on the empowerment of unemployed youth by providing skill training.

The AP CID started an investigation into an alleged scam worth ₹3,300 crore in March 2023 which revealed that the project was initiated without following a proper tendering process.

According to reports Investigations revealed irregularities such as:

1. Before any expenditure by private entities, the GoAP/APSSDC provided an advance of Rs. 371 Crores, representing the entire 10% commitment by the government, according to an official statement.

2. Most of the money advanced by the government was diverted to shell companies through fake invoices, with no actual delivery or sale of the items mentioned in the invoices.

3. A portion of the funds was used to create the Certificate of Entitlement (COE) clusters, a departure from the official procedure, while the rest was routed through shell companies, the statement read.

4. The investigation implicates prime accused Nara Chandrababu Naidu, along with the Telugu Desam Party, as beneficiaries of the misappropriated funds.

5. Naidu is considered the principal conspirator behind the scheme, orchestrating the transfer of public funds to private entities via shell companies, resulting in a loss to the public exchequer and private gains.
6. The ultimate use of the misappropriated funds, including cash holdings with individuals like Vikas Khanvilkar, requires further examination, the statement said.
7. Key documents related to the case have gone missing, with Naidu and other individuals being primary suspects.

12. The Fodder Scam

The fodder scam, popularly known as *chaara ghotala*, refers to dozens of cases of financial irregularities to the tune of around Rs 930 crore in the animal husbandry department of the undivided Bihar between 1985-1995.

According to a media report the Doranda treasury scam is a bizarre case where documents showed that cattle were transported from Haryana and Punjab to Bihar on scooters during the years 1990-92.

In 1996, deputy commissioner Amit Khare of the animal husbandry department ordered a raid. The documents that were seized indicated embezzlement of money in the pretext of supplying fodder. It started with small-scale fraud by low-level government employees but grew to involve businesses and politicians.

After the raids, the state government set up two commissions. One of them was headed by state development commissioner Phoolchand Singh – whose involvement in the scam later emerged. This forced the commission to be aborted.

Meanwhile, the Bihar police also filed multiple FIRs on the instructions of the state government.

On the other hand, multiple public interest litigations (PIL) were filed in the Patna high court to hand the case over to the CBI.

Hearing the petitions, the Patna high court in a March 11, 1996 directed by an order CBI to enquire and scrutinize all cases of excess drawings and expenditure in the department of Animal Husbandry in the State of Bihar during the period 1977-78 to 1995-96 and lodge cases where the drawls are found to be fraudulent in character, and take the investigation in those cases to its logical end, as early as possible preferable, within four months.'

As the CBI began investigating, the roles of Lalu, former chief minister Jagannath Mishra and top bureaucrats came under the scanner.

The agency took up the investigation of 41 cases already registered by the state Police, and 23 cases were registered on the basis of intelligence reports and complaints following the order of the Patna high court.

On March 27, 1996, the CBI registered the first FIR in the Chaibasa treasury case. That year, the CBI requested the governor of Bihar permission to prosecute Lalu, who was the chief minister, and filed a chargesheet against him and 55 others in June 1997 under Sections 420 (forgery) and 120 (b) (criminal conspiracy) of the Indian Penal Code and Section 13 (b) of the Prevention of Corruption Act.

Lalu Prasad Yadav, former chief minister of Bihar and the Rashtriya Janata Dal (RJD) supremo, was on found guilty in February 2018 in the Rs 139 crore scam from the Doranda (Jharkhand) treasury.

He resigned from the chief minister's post but installed his wife Rabri Devi as his replacement. She won the vote of confidence. In 2001, Jharkhand was created and the cases were transferred to that state.

In March 2012, charges were framed against Lalu and Mishra in fraudulent withdrawal of money from Banka and Bhagalpur districts.

On September 30, 2013 he and Mishra along with 45 others were convicted by a CBI court in the Chaibasa case and sentenced to five years in prison. He was an MP at the time and was disqualified from contesting any election for eleven years.

In December 2017, he was convicted in another case, where he was sentenced to three-and-a-half years in jail and Rs 10 lakh in fine for illegal withdrawal from the Deoghar treasury. But Jagannath Mishra was acquitted.

In January 2018, he was convicted in another Chaibasa treasury case for illegal withdrawal of ₹ 33.67 crore and awarded a five-year jail term and in March the same year, sentenced to seven years in jail in a case related to the fraudulent withdrawal of ₹ 3.13 crore from the Dumka treasury.

Apart from Lalu Yadav and Jagannath Mishra, hundreds of persons have been convicted in the scam.

Till February 2018, 295 accused persons on single counts and 821 accused persons on repeated counts have been convicted and fines ranging from ₹ 20,000 to ₹ 1.2 crore were imposed on them by courts.

Lalu was involved with many corruption cases, apart from the several Fodder Scam such as Indian Railway Tender Scam (2005), Delight Properties Case {2017), AB Exports Case (2017), Patna Zoo Sil Scam (2017),

In April 2022, the Jharkhand High court granted bail to Yadav as he had served 41 months in jail in this case.

13. Tatra truck scam: 2011

Top officials of Bharat Earth Movers Ltd (BEML), a defense public sector undertaking, and the defense ministry siphoned off Rs750 crore in bribes and commissions over the past 14 years in the purchase of components for Tatra trucks.

For over a decade, the BEML flouted defense procurement guidelines and sold Tatra trucks to the army at an inflated price.

Flouting defense ministry guidelines, BEML, formerly Bharat Earth Movers Limited, a Rs3,500 crore company in which the government of India is the majority shareholder, has been buying components for the 6x6 and 8x8 trucks from a middleman in London.

The defense procurement guidelines clearly mention that all purchases are to be made from the original equipment manufacturer (OEM).

However, investigation revealed that BEML, was dealing with Tatra Sipox (UK) Ltd, which is neither the OEM nor a subsidiary of the OEM.

However, no action was taken by the government until former Army Chief General VK Singh, in an interview, admitted that he was offered bribe of Rs14 crore for clearing the purchase of 600 substandard Tatra-all-terrain vehicles.

Following this revelation, Defense Minister AK Antony was forced to order a CBI probe into the scam.

On 26th. August 26, 2014 CBI filed a closure report on the cam saying that there was insufficient evidence to file a charge sheet.

14. Antrix Devas deal

In January 2005, Antrix Corporation signed an agreement with Devas Multimedia (a private company formed by former ISRO employees and Venture Capitalists from USA) for lease of S band transponders on two ISRO satellites (GSAT 6 and GSAT 6A) for a price of ₹14 billion (US$180 million), a huge amount lower than market price, to be paid over a period of 12 years. Devas shares were sold at a premium of ₹1,226,000 (US$15,000), taking the accumulated share premium to ₹5.78 billion (US$72 million), thus getting a high profit. In July 2008, Devas offloaded 17% of its stake to German company Deutsche Telekom for US$75 million, and by 2010 had 17 investors, including former ISRO scientists.

In late 2009, some ISRO insiders exposed information about the Devas-Antrix deal, and the ensuing investigations resulted in the deal being annulled. G. Madhavan Nair (ISRO Chairperson when the agreement was signed) was barred from holding any post under the Department of Space. Some former scientists were found guilty of "acts of commission" or "acts of omission". Devas and Deutsche Telekom demanded US$2 billion and US$1 billion, respectively, in damages.

The Central Bureau of Investigation concluded investigations into the Antrix-Devas scam and registered a case against the accused in the Antrix-Devas deal under Section 120-B, besides Section 420 of IPC and Section 13(2) read with 13(1)(d) of Prevention of Corruption Act, 1988 on 18 March 2015 against the then executive director, Antrix Corporation Limited, Bengaluru; two officials of USA-based company; Bengaluru based private multi-media company and other unknown officials of Antrix Corporation Limited /ISRO/Department of Space.

In Aug 2016: Former ISRO chief G Madhavan Nair and other senior officials were chargesheet by the CBI as they were accused of facilitating "wrongful" gain of Rs 578 crore to Devas.

In Sept 2017: International Chamber of Commerce (ICC) awarded Devas a compensation worth $1.3 billion on the appeal of foreign investors in Devas.

In Jan 2021: Ministry of corporate affairs directed Antrix to initiate a winding up petition against Devas under Companies Act. NLCT admitted Antrix petition against Devas and appointed provisional liquidator.

In Sept 2021: NCLAT upheld NCLT order to wind up Devas Multimedia.

Chapter VI

Corruption in Judiciary and Professional Bodies

A. Judiciary in India

(i) ***Background Note

A non-corrupt judiciary is a *sine qua non* for democracy to function successfully and for a guaranteed assurance on basic human rights to a Society.

The judiciary must therefore be an independent and fair body that is not influenced by corruption. Unfortunately, due to human deficient qualities, there have been cases where the judges failed to discharge their sworn duty by misusing their position while delivering justice.

The justice delivery is slow, the appointment of judges is mired in controversy, disciplinary mechanisms scarcely work, hierarchy rather than merit is preferred, women are severely under-represented, and constitutional matters often languish in the Supreme Court for years

It is also feared that some judges are influenced by the debates on electronic media on crime investigations fearing public criticism.

Instances of corruption and bribery in the lower rungs of judiciary are reported from across the country that only add to an overall negative narrative against the judiciary. For example, in April 2018, three judges of lower courts in Telangana were arrested for possessing assets disproportionate to their known sources of income. Similarly, in Gujarat, two judges of the lower judiciary were arrested for allegedly taking money to settle cases during their posting at Vapi court in 2014. In January 2018, four sitting Supreme Court judges held a news conference to highlight alleged rot that they claimed had set in the judiciary.

(ii) Appointment of Judges to Supreme Court

The appointment of judges is another controversial topic where the judiciary is resisting transparency from the longest of times. The appointment of the Supreme Court judges is made by the Chief Justice of India and four other judges on whose recommendations the President appoints the Supreme Court judge. This is where the appointment becomes controversial. On the contrary, the political leaders are not selected but democratically elected.

****{Legal Services India}*

According to Chief Justice of India DY Chandrachud, the process of appointment of judges is expected to become more transparent. Objective parameters will be laid down for the appointment of judges to the high courts and the Supreme Court. The Chief Justice has shared that the center for planning and research has begun working on a broad platform to assess the top judges of the country who are eligible for appointments. The assessment will be done based on data available on the judges and judgments delivered by them[1]. A dossier will be prepared with objective criteria for appointments to the high courts and the Supreme Court[1]. This move aims to make the appointment process more transparent and ensure that deserving candidates are considered for these positions. *{India Today 15 Sep. 2023}*

(iii) Mountain of Pending Cases

The National Judicial Data Grid (NJDG) - Department of Justice reflects the following statistics on its web site of cases pending with 8,735 District & Subordinate Courts and High Courts as on April 8, 2023:

	Nature	Total cases	More than 1 year
1.	Civil Cases	1,10,57,002	68,92,891 {% 62.34}
2.	Criminal Cases	3,33,50,202	2,15,27,167 {%64.55}
Total		**4,44,07,204**	

In a written reply the Law Minister Arjun Ram Meghwal said that as on July 24,2023 - 71,204 cases were pending in high courts for more than thirty years. Similarly, 1,01,837 cases were pending for over 30 years in district and subordinate courts.

India's Justice Report 2022 *{Initiative of TATA Trusts}*

(iv) Shortage of Judges

The judiciary is facing a severe shortage of judges and infrastructure, leading to rising pendency, increasing caseloads, and declining case clearance rates (CCR) in lower courts.

As of December 2022, the High Courts were functioning with only 778 judges against a sanctioned strength of 1,108 judges.

(v) Court Halls

Nationally, the number of court halls will become a problem if all the sanctioned posts are filled.

In August 2022, there were 21,014 court halls for the 24,631 sanctioned judges' posts, a shortfall of 14.7%.

(vi) National Deficits

Police

SC/ST/OBCs - Every State has statutorily mandated quotas for these classes. Only Karnataka has been able to fulfil these reservations.

Women

Not a single State/UT meets with their own reserved quotas for women in police.

Rural-Urban Divide

In 19 States/UTs Urban police stations serve greater population than their rural counter parts. Kerala's urban police stations serve 10 times the population of a rural one and Gujarat's 4 times.

SHRC - 33312

Total number of pending cases across all State Human Rights Commissions in March 2021

44% National average vacancy across 25 NHRCs.

CCTVs

Compliance with Supreme Court Judgment on installation of CCTVs

Only Arunachal Pradesh reports having cameras in all 14 spots in all of its 24 police stations. Only 8 States/UTs reported having night-vision equipped CCTVs.

Legal Aid - 9417

Reduction in the number of Legal Services clinics dropping to 4742 (2022) from 14,159(2021).

Prisons

32/UTs States where share of undertrials is more than 60%.

24 States/UTs that provided education to less than 5% inmates during 2021.

5 States that did not provide any vocational training to inmates in 2021.

(vii) Reforms Recommended for Judiciary

In August 2023, the Parliamentary Standing Committee on Personnel, Public Grievances, Law and Justice, chaired by BJP MP Sushil Kumar Modi, presented their 133rd. report on "Judicial Process and Reforms," said that adequate representation of backward classes, women and minorities will further strengthen the trust, credibility, and acceptability of the Judiciary among the citizens." Thus, it suffers from "Diversity Deficit".

The panel recommended bringing a law making it mandatory for Supreme Court and high court judges to disclose their assets annually to an appropriate authority.

The report pointed out that out of the 601 high court appointments since 2018, 457 were from the general category, 18 from Scheduled Classes, 9 from Scheduled Tribes. 72 from Other Backward Classes, 32 from minority communities and 91 women.

The committee also flagged vacations of judges and recommended that judges follow a rotational model instead of courts shutting for vacations. It said pendency of cases was piling up due to the long vacations of courts.

It said there is a need to institutionalize the mechanism of regular filing of assets by the judges and putting it in the public domain and the government must bring an appropriate legislation to make it mandatory for judges of the higher judiciary (Supreme Court and High Courts) to furnish their property returns on an annual basis to the appropriate authority.

(viii) Some of the Controversies concerning Judges

1,622 complaints were received in the Centralised Public Grievance Redress and Monitoring System (CPGRAMS) on the functioning of the judiciary, including judicial corruption, during the last five years, the Rajya Sabha was informed on December 2, 2021. These were forwarded to the Chief Justice of India or concerned Chief Justices of the respective high courts as per the established "in-house mechanism. Accountability in higher judiciary is maintained through "in-house mechanism", the Minister said.

1. Justice S Karnan

This is the tale of an infamous high court judge, who has the dubious distinction of being the first sitting high court judge to be imprisoned for six months on a charge of contempt of court. He also became the first high court judge who could not give his farewell speech.

Karnan, with his unprecedented moves, shook the Indian Judiciary to its core. These involved challenging the appointment of a judge alleging that he had fake academic qualifications. He accused some judges of giving decisions which reflected upon them being corrupt, not independent and impartial. He accused the Chief Justice of Madras High Court for approaching the Supreme Court in retaliation for an order which was passed by Justice C.S. Karnan. He even accused the Chief Justice Of Madras of caste-based discrimination against him. Karnan went on to accuse some judges of having illicit relations amongst themselves.

Combining all these issues, the Supreme Court constituted seniormost seven-judge bench to adjudge a case on contempt of court against Justice C.S. Karnan.

The seven-judge bench held that he was guilty of hurling unpalatable accusations on Chief Justices of various High Courts, Justices of Supreme Court and the Madras High Court, which were all held to be false. The judge, shielding himself with his Dalit card, made a completely unacceptable public statement and dishonored the decorum of the court. His actions were a disrespect towards the Indian judiciary. Therefore, it was held that this sitting judge of the Calcutta High Court was guilty of contempt of court and the Indian judiciary, and was sentenced to six years imprisonment. He retired on 12 June and subsequently after a week of his retirement, was arrested by the Kolkata Police on 21 June 2017.

2. Former CJI Shri Ranjan Gogoi

A Supreme Court staffer, who worked as a junior court assistant, had alleged that she had been sexually harassed by then CJI Ranjan Gogoi. In her representation to the Supreme Court judges, she sought an inquiry against Justice Gogoi.

The suo motu case began in April 2019 after the publication of details of the complaint filed by a Supreme Court staffer against Justice Ranjan Gogoi by four news outlets. But the matter relates to an alleged incident that took place in October 2018.

After the allegations were published, the Supreme Court took a suo motu cognizance of the matter and listed the case in an open court on a non-working day for the court. Justice Gogoi headed the bench that took strong exception to the reports. He also denied the allegations levelled by the woman.

After she filed an affidavit on 19 April detailing the alleged harassment, the Supreme Court set up an "in-house committee" with three judges, including two women, to look into the allegations.

Former Chief Justice of India Ranjan Gogoi could have been a victim of a conspiracy to target him for taking a tough stand on judicial and administrative side during his tenure as the Supreme Court head. A three-judge bench of the Supreme Court said this as it closed the suo motu proceeding in the case of sexual harassment charge levelled by a staffer against Justice Ranjan Gogoi.

Supreme Court lawyer Indira Jaising called the ruling a "scandal" on Twitter and demanded the court release the report.

3. Attempt to impeach CJI Dipak Misra by Opposition in April 2018

The case was moved by the Congress and six opposition parties through a notice for removal of the CJI on five counts of "misbehaviour" and "misusing" authority. The five charges levelled include conspiracy to pay illegal gratification in the Prasad Education Trust case; denial of permission to proceed against a retired high court judge in the same matter; a piece of land which the CJI acquired as an advocate by giving a false affidavit.

Listing five allegations of "mis-behavior" a Congress leader Kapil Sibal said the notice for impeachment of the CJI has been moved with a heavy heart. "As representatives of the people, we are entitled to hold the Chief Justice accountable, just as we are accountable to the people. The majesty of the law is more important than the majesty of any office," Sibal said.

Rajya Sabha chairman Venkaiah Naidu, in June 2018 rejected the petition by observing: I have applied my mind to all five charges made out in impeachment motion and examined all annexed documents. All facts as stated in motion don't make out a case which can lead any reasonable mind to conclude that CJI on these facts can be ever held guilty of misbehavior.

4. **Mr S N Shukla** - A three-judge in-house committee found substance in the allegations against the Allahabad High Court judge, in the medical admissions scam, and has recommended his removal to Chief Justice of India Dipak Misra.

   On the committee's recommendation, the Chief Justice advised Justice Shukla to either resign or take voluntary retirement – an option the Allahabad HC judge refused to take. Left with no other option, the CJI advised the Chief Justice of Allahabad HC to withdraw work from Shukla. This cleared the way for the CBI to register a case against Justice Shukla in connection with the scam that rocked the judiciary.

   Justice Shukla, while heading a division bench in the High Court, allegedly defied categorical restraint orders passed by a CJI-led bench in 2017 to permit private colleges to admit students for the 2017-18 academic year.

   The inquiry committee said Justice Shukla had "disgraced the values of judicial life, acted in a manner unbecoming of a judge," lowered the "majesty, dignity and credibility of his office" and acted in breach of his oath of office.

After inquiring into the allegations of favours granted by Justice Shukla to private medical colleges through judicial orders, the committee headed by Justice Banerjee gave a scathing report against the Allahabad HC judge. The report states that "the committee concluded there is sufficient substance in the allegations" against Shukla and aberrations on his part were sufficient to warrant a removal.

This alleged aberration by the HC judge led to a CBI probe and the subsequent arrest of former Orissa HC Judge Justice IM Quddusi.

5. **Former High Court Judge Ishrat Masroor Quddusi**

He is a Retired Odisha High Court Judge. Earlier he was judge in the Allahabad High Court and Chhattisgarh High Court. He was arrested by the CBI on charges of attempting to help an Uttar Pradesh based Prasad Education Trust, educational trust barred from admitting students by the Government and Medical council of India.

*** ***Bar & Bench***

6. **Justice AK Ganguly**

While releasing a book on corruption in 2011, Supreme Court judge Justice Ganguly said:

"I am happy that Prof. Raj Kumar has also talked about corruption in the judiciary. He has referred to recent cases of impeachment. Both the learned Judges referred to; I cannot defend them. I feel sorry for them. If the judges of the high court today are accused of this kind of things, then what will happen to elimination of corruption? Even then I appreciate the candor and the courage with which Prof. Raj Kumar has attempted this book. This is a very valiant effort."

7. Justice J S Verma

"I cannot say that there has not been a single corrupt judge even in the Supreme Court. You have that in public knowledge," Justice JS Verma, who was CJI from March 1997 to January 1998, told CNN-IBN. He agreed that the rot ran deep in the judicial system.

Justice Verma also revealed that his successor, CJI MM Punchhi, was sworn in despite his reservations because the then Prime Minister IK Gujral did not order an inquiry into the allegations which he had forwarded to him, requesting a probe. He said,

"When I joined the bar 40 years back, no one talked about corruption even in the district judges. Now when people talk about corruption even in the apex court, I feel like it is a slap on my face."

8. Justice V R Krishna Iyer

Justice Iyer was among those who demanded former CJI KG Balakrishnan's resignation as the Chairperson of the National Human Rights Commission following allegations of corruption. Two former judges of the Kerala high court, Justice PK Shamsuddin and Justice K Sukumaran, also made serious allegations against Justice Balakrishnan.

Justice Krishna Iyer wrote an open letter to then Congress General Secretary Rahul Gandhi in 2011, saying:

"The judicature, a sacred instrument with great powers to punish corruption, is itself corrupt. Not a single corrupt judge has been caught or punished."

In 2013, he wrote to then President Pranab Mukherjee, seeking a probe and action against some senior Supreme Court judges who, he said, are "suspect of moral deviance". He told the President that the scourge of bribery tainting politics had not polluted the judiciary for long, but that was "becoming a matter of the past".

9. Justice MN Venkatachaliah

"There are just 25 judges in the Supreme Court in a country with a population of a billion-plus. And even there, some of them turn out corrupt," former CJI Venkatachaliah told Anuradha Raman of Outlook in 2011. "The most heinous crime is the CJI incurring criticism, or giving room for doubts that his hands are dirty."

10. Justice J Chelameswar

In an interview to the *Economic Times*, Justice Chelameswar said:

"Corruption does exist. Why was Quddusi arrested? A former judge of a high court in this country was arrested…If this institution is discredited, democracy is not safe. All my effort was to preserve the institution, strengthen it by creating a greater degree of credibility which can only come through transparent functioning. That was my whole effort….Judges will be politically influenced. To say that judges are not touched by politics, I think is not an honest statement. And mind you, I am not talking of party politics. The question is how dispassionately can judges handle the current political events….No direct pressure, but there are subtle ways of putting the pressure (in answer to the question whether there is more political pressure now)."

At a press conference held with Justices **Ranjan Gogoi, Madan B Lokur** and **Kurian Joseph** on January 12, 2018, Chelameswar J said,

"Twenty years later some wise men shouldn't say judges sold their souls."

11. Justice Markandey Katju

During his term as Chairman of the Press Council of India, Justice Katju alleged corruption in the Supreme Court. He said three former Chief Justices of India had compromised in giving an extension to an additional judge of the Madras High Court at the insistence of the then UPA government at the Centre, under pressure from one of its allies, the DMK.

"By rejecting *Mr. Shanti Bhushan's petition seeking registration of an FIR against Justice C.K.Prasad for gross corruption, the Indian Supreme Court has once again sought to bury corruption by one of its own members under the carpet, forgetting that however much one may seek to conceal it, the bulge will show.*

I accuse the Indian judiciary of repeatedly burying corruption by its own members under the carpet. I accuse it of being hypocritical by speaking against corruption by politicians and bureaucrats, but deliberately protecting its own corrupt brethren."

12. Justice Michael Saldanha

Justice Saldanha of the Karnataka High Court has been quoted as saying that 33% of the judiciary is corrupt.

13. Justice SP Bharucha

In a speech in 2001, Justice Bharucha, the then CJI, lamented that 20% of the judges in India were corrupt. He made this speech during the Law Day function on November 26, 2001 on the lawns of the Supreme Court. In his speech, he refers to what he said in public before assuming office as the CJI.

A petition seeking to initiate contempt proceedings against the former CJI for making this speech was dismissed by the Rajasthan High Court later.

14. Justice ES Venkataramiah – 19th. CJI {June 1989 – December 1989}

He told journalist Kuldip Nayar on the eve of his retirement:

"The judiciary in India has deteriorated in its standards because such judges are appointed as are willing to be 'influenced by lavish parties and whisky bottles.'"

He reminded the sitting judges of former Union Minister of Law and Justice P Shiv Shankar's pungent statement:

"Anti-social elements, that is FERA violators, bride burners and a whole horde of reactionaries, found their haven in the Supreme Court."

Contempt proceedings were sought to be initiated in 1990 against Justice Venkataramiah before the Bombay High Court. The complainant, one Vishwanath, son of Gopal Palshikar, claimed that the judge had scandalised the Court by this statement, which was attributed to him in the interview:

"In every high court, there were at least four to five judges who were practically out every evening, wining and dining either at a lawyer's house or a foreign embassy and that the estimate of the number of such judges was

around 90 and that practically in all the 22 high courts in the country, close relations of the judges were thriving."

Justice Venkataramiah favoured transferring such judges to other high courts.

He reiterated that close relatives of judges should be debarred from practicing in the same high courts. He expressed himself strongly against sons, sons-in-law and brothers of judges appearing in the courts where the latter are on the bench. He said that most judges' relatives are practicing in the High Courts of Allahabad, Chandigarh, Delhi and Patna.

In an interview, former CJI Venkataramiah said that in practically all (then) 22 high courts in the country, close relatives of judges were thriving. There were allegations that certain judgments have been influenced through them even though they have not been directly engaged as lawyers in such cases, he said.

"It is hard to disregard the reports that every brother, son or son-in-law of a judge, whatever his merit or lack of it as a lawyer, can be sure of earning an income of more than Rs 10,000 a month," he said in that interview.

Nayar said in the preface to that interview:

"Sad and somber, Chief Justice Venkataramiah said that he had vainly tried to bring to the notice of Judges the Law Commission Report which has cited examples to

prove how Judges compromise their position and prefer to be seen in the precincts of government houses and elsewhere."

The government pleader, Badar, citing this portion of the interview, told the Court that the entire judgment had to be judged and appreciated in light of the fact that the former CJI's motive was to improve the judiciary. According to Badar, Nayar did not fail to notice that the former CJI felt hurt while expressing his feelings.

A similar petition was filed in the Supreme Court by then Chairman of the Jammu and Kashmir Legal Aid Committee, Bhim Singh. He sought a direction from the Supreme Court to disclose the names of 90 judges of the different high courts as mentioned by the former CJI. The petition was dismissed by the Supreme Court on February 1, 1990.

The petitioner before the Bombay High Court contended that had the former CJI disclosed the names of 90 judges, it would have been a different matter. But that not having been done, every judge of the High Court became a suspect.

The Bench, however, disagreed, and reminded him of a Chinese proverb *"As long as you are up-right, do not care if your shadow is crooked."* It reasoned that the former CJI's statement referred only to such judges who were indulging in 'wining and dining' at lawyers' houses or foreign embassies or whose sons, sons-in-law, and brothers were minting money by abusing their position.

Without getting the Advocate General's consent, the petitioner sought *suo motu* action by the Court in the matter, in view of the grave nature of the contempt. Despite the Court asking the petitioner to seek the AG's consent, he refused to do so, and requested the Court to take *suo motu* action on the basis of the facts he brought to its notice.

The interview was published in several newspapers including *Lokmat* and *Dainik Rashtradoot* in Nagpur. Both Justice Venkataramaiah and Nayar were made respondents.

On March 2, 1990, Justices MM Qazi and BU Wahane of the Nagpur Bench of the High Court dismissed the petition.

*[***Bar & Bench]*

B. Some Orders by the NFRA on Audit Quality and Independence of Auditors {Sec 134(4) of the Companies Act, 2013

National Financial Reporting Authority has passed 34 Orders as on 21 Aug 2023, of which 28 orders were passed in 2023 itself against the auditors on the professional misconduct or quality of work or their lack of independence and in the process helping their clients. Just a few instances have been extracted from NFRA Order and summarized as under:

1. **Company: Burnpur Cement Ltd.**

Auditor K Pandeya &Co. Engagement Partner (CA Manjeet Kumar Verma)

NFRA Order 29/2023 Aug 21,2023 *{SEBI letter dated 11.03.2022}*

Punishment:

Audit Firm - **Penalty** of Rupees Twenty-Five Lakhs.

Engagement Partner: **Penalty** of Rupees Five Lakhs. Also **debarred** for Five Years from being appointed as an auditor or internal auditor or from undertaking any audit in respect of financial statements or internal audit of the functions and activities of any company or body corporate.

Sec 132(4) of C A, 2013 - Findings

The Auditors failed to meet the relevant requirements of the Standards on Auditing ('SA' hereafter) in respect of several significant areas, reflecting a serious lack of professional competence to perform audit of a Public Interest Entity (PIE). In the identified areas of audit, the Auditors were grossly negligent and failed to apply professional skepticism and due diligence sufficiently and adequately to challenge the management assertions

The Auditors failed in applying sufficient appropriate audit procedure and professional skepticism in identifying and reporting of material misstatements in the financial statements.

The Auditors were grossly negligent in the conduct of the audit, which led to erroneous reporting and portraying a misleading picture of the company to the investors and stakeholders

2. **Tanglin Developments Ltd. Auditors (M/s Sundaresha & Associates, CA C. Ramesh, and CA Chaitanya G. Deshpande**

   NFRA Order 28/2023 Aug 21,2023 *{SEBI letter dated 1April 2022}*

Punishment

Audit Firm - **Penalty** of Rupees One Crore + total **debar** for four years concurrently .

Engagement Partner: **Penalty** of Rupees Five Lakhs. Also **debarred** for Five Years from to run concurrently with earlier two orders as an auditor or internal auditor or from undertaking any audit in respect of financial statements or internal audit of the functions and activities of any company or body corporate.

Sec 132(4) of C A, 2013 - Findings

Auditors for the FY 2019-20 failed to meet requirements of the 'SA', provisions of the Companies Act 2013; and demonstrated serious lapse and absence of due diligence.

They failed to exercise professional judgement where borrowings of Rs 2027.46 crores, was used in fraudulent diversion of funds to MACE; Rs 2073.23 crores through its Group entities, given without any business rationale or agreement and the money ultimately moved to promoters' entity MACEL.

The Auditors failed to exercise professional judgement of fraudulent diversion of funds in the name of land advances - (a) Rs 275 crores to mother of the Chairman of Holding company and (b) Rs 100 crores to a Director of a subsidiary, which was provided for write off in the same year. The Auditors failed to report that Internal Financial Control over Financial Reporting was completely absent despite large scale evergreening of loans through structured circulation of funds and use of pre-signed blank cheques for diversion and circulation of funds.

They failed to evaluate their potential conflict of interest and failed to maintain their independence.

They had audit and non-audit relationships with a large number of Coffee Day Group companies and the promoters' family members They also made an attempt to mislead NFRA by adding more documents to as well as altering the documents in their audit file which amounted to tampering with the Audit File.

3. Bartonic India Ltd. Auditor Mis T. Raghavendra & Associates. CAT. Raghavendra

NFRA Order 27/2023 Aug 3,2023 *{MCA Information}*

Punishment:

Penalty - Rupees Five Lakhs on CAT. Raghavendra;

Debarment of CA T Raghavendra for **ten years** from being appointed as an auditor or internal auditor or from undertaking any audit in respect of financial statements or internal audit of the functions and activities of any company or body corporate

Sec 132(4) of C A, 2013 - Findings {1.10.2013 to 31.3.2015}

Professional misconduct by misusing the Emphasis of Matter for covering up misstatements in the financial statements and including under the "Emphasis of Matter" the matters that warranted consideration for modifying his audit opinion.

These matters included non-provision of interest on loans, doubtful capital advances etc.

Various other lapses in the Statutory Audit such as not reporting the failure of the Company to report under the Companies Act, 1956, and wrong recognition of deferred tax assets etc.

4. Coffee Day Global Ltd. Auditor M/s ASRMP & CO. CA A S Sundaresha and CA Madhusudan

NFRA Order 24/2023 28.7.2023 {SEBI April 2022}

Punishment:

Penalty - Rupees Two Crore on ASRMP & CO.

Debarment of Firm for four years from being appointed as an auditor or internal auditor or from undertaking any audit in respect of financial statements or internal audit of the functions and activities of any company or body corporate

Penalty: Ten Lakh on CA A S Sundaresha . In addition, he is Debarred for ten years from being appointed as an auditor or internal auditor or from undertaking any audit in respect of financial statements or internal audit of the functions and activities of any company or body corporate

Penalty: Five Lakh on CA Madhusudan UA . In addition, he is Debarred for five years from being appointed as an auditor or internal auditor or from undertaking any audit in respect of financial statements or internal audit of the functions and activities of any company or body corporate

Sec 132(4) of C A, 2013 - Findings {1.10.2013 to 31.3.2015}

Auditors for the FY 2019-20 failed to meet requirements of the 'SA', provisions of the Companies Act 2013; and demonstrated serious lapse and absence of due diligence.

They failed to evaluate their potential conflict of interest and maintain their independence from CDGL by having audit and non-audit relationships with a large number of Coffee Day Group Companies and the promoter's family and thus violated the Code of Ethics issued by the ICAI as the fee received from the Group exceeded 40% of their total fees

They also attempted to mislead NFRA by adding and altering documents in their audit file which amounted to tampering with audit file.

Auditors failed to exercise professional skepticism and judgement where there was-

(a) Fraudulent diversion of funds.

(b) Evergreening of loans.

(c) Roundtripping of CDGL's own funds.

(d) Misstatement of Sale price.

(e) Failure to obtain appropriate audit evidence.

(f) Misstatements.

5. **Mann Industries (India) Limited. Auditor M/s M H Dalal & Associates. And CA Devang Dalal**

NFRA Order 021/2023 28.6.2023 {SEBI 23.6.2022}

Punishment:

Penalty - Rupees Fifty lakh on M H Dalal & CO.

Penalty: Ten Lakh on CA Devang Dalal. In addition, he is Debarred for five years from being appointed as an auditor or internal auditor or from undertaking any audit in respect of financial statements or internal audit of the functions and activities of any company or body corporate

Sec 132(4) of C A, 2013 - Findings {1.10.2013 to 31.3.2015}

1. Financial Statements did not contain disclosures under Ind24 and the Act.
2. Disclosure on Credit Risk Profile of Trae Receivables were erroneous and bon compliance with AS 107
3. Impairment losses were not recognized . Otherwise PBT would have turned into loss.\
4. Qualified Opinion on Consolidated Financials was erroneous.
5. Appropriate and sufficient Audit Evidence were missing for Trade Recivables, Impairments, Valuation of Subsidiary.
6. Audit Report on Internal Control over Financial Reporting was false.
7. Auditors collected only reams of photocopies of documents reflecting on dismal quality of work.

8. **CA Lavitha Shetty {Lavitha & Associates} - NF-23/14/2023 dated 25.04.2023**

Mysore Amalgamated Coffee Estates Limited, ('MACEL}

Punishment:

(a) Imposition of a monetary penalty of Rs Ten Lakhs;

(b) Debarment for a period of Ten years from being appointed as an auditor or internal auditor or from undertaking any audit in respect of financial statements or internal audit of the functions and activities of any company or body corporate.

The first five years out of the ten years debarment ordered, would run concurrently with the period of debarment ordered vide NFRA order dated 13.04.2023 in the case of CA Lavitha Shetty

Sec 132(4) of C A, 2013 - Major Findings {1.10.2013 to 31.3.2015}

(a) Failure to meet the relevant requirements of the Standards on Auditing in a number of significant aspects and demonstrated a serious lack of competence.

(b) The EP failed to exercise professional judgement & scepticism during audit of fraudulent borrowings of Rs. 4,438.37 crore from Banks & Related Parties and its use for fraudulent diversion of Rs. 4,176.67 crore to personal accounts of promoters, their relatives, entities controlled by them and other Related Parties.

(c) The EP failed to exercise professional scepticism during audit of Related Party Transactions involving an Order in the matter of MACEL (A Coffee Day Group case) for FY 2019-20 Page 1 of 35 accounting fraud orchestrated by issue of cheques at the end of FY 2018-19 without adequate bank balance or bank credit limit, with the ulterior motive to conceal huge amount of Related Party balances. These cheques were cleared in the subsequent year i.e., FY 2019-20 by evergreening of loans through structured circular transactions of funds among Coffee Day Group Companies.

(d) The EP failed to exercise professional scepticism during the audit of inappropriate recognition of finance cost of Rs 40.47 crores for the borrowings that were not used for any business purpose of MACEL. The EP failed to perform sufficient and appropriate audit procedure during audit of Cash Flow Statement, which had material misstatement of Rs 1,938.87 crores. The EP failed to evaluate corporate guarantees issued by MACEL and creation of charges on its assets to facilitate borrowings of Rs 130 crores taken by the wife of V.G. Siddhartha (chairman of CDEL, the listed company of the coffee Day group) and one other related party.

(e) The EP did not report that Internal Financial Control over Financial Reporting was absent, despite pre-signed blank cheques being used by V.G. Siddhartha ('VGS' hereafter), who was neither a shareholder nor a director nor an employee of MACEL, for diversion of funds to other group entities.

6. **Other notable NFRA's orders** were against about a dozen branch auditors of DHFL; three auditors of IL&FS Financial Services Ltd., Few more auditors of SRS Limited; Few more auditors of Coffee Day Global Limited.

7. **Partners of Price Waterhouse**

Within days of Sebi passing order against Price Waterhouse network entities in the Satyam scam, ICAI, in January, 2012 awarded maximum punishment to individual auditors {Engaging Partners} involved but it has no powers to initiate disciplinary action against the CA firm.

Sebi imposed a two-year ban on Price Waterhouse network entities from issuing audit certificates to any listed company in India

ICAI cancelled the membership of six chartered accountants with respect to the accounting fraud at Satyam Computer Services and monetary punishment.

8. Deloitte Haskins & Sells and BSR& Associates - affiliate of KPMG

The Supreme Court of India on May 3, 2023 has allowed the Serious Fraud Investigation Office (SFIO) to resume criminal proceedings against former auditors of IL&FS Financial Services, Deloitte Haskins and Sells LLP, and BSR & Associates LLP, for their alleged role in financial irregularities at the firm . The Bombay High Court had earlier quashed the Ministry of Corporate Affairs (MCA) proceedings to prosecute the auditors involved in the case.

The firms are accused of "deliberately" failing to report fraudulent activity, and the Serious Fraud Investigation Office (SFIO) said that both "miserably failed to fulfill the duty entrusted to them," and also colluded with IFIN to perpetrate the malfeasance.

"Simply put, the fraud committed at IFIN is nothing short of organized crime, actively aided and abetted by the statutory auditors," the ministry filing said.

The investigation in IFIN showed that the organization loaned money to companies that didn't repay the debt, and then instead of calling those bad loans, IFIN loaned money to the defaulters' group companies that they used to repay earlier loans.

"The auditors, despite being aware of this modus operandi of fraudulently funding principal and interest to the defaulting borrowers, had not reported the same in the audit report," the government alleged.

C. Few Medical Scams

1. Medical Services Fraud

The Enforcement Directorate (ED) has filed a prosecution complaint (chargesheet) in the Rs 211 crore Insurance Medical Services (IMS) fraud under the Prevention of Money Laundering Act (PMLA) in August 2023.

Charges have been filed against the then IMS director Dr Devika Rani and 15 other accused, including representatives of several drug firms and pharma company owners.

ED had already attached properties worth Rs 144 crore. The accused had allegedly resorted to financial irregularities in the supply of medicines and other surgical kits to dispensaries and Employee's State Insurance (ESI) hospital across Telengana. ..

ED's PMLA case is based on eight FIRs registered by the Anti-Corruption Bureau (ACB) against the accused for violations in the tender process, misappropriation of public funds and causing loss to the state exchequer. Dr Devika Rani and others are alleged to have conspired with medicine and medical equipment suppliers and issued purchase orders in violation of norms.

The chargesheet alleges that Dr Rani, in collusion with other IMS staff, violated all norms with supplier K Srihari Babu and also benami firms set up by the IMS chief and P Rajeshwar Reddy.

The prices of medical items were inflated, and indents and stock registers were fabricated. Another key accused Dr K Padma, who was joint director IMS, was found to be siphoning off medicines and supplies in the name of medical camps.

Dr Rani and pharmacist Nagalaxmi allegedly conspired with PMJ Jewelers and purchased jewelry worth around Rs.6.3 crore without bills using the scam money. The accused also invested in real estate. The scam mostly took place between 2015-16 and 2018-19. Several shell firms were floated to layer the money. The ED had attached villas, open plots, commercial shops and agricultural land parcels in Hyderabad, Bengaluru, and Noida.

2. Corona Virus Vaccine Scam

Thousands of people have fallen prey to an elaborate wide-ranging scam selling fake coronavirus vaccines, with doctors and medical workers among those arrested for their involvement.

At least 12 fake vaccination drives were held, where reportedly they were using saline water and injecting it. An estimated 2,500 people were given fake shots and the organizers charged their victims fees for the shots, earning up to $28,000 in total, said Vishal Thakur, a senior official of the Mumbai police department.

He also said, doctors were arrested. They were using a hospital which was producing the fake certificates, vials, syringes.

In July 2021, 14 people were arrested on suspicion of cheating, attempts at culpable homicide, criminal conspiracy, and other charges.

The fake vaccination drives took place between late May and early June 2021, when authorities began investigating after some of the scam victims, suspicious of the vaccination certificates they received, reported it to police.

As police began investigating, others took legal action of their own. Siddharth Chandrashekhar, a lawyer in Mumbai, filed a public interest lawsuit on June 24 – by which point the public prosecutor had already confirmed more than 2,000 victims of the scams. The allegations are "really shocking," said the Bombay High Court in the filing, urging state and local authorities to take action "so that innocent individuals are not duped in future."

3. Civic Body Bag Scam

A private company Vedanta Innotech which is under scanner had allegedly supplied body bags for deceased patients to the BMC at Rs 6,719 a piece, which was over three times (Rs 1,500 per piece) of what it had charged other private hospitals or government authorities during the same period, an earlier ED inquiry has reportedly found. EOW's case was registered based on the July 18 complaint of former BJP MP Kirit Somaiya, alleging irregularities in expenditure during the pandemic.

The ED has registered a case under the Prevention of Money Laundering Act (PMLA) against ex-mayor and Shiv Sena (UBT) leader Kishori Pednekar, a former additional municipal commissioner (projects) and a former deputy municipal commissioner (purchase/CPD), private contractor Vedanta Innotech, and unknown other government servants in the alleged scam involving the purchase of body bags at inflated rates during the Covid pandemic in September 2023.

The money involved in the alleged fraud has been mentioned as Rs 49.63 lakh. The ED may soon summon the accused civic officials and others for questioning.

An agency source confirmed the development saying the ED has recently registered an Enforcement Case Information Report (ECIR) in the body bag scam case. This is the second money laundering case registered by the ED in connection with the irregularities in the functioning of BMC during pandemic.

Earlier, it registered a PMLA case in the Covid Jumbo Centre scam, and in July 2023, it arrested Shiv Sena (UBT) leader Sanjay Raut's close aide and a civic doctor, in connection with the alleged multi-crore scam.

ED's current case is based on the FIR registered by Mumbai Police's Economic Offences Wing on August 4 against Pednekar, civic officials, and others. The case was filed to probe the alleged irregularities in purchasing body bags for deceased Covid patients.

Pednekar and other senior civic officials were booked under Sections 409 (criminal breach of trust by a public servant or by a banker, merchant, or agent), 420 (cheating), and 120B (criminal conspiracy) of IPC. The ED will probe the money laundering aspect of the alleged scam, while the EOW is looking into the criminal aspect of the scam, said an officer.

4. Rs 200-cr SC, ST scholarship scam

The ED in September 2023 arrested four people, including a former official of the Himachal Pradesh higher education directorate, under provisions of the Prevention of Money Laundering Act (PMLA) in a case linked to the alleged Rs 200-crore scam in grant of scholarships to SC, ST and OBC students of the state.

Rajdeep Josan and Krishan Kumar, partners at ASAMS education group, Hitesh Gandhi, vice chairman of KC group of institutions (located in Pandoga), and Arvind

Rajta, a former official of the Himachal Pradesh Directorate of Higher Education's scholarship branch, were taken into custody.

Josan and Kumar through ASAMS education group and skill development society claimed scholarship under the post-matric scheme for Scheduled Castes (SC), Scheduled Tribes (ST) and Other Backward Classes (OBC) students by presenting "fabricated" documents, it alleged.

Similarly, the ED said, the KC group of institutions headed by Gandhi made "bogus" claims for scholarship, which were verified by Rajta. Gandhi transferred the scholarship disbursed in the bank account of students to the bank accounts of KC group of institutions, the ED said.

The ED's case under provisions of the PMLA is based on an FIR of the CBI in which it was alleged that officials of Himachal Pradesh education department, private institutions and banks were involved in large-scale misappropriation of disbursement of scholarship funds of more than Rs 200 crore.

The ED had carried out raids on August 29 in the case at 24 locations in Himachal Pradesh, Haryana, Punjab and Delhi. It had seized unaccounted cash of Rs 75 lakh and froze Rs 2.55 crore lying in bank accounts during these raids, the agency said.

5. The Minority Scholarship Scam Unearthed in 21 States {August 2023} *{News 18}*

Several states have witnessed irregularities in the implementation of the Centre's Pre-Matric Scholarship, Post-Matric Scholarship, and Merit cum-Means schemes for students of six minority communities—Muslims, Christians, Sikhs, Jains, Buddhists, and Parsis. After receiving initial complaints about embezzlement of funds, the government asked the National Council of Applied Economic Research (NCAER) to carry out a third-party evaluation.

A total of 1,572 institutes were identified for evaluation based on red flags generated on the National Scholarship Portal (NSP). Of these, 830 institutes from 21 states were found to be either non-operational, fake, or partially fake, it is said.

"Fake" means there is possible irregularity as the students in the list of beneficiaries provided by the ministry turn out to be non-beneficiaries as they either do not belong to the said school, or are from a non-operational school, or they never applied for the scholarship.

It appears that the verifications were compromised at the level of the institute nodal officer (INO) and district nodal officer (DNO) and the scholarship was syphoned off by them in collusion and connivance with the institutes, banks, and cybercafe owners, said sources.

The most common irregularities found at the school/ institution level are:

- Some institutions with enlisted beneficiaries were found to be completely non-operational, but are availing the benefits of the scheme.
- The enlisted beneficiaries were found 'fake' in some operational schools.
- There are some fake schools, under which scholarships are being transferred to minority students, who either do not exist or belong to other institutions, but never benefit from the scheme.
- In Kanker, Chhattisgarh, one specific government school is functional only for primary classes, i.e., for classes I to V for Scheduled Tribe girl students only and there are no minority students. However, it has been found that a significant number of fake students enrolled in the said school are availing of the Post-Matric Scholarship.
- Bihar: It has been reported that the registered Institute Nodal Officer (INO) in the Ministry of Minority Affairs list are cybercafe owners, who probably made fake applications for coaching Centre students. Most INOs seek help from cybercafes, due to a lack of computer literacy and skills to operate one.
- Many schools from Madhya Pradesh reported that they are not recognised for the 8th class and above but

still, a large number of applications have been filled for these classes. Schools have reported misuse of school user IDs and passwords.

- Many schools from states like West Bengal have most applicants listed as fake, are either from primary or pre-primary classes, or have no minority students studying in the schools.
- In states like Gujarat, Meghalaya, Uttarakhand, Punjab, and Maharashtra, when schools get upgraded from middle level to secondary or higher secondary level, they are allotted multiple Unified District Information System (UDISE) codes for different levels. But on the NSP portal, usually, the first allotted code is displayed. This causes recognition discrepancies.
- Delay in updating the school status on the UDISE portal.
- One institute has 4 colleges with separate UDISE codes, but students from these colleges unknowingly filled out applications from a single code.
- In regions like Jammu and Kashmir, 'renewal candidates' applied as fresh candidates, because of the perception that fresh candidates get accepted easily.
- In states like Telangana, Andhra Pradesh, and Bihar, schools have not disabled their old UDISE codes and

are using both old and new ones to fill out applications.

- Schools have different UDISE codes for different levels of education provided by them.
- DNOs are not performing due diligence during the verification of applications, maybe due to staff shortage. However, DNOs are aware of fake INOs as the KYC process for each INO is being done by the DNO only.

D. Some Scandals of Indian Army

(i) Frozen Meat Scam

An Army Service Corps top officer, Lt. Gen. S.K. Dahiya, was indicted in a case involving irregularities in the procurement of frozen meat for troops posted in Ladakh and discrepancies in procurement of dry rations in early 2007.

(ii) Ration Supplies Scam

The case of a scam in ration supplies to army personnel in high altitude areas broke out in 2007 and then Army Service Corps chief Lt. Gen. S.K. Sahni was found guilty and dismissed from service. Sahni had retired from service when he was court martialled and cashiered from service.

(iii) Sukna Land Scandal

A 70-acre land adjacent to Sukna military station in Siliguri, West Bengal, was converted into an educational institution by handing it over to a private trust. Then army chief Gen. Deepak Kapoor's military secretary Lt. Gen. Avadesh Prakash and then 33 Corps commander Lt. Gen. P.K. Rath were court martialed in the case and punished for their involvement.

Chapter VII

Corporate Failures

i. Corporate - Failure, Collapse and Scandal

The term corporate failure entails discontinuation of company's operations leading to inability to reap sufficient profit or revenue to pay the business expenses. It may happen due to a variety of factors such as poor management, incompetence, and bad marketing strategies etc.

A corporate collapse typically involves the insolvency or bankruptcy.

A corporate scandal involves alleged or actual unethical behavior by people acting within or on behalf of a corporation.

Fraud does not always result in corporate failure, nor do corporate failures occur only as a result of fraud. However, in some of the biggest corporate failures across the globe, fraud was involved.

ii. Warning symptoms of Corporate Failure

Low profitability and consequent fall in profitability ratios. Profitability ratios reflect the efficiency of the company to generate profit and value for shareholders.

High Gearing - the company has large proportion of debt versus equity.

Low Liquidity - the ease with which an asset can be converted into ready cash without affecting its market price,

iii. Common tendencies in most corporate failures

(a) Companies in Overexpansion Drive

(b) Failure to adapt to changing market environments despite realising the need for change. Such managements were unable to change the previously well-established business model that had made them so successful.

(c) Companies turning into bad ones to achieve ambitious goals by increasingly engaging in unethical business practices.

iv. Causes of Corporate Failure

Economic Distress: The decline in the economy - global or domestic.

Mismanagement: Mismanagement means a pattern of incompetent management actions which are wrongful, negligent or arbitrary and capricious and which adversely affect the efficient accomplishment of desired results.

Financial mismanagement: is management that deliberately or not, is handled in a way that can be characterized as "wrong, bad, reckless, inefficient or incompetent" that go to reflect negatively upon the financial standing. For example, Financial mismanagement may arise out of wrong distribution of responsibility neglecting responsibility, loose controls etc.

Accounting scandals: are business scandals which arise from intentional manipulation of financial statements with the disclosure of financial misdeeds by trusted executives of corporations or governments. Such misdeeds typically involve complex methods for misusing or misdirecting funds, overstating revenues, understating expenses, overstating the value of corporate assets, or underreporting the existence of liabilities. It involves an employee, account, or corporation itself and is misleading to investors and shareholders.

Management Failure: is associated with a host of factors, some external and others internal to the organization. Management failure can occur when it fails to manage its affairs through adoption of sound direction, monitoring and control mechanisms directed at attainment of the laid-down objectives and Vision.

Technological Causes: If an industry fails to improve constantly its technological capabilities to satisfy its customers; improve working efficiency and be cost effective; at least match the competition sooner or later it may cause its failure.

Working Capital Problems: Insufficiency of funds in an organization hurting its' capacity to run the day-to-day operations effectively are an indication of liquidity issues.

Fraudulent Management: Often personal greed influences managers to use unfair means such as falsification in the financial statements and accounting reports of the company which ultimately causes corporates to fail.

Corporate governance failures

Corporate governance was also touted in many instances as the main reason for corporate failures. Attempts at curbing these failures in the form of more stringent legislation and regulation does not appear to have had the desired impact.

Following are some of the governance issues contributing to corporate failure:

1. Incompetent or ineffective boards and board committees.
2. Non-independent board and audit committee members. Example where a CEO fulfilled multiple roles in various committees
3. Inadequate governance structures. Example, lack of board committees or committees consisting of a single member
4. Inappropriately qualified members. Example, family members holding board positions or audit committee members not having appropriate accounting and

financial qualifications or experience to analyze key business transactions

5. Ignorance by auditors, regulators, analysts etc., of the financial results and red flags

6. Management, who deliberately undermines the role of the various governance structures through the circumventing of internal financial controls.

7. Implementing the regulatory and best practice guidelines for good corporate governance is considered as a costly and cumbersome exercise for most companies.

8. The implementation of "good" governance structures has become only a checklist exercise to ensure compliance.

9. Some members of governance structures are not aware of the onerous positions that they hold and the full extent of the responsibility and accountability ascribed to them.

10. Tendency of the leaders of organizations suffering corporate failures, placing major responsibility at the door of each stakeholder, banking institution, analyst and the public that missed the red flags.

11. The committing of fraud is intended to overstate profits to benefit management through bonuses, stock options etc., based on profitability.

12. CEOs and CFOs commit accounting fraud to conceal poor financial performance, preserve their personal status and control and to maintain their personal income through performance-based bonuses.

13. Most important cause for the shortcomings is poor ethics, ethos and culture of persons managing the affairs of companies.

Considering the wide variety of causes, the challenge of detecting and deterring fraud is not easy due to the numerous players. Possible causes are attributed in general to:

(a) Non-independence of auditors

(b) Compromised quality of audit work due to reduced fees

(c) Deliberate actions and misrepresentations by management to delay or divert auditors' attention from problematic areas

(d) Misconception of the role of an auditor and to what extent they are able to identify fraud through their audit procedures

(e) Poor or lack of corporate governance despite legislation and regulation, including non-independent and inadequately qualified board or committee members, lack of debate of business issues at board level and a deliberate disregard of legislation by management

(f) Unrealistic expectations of stakeholders for performance and growth or the fear of management to look like a failure and thereby camouflaging the true financial status of the company

The mind-sets of management and those tasked with governance have not fully changed. Some members of governance structures are not aware of the onerous positions that they hold and the full extent of the responsibility and accountability ascribed to them

v. Attributes of Management Failure:

(i) Mismanagement

- Relaxed control over the persons who manage the Company's business.
- The control is entrusted to a weak person of poor capabilities and skill.
- When there is lack of strained team work.
- When the leadership lacks foresightedness.
- When the Company has weak or non-robust review systems.
- When the Organisation is plagued with all-round complacency or low motivation. and recognitions and such other causes contribute to management failure.

(ii) Mismanagement may take forms such as-

- Non-discharge of Fiduciary responsibility towards customers, investors, employees, communities, shareholders and others. This happens when one serves own interests using the resources of the Organisation.
- Weak internal controls aids mismanagement.
- Poor Management of Risks in the organisation.
- Faulty/Weak Communication and Reporting-
- Poor Compliance with laws and regulations
- Low productivity and efficiency
- Loss of tangible or intangible value – goodwill, brand value, capital etc.
- Delegation of responsibility without proper accountability.
- Disconnection with the job as to not knowing the information basic to the job.

(iii) Mind-set of Defeatism

This occurs when pessimism about strategy or decisions overtakes the beliefs. As a result, Managers may tend to work against the set goals resulting in decision paralysis.

(iv) Shortfalls in performance measured on all key parameters.

(a) Poor Planning causing the team members not be aware of clear expectations from them with definite time schedules for completion of assigned work.

Realistic Corporate and Operations Budget may not be in place. The situation will inevitably result in lack of timely cash availability for efficient operations.

(d) Erosion of Customer-base due to dissatisfaction.

(e) Lack of support from stakeholders including lenders, vendors, financiers

(f) Erosion of reputation, loss of goodwill, poor credit rating and declined investor perceptions.

(v) Leader Attributes for failures

- Authoritarianism of the leader
- Neglect of Organization Culture, Code of Conduct/Ethics
- Incompetent promoters or leaders or rude obnoxious or annoying person
- Adamant attitude to adapt to changing work or market environment
- Narcissism Mentality of managers

- Over expansion and unrelated diversification of activities

vi. Recapitulation of Causes - Corporate governance failures

The ineffectiveness arises out of factors such as:

Limitation on skills; lack of experience in desired business areas; poor training and knowledge levels of non-executive directors (NEDs);

Complexity

Risk blindness driven by notion that time will on its own fix the problem.

Unhealthy company culture

Technological disruption

Information glass ceiling

vii. Corporate Scandal and the Board

It is often seen that on eruption of a corporate scandal the first question that is asked is, how could the board of directors let this happen? In other words, failure in corporate governance is mostly attributed to the role played by the board members.

The justifications would rest on factors such as-

- Did the directors, however successful and busy they may be, allot reasonable time and commitment to play their envisaged role for the Company?
- Did the directors have the experience, skill and knowledge required to make effective decisions for the Company's complex issues, business environment?
- Was the structure of the Board compact, diverse, cohesive, well informed with transparent information, trusted, experienced, really independent of the Chairman/CEO etc?

viii. Attributes of bad managers who fail the Companies

Poor leaders – Do not assume total responsibility, trust the team players, weak communicators with the team and overall poor managers. They do not take the employees into consideration.

Lack empathy - and thereby fail to understand each team member and their work - related problems.

Non-involvement attitude – Resulting in inability to solve problems or help in overcoming issues.

Over-involvement attitude – Managers who are at the extreme end get themselves over involved themselves with management of issues causing employees to turn unsatisfied or frustrated.

Stumbling Block attitude – Gets involved only at the time of completion of a task and starts making changes to the task which may derail the ultimate product.

Vindictive attitude – towards employees due to jealousy or have overbearing attitude, The quality frustrates employees right through.

Incompetent managers – Such persons cause serious damage to the business.

Chapter VIII

Fraud and Punishments in India

A. Introduction

Corporate frauds have emerged as the biggest risks which companies are exposed to, and are increasingly becoming a big threat. Incidents of frauds are increasingly at an alarming rate in terms of amounts involved and in the process they:

- Destroy the confidence of investors in stock markets
- Results in enormous destruction in wealth of investors
- Damage the reputation of the affected company, its management and board of directors
- Erode ability of affected company to borrow and thus creating financial stress.
- Creates concerns on "going concern" issues (raising doubts in the ability of the company to continue its operation in the near - future)-
- Have a widespread impact because of the huge number of stakeholders involved - customers,

vendors, employees, investors, Regulators, Banks, and lenders.

- Encourage new fraudsters to indulge in innovative frauds

Regulations are being regularly tightened to ensure monitoring, vigilance and disclosure mechanisms including whistle blowers' complaints. Yet, It is a reality that fraudsters always invent ways to remain a step ahead of regulators.

To shield against occurrence or recurrence of the frauds, their impact and incidence, it is essential for companies to strengthen and constantly keep reviewing the mechanisms to minimize their risk exposures. This can be done through - strong systems, processes, corporate governance practices and a robust recruitment process to ensure that right people with integrity and value systems are hired.

It is also important to create awareness among employees through rigorous training mechanisms, as to areas exposed to fraud and ensure that frauds are impartially investigated and culprits are punished, in time.

Whenever the frauds are detected or corporates fail, it is observed that frauds are perpetuated generally by collective body of individuals and seldom by the acts of a single person.

The hard truth of fraud is that it is deliberate and exploitive in a number of ways. Vigilant and concerted effort at numerous levels has to be an inbuilt feature in the framework to effectively flag or combat the occurrence of fraud.

A company may consider mandating a "fraud prevention and detection policy" and give training on the policy to employees at all levels on constant basis. Particular care and attention must always be focused on the specific vulnerable areas in a company where chances of occurrence of fraud are perceived to exist.

Corporate scams or scandals typically involve complex methods for misusing or misdirecting funds, overstating revenues, understating expenses, overstating the value of corporate assets or underreporting the existence of liabilities.

Fraud is often used to hide the truth to convince investors and analysts that all was well, by: hiding excessive debt, poor strategic decisions and the liquidity.

Creative and aggressive accounting, fraud and coercion can disguise the truth only for a while, until the underlying problems become so enormous that it cannot be hidden any longer.

It is the responsibility of any management, in their fiduciary capacity, to prevent and detect fraud. But, when they themselves wish to indulge in the crime, their ability to influence people and to disguise the true nature of the events facilitates the occurrence of fraud.

It therefore requires a concerted effort at numerous levels to be vigilant and ask appropriate questions in order to properly unpack red flags before they are disregarded.

It must be understood that fraud does not always result in corporate failure, nor do corporate failures occur only as a result of fraud. However, in some of the biggest corporate failures across the globe, fraud was involved.

B. What is Corporate Fraud?

Corporate fraud is an end result of illegal or unethical or deceptive actions committed either by a company or an individual. The design is to give an advantage to the perpetrator with or without involvement of an outsider.

Companies adopt various modus-operandi to commit corporate frauds, which may include mis-information in the prospectus, manipulation of accounting records, debt hiding etc. The aspect of falsification of financial information includes false accounting entries, false transactions for inflation of profits, disclosure of price sensitive information which comes under the ambit of insider trading. understatement of liabilities, overstatement of assets etc.,

C. Factors contributing to commit corporate Fraud

Greed: Ambitious corporate growth; Deceptive reporting practices and lack of transparency; Excessive interest in maintaining stock prices and valuation; Executive incentives; Stock market expectations; High risk deals that went sour; Aggressiveness of investment and commercial banks, rating agencies and investors; Weak independent directors and audit committee; Ineffective whistle-blower policy etc.

Poor strategic decisions: Overexpansion and misguided acquisitions; Dominant CEOs; Greed, arrogance, resort extensively to Related Party Transactions; pride and the desire for power; Failure of internal controls at all levels; Incompetent or ineffective boards; Lack of independence of Auditors; undesirable quality of audit work; integrity and professionalism of auditors;

Typically, the profile of the person indulging in fraud is not the one who is struggling to make ends meet. On the contrary, the fraudster is a well-off individual in life.

Some promoters consider themselves to be an extension of the Company. They regard themselves as exceptional leaders. Such persons go to the extent of using corporate funds for personal purposes without any shame. They do not shy away from mercilessly removing anyone who comes on their way in any manner.

The long list of some of the Corporate Failures and frauds covered in later Chapters suggest presence of the following elements in isolation or in combination, and not necessarily in this order:

- ❖ The capability of individuals to commit fraud by circumventing internal controls, using company finances for their personal benefit.
- ❖ Dominance by the chairman or CEO
- ❖ Poor or lack of corporate governance despite legislation and regulation, including non-independent

and inadequately qualified board or committee members, lack of debate of business issues at board level and a deliberate disregard of statutory or regulatory compliances by some managements

- Poor Ethics and values or lack thereof
- Believing in their own magic by Promoter or authoritarian CEO
- Inappropriately qualified board members
- Weak Internal Audits
- Lack of training to independent directors on their role especially related to their duty; accountability; rights etc.
- Misrepresentations to Auditors and Board by the Company management
- Poor strategic decisions
- Manipulation of financial records and/or fraudulent financial reporting to hide or window dress the true nature of underlying realities
- Pressure from Promoters or CEOs to achieve targets beyond the capacity of the Organisation for own benefits
- Pressure to pay higher Returns to Investors
- Questionable and non-compliant Related Party regulations

- Insider Trading
- To attract investment funds into the Company from Investors, Banks and FIs at high valuations.
- Desire to boost equity price or to command high premiums from new Shareholders
- Greed, arrogance, pride the desire for power and quest to make quick money.
- Overexpansion and misguided acquisitions
- Abuse of Authority
- Excessive debt to fund expansions
- Incentives to people to become accomplice for commitment of fraud
- Questionable role of Auditors, Rating Agencies, Investment Bankers in abetting frauds by management with attraction of high remuneration
- Compromised quality of audit work due to poor fees
- Misconception of the role of an auditor to detect fraud through their audit procedures
- Weak or outdated or no Risk management practices
- Subservient CEOs to promoters
- Low moral and ethical values of leaders in the Organisations

- Corruption at the level of investigating agencies which allow the promoters to avoid punishments by closure of complaints in abrupt manner with or without interference by politicians.
- Unrealistic expectations of stakeholders for performance and growth
- Ineffective whistle-blower policy
- Stock market expectations

D. Types and Elements of Corporate Frauds

Most common types are: Financial and Accounting Frauds, Misappropriation of Assets, employee fraud, vendor fraud, customer fraud. investment scams, money laundering, compliance failure frauds etc.

Accounting fraud is the intentional manipulation of financial statements to create a false appearance of corporate financial health. The fraud is generally committed by misusing or misdirecting funds, inflating the revenue, suppressing expenses, and overstating the value of assets, understating liabilities etc.

Following are the **general elements of fraud:**

(a) Non-adherence to accounting standards

(b) Manipulation of accounts

(c) Misrepresentation or omission of facts

(d) Misappropriation of funds and assets

(e) Forging of documents

(f) Corruption, bribes or kickbacks

(g) Theft/ misuse in assets

(h) Breach of Trust

(i) FEMA violations

Effective corporate governance, knowledgeable proactive audit committees, strong internal audit set-up and regular interactions with Statutory auditors on review of fraud prone sensitive areas can protect an Organization from areas of significant frauds.

Creative and aggressive accounting, fraud and coercion can disguise the truth only for a while, until the underlying problems become so enormous that it cannot be hidden any longer.

E. Some of the habits of Leaders of failed corporates

Sydney Finkelstein, Professor of Management at Tuck School of Business at Dartmouth, summarized the following seven habits of leaders who presided for major corporate failures:

ONE - The leaders vastly overestimate the level of control they have over circumstances and believe that they are personally able to control things to ensure the company's success. Such business leaders may use intimidating or excessive behavior to dominate those around them.

TWO - These leaders do not treat the company as something to be nurtured, protected and cared for but rather as an extension of themselves. Such leaders are described as people who feel personally responsible for the company's success and that they could develop a "private empire" mentality, causing them to behave as if it's their own company and act as though they have the right to do anything with the company. Such leaders, may be inclined to use corporate funds for personal reasons due to the rationalization that everything they do is for the company.

THREE - They think they have all the answers to everything under the sun. Such leaders exhibit this habit as a means of protecting themselves from their personal lack of control over every situation

FOUR - They ruthlessly eliminate anyone who is not fully behind them These leaders, believe that their vision should be instilled throughout the company to get everyone to work together to achieve their set goals. Leaders who have presided over major corporate failures often implemented a policy of removing those who were seen to undermine their vision and were likely to raise opposing views.

FIVE - They are consummate company spokespersons, obsessed with the company image. These leaders are constantly in the public eye and have the ability to inspire confidence among the public, employees and particularly investors. The public tendency to judge a CEO's success by the current price of the company's stock greatly reinforces this habit because the fastest and easiest way to improve the share price is to put on a good show for the media and investors.

SIX - They underestimate major obstacles. Such leaders become so obsessed with their vision that they see every challenge as minor and therefore neglect to consider the difficulties of actually achieving the goal. The leaders assume that all problems can be solved.

SEVEN - They stubbornly rely on what worked for them in the past. Unsuccessful leaders often revert to what worked for them in the past in an effort to maintain control. Finkelstein stated that these leaders reach this "defining moment" at some point during their career when they achieved particular success. Their "defining moment" becomes their definition of success throughout their careers and to some extent they let it define their company as well.

F. Fraud and their Reporting Requirements under Companies Act, 2013

(i) By the Auditors *{The Act and Guidance Note on reporting issued by ICAI}*

✓ **Section 143 (12) of the Companies Act, 2013**

Section 143(12) states that "Notwithstanding anything contained in this section, if an auditor of a company, in the course of the performance of his duties as auditor, has reason to believe that an offence of fraud involving rupees one crore of more is being or has been committed in the company by its officers or employees, the auditor shall report the matter to the Central Government, the Board or the Audit Committee, as the case may be, immediately but not later than two days of his knowledge of the fraud.

Where the fraud involving lesser than one crore rupees, the auditor shall report the matter to the audit committee constituted under section 177 or to the Board immediately but not later than two days his knowledge of the fraud, seeking their reply or observations within forty-five days;

The companies, whose auditors have reported frauds to the audit committee or the Board but not reported to the Central Government, shall disclose the details about such frauds in the Board's report in such manner as may be prescribed."

The reporting requirement under Section 143(12) is for the statutory auditors of the company and also equally applies to the cost accountant in practice, conducting cost audit under Section 148 of the Act; and to the company secretary in practice, conducting secretarial audit under Section 204 of the Act.

However, the provisions of Section 143(12) do not apply to other professionals who are rendering other services to the company. For example, Section 143(12) does not apply to auditors appointed under other statutes for rendering other services such as tax auditor appointed for audit under Income-tax Act; Sales Tax or VAT auditors appointed for audit under the respective Sales Tax or VAT legislations.

It may also be noted that internal auditors covered under Section 138 are not specified as persons who are required to report under Section 143(12). As per sub-rule (3) of Rule 12 of the Companies (Audit and Auditors) Rules, 2014, the provisions of sub-section (12) of Section 143 read with Rule 13 of the Companies (Audit and Auditors) Rules, 2014 regarding reporting of frauds by the auditor shall also extend to a branch auditor appointed under Section 139 to the extent it relates to the concerned branch. It may be noted that Section 143(12) includes only fraud by officers or employees of the company and does not include fraud by third parties such as vendors and customers.

The Companies (Audit and Auditors) Amendment Rules, 2015, provides the manner of reporting to Central Government as under:

On receipt of such reply or observations the auditor shall forward his report on his letter head duly signed with his membership number and seal and the reply or observations of the Board or the Audit Committee along with his comments (on such reply or observations of the Board or the Audit Overview

Committee) to the Secretary, Ministry of Corporate Affairs, Central Government by Registered/Speed Post within fifteen days from the date of receipt of such reply or observations followed by an email in confirmation of the same.;

In case the auditor fails to get any reply or observations from the Board or the Audit Committee within the stipulated period of forty-five days, he shall forward his report to the Central Government along with a note containing the details of his report that was earlier forwarded to the Board or the Audit Committee for which he has not received any reply or observations;

The audit report shall be in Form ADT-4.

The following details of each of the fraud reported to the Audit Committee or the Board under sub-rule (3) of amended Rule 13 during the year shall be disclosed in the Board's Report:-

(a) Nature of Fraud with description;

(b) Approximate Amount involved;

(c) Parties involved, if remedial action not taken; and

(d) Remedial action taken.

Auditors' Responsibility for Consideration of Fraud in an Audit of Financial Statements

The auditor shall consider the requirements of the Standards on Auditing (SA) 240 on documentation of their understanding of the entity and its environment and the assessment of fraud risks must include significant decisions made during the discussions among the engagement team regarding the susceptibility of the entity's financial statements to material misstatement due to fraud, as well as identified and assessed risks of material misstatement due to fraud at both the financial statement level and the assertion level.

If an offence of fraud in the company by its officers or employees that is identified/noted by the auditor in the course of providing any attest or non-attest services, which the auditor uses or intends to use the information that is obtained in the course of performing such attest or non-attest services when performing the audit under the 2013 Act, then in such cases, the matter may become reportable under Section 143(12), read with the Rules thereunder.

Accordingly, in case a fraud has already been reported or has been identified/detected by the management or through the company's vigil/whistle blower mechanism and has been/is being remediated/dealt with by them and such case is informed to the auditor, he will not be required to report the same under Section 143(12) since he has not per se identified the fraud. The auditor should apply professional skepticism to evaluate/verify that the fraud was indeed identified/detected in all aspects by the management or through the company's vigil/whistle blower mechanism so that distinction can be clearly made with respect to frauds identified/detected due to matters raised by the auditor vis-à-vis those identified/detected by the company through its internal control mechanism.

However, in case of a fraud which involves or is expected to involve individually, an amount of rupees one crore or more, the auditor should review the steps taken by the management/those charged with governance with respect to the reported instance of suspected offence of fraud stated above, and if he is not satisfied with such steps, he should state the reasons for his dissatisfaction in writing and request the management/those charged with governance to perform additional procedures to enable the auditor to satisfy himself that the matter has been appropriately addressed.

If the management/those charged with governance fail to undertake appropriate additional procedures within 45 days of his request, the auditor would need to evaluate if he should report the matter to the Central Government in accordance with Rule 13 of the Companies (Audit and Auditors) Amendment Rules, 2015.

The auditor of the parent company in India will be required to report on suspected offence involving frauds in the components of the parent company, if the suspected offence of fraud in the component is being or has been committed by employees or officers of the parent company and if such suspected offence involving fraud in the component is against the parent company

In case of corruption, bribery and money laundering, the direct effect of such act (benefit or penal consequence) is on the company. The auditor should comply with the relevant SAs with regard to illegal acts (SA 240 and SA 250, "Consideration of Laws and Regulations in an Audit of Financial Statements") when performing the audit. If the auditor, in the course of performance of his/her duties as the auditor, comes across instances of corruption, bribery and money laundering and other intentional non-Guidance Note on Reporting on Fraud compliances with laws and regulations, the auditor would need to evaluate the impact of the same in accordance with SA 250 to determine whether the same would have a material effect on the financial statements.

The proviso to Section 147(2) in the context of punishment to auditors for contravention with the provisions, inter alia, of Section 143 of the 2013 Act, states, "if an auditor has contravened such provisions knowingly or willfully with the intention to deceive the company or its shareholders or creditors or tax authorities, he shall be punishable with imprisonment for a term which may extend to one year and with fine which shall not be less than one lakh rupees but which may extend to twenty-five lakh rupees."

(ii) Report of Board of Directors on Fraud

Section 134 3(ca) read with Section 143(12) shall, *inter alia* include-

(ca) The details of the fraud that has been reported by the auditor, in the following format, must be disclosed in the board report:

- Description and nature of fraud reported.
- The estimated amount of fraud.
- If remedial action not taken then the Parties involved.
- In the case of remedial action taken, then the details of such action.

G. Responsibility for Fraud Prevention and Detection

- **Prime Responsibility:** The primary responsibility for the prevention and detection of fraud rests with both those charged with governance of the entity and management. It is important that management, with the oversight of those charged with governance, place a strong emphasis on fraud prevention, which may reduce opportunities for fraud to take place, and fraud deterrence, which could persuade individuals not to commit fraud because of the likelihood of detection and punishment.

- **Role of the Auditor:** An auditor conducting an audit is responsible for obtaining reasonable assurance that the financial statements taken as a whole are free from material misstatement, whether caused by fraud or error. Owing to the inherent limitations of an audit, there is an unavoidable risk that some material misstatements of the financial statements may not be detected, even though the audit is properly planned and performed in accordance with the SAs.

The potential effects of inherent limitations are particularly significant in the case of misstatement resulting from fraud. The risk of not detecting a material misstatement resulting from fraud is higher than the risk of not detecting one resulting from error. This is because fraud may involve sophisticated and carefully organized schemes designed to conceal it, such as forgery, deliberate failure to record transactions, or intentional misrepresentations being made to the auditor. Such attempts at concealment may be even more difficult to detect when accompanied by collusion. Collusion may cause the auditor to believe that audit evidence is persuasive when it is, in fact, false. The auditor's ability to detect a fraud depends on factors such as the skilfulness of the perpetrator, the frequency and extent of manipulation, the degree of collusion involved, the relative size of individual amounts manipulated, and the seniority of those individuals involved. While the auditor may be able to identify potential opportunities for fraud to be perpetrated, it is difficult for the auditor to determine whether misstatements in judgment areas such as accounting estimates are caused by fraud or error.

Furthermore, the risk of the auditor not detecting a material misstatement resulting from management fraud is greater than for employee fraud, because management is frequently in a position to directly or indirectly manipulate accounting records, present fraudulent financial information or override control procedures designed to prevent similar frauds by other employees.

When obtaining reasonable assurance, the auditor is responsible for maintaining professional scepticism throughout the audit, considering the potential for management override of controls and recognizing the fact that audit procedures that are effective for detecting error may not be effective in detecting fraud.

H. Role of Board of Directors /Audit Committee on Fraud under the Act and Listing Agreement

When a suspicion of fraud is reported by the auditor, the Board or Audit Committee is required to evaluate the matter and take appropriate action including, conducting an investigation or a forensic audit. Further the Board or Audit

Committee is expected to respond to the auditor within 45 days of the suspected fraud being highlighted.

Where it is not possible to conclude the investigation in forty-five days, because of the nature of the fraud, the MCA notification suggests that the company may respond by providing information on the steps taken – such as commencement of the investigation and the case status - and any other observations by the Board or Audit Committee on the matter, within 45 days to the auditor.

Section 177 - Audit Committee under Companies Act, 2013

Every listed company and other public companies with a paid-up capital of more than Rs. 10 Crores or a turnover of INR 100 crores or outstanding loans or borrowing exceeding INR 50 crores (as per the latest audited accounts) to form an audit committee comprising at least 3 directors, the majority of whom have to be independent,

Majority of members of Audit Committee including its Chairperson must have the ability to read and understand the financial statement.

The board shall lay down in writing the terms of reference for the Audit Committee.

The terms of reference to include: –

Recommendation for appointment, remuneration and terms of appointment of the auditors;

Review and monitor auditor's independence and performance and effectiveness of the audit process; Examination of the financial statement and auditor's report;

Approval or modification of related party transactions;

Scrutiny of inter corporate loans and investments;

Valuation of assets;

Evaluation of internal financial controls and risk management systems;

Monitoring of end use of funds of the public offers;

Establish Vigil Mechanism:

Under Section 177(9) of the Act - Every listed company and the companies which accept deposits from the public or Companies which have borrowed money from banks and public financial institutions in excess of fifty crore rupees.

shall establish a vigil mechanism for directors and employees to report genuine concerns in such manner as may be prescribed.

Sub-section (10) provides for adequate safeguards against victimization of persons who use such mechanism and make provision for direct access to the chairperson of the Audit Committee in appropriate or exceptional cases. Details of establishment of such mechanism shall be disclosed by the company on its website, if any, and in the Board's report.

Part C of Schedule II Regulation 18(3) of the SEBI (Listing Obligations and Disclosure Requirements) Regulations, 2015

The Regulation has, *inter alia*, stipulated the following role for the Audit Committee for the review of information:

1. oversight of the entity's financial reporting process and the disclosure of its financial information to ensure that the financial statement is correct, sufficient and credible;
2. recommendation for appointment, remuneration and terms of appointment of auditors of the listed entity;
3. approval of payment to statutory auditors for any other services rendered by the statutory auditors
4. reviewing with the management, the annual financial statements and auditor's report thereon before submission to the board for approval, with particular reference to:

(a) matters required to be included in the director's responsibility statement to be included in the board's report in terms of clause (c) of sub-section (3) of Section 134 of the Companies Act, 2013;

(b) changes, if any, in accounting policies and practices and reasons for the same;

(c) major accounting entries involving estimates based on the exercise of judgment by management;

(d) significant adjustments made in the financial statements arising out of audit findings;

(e) Compliance with listing and other legal requirements relating to financial statements;

(f) Disclosure of any related party transactions;

(g) Modified opinion(s) in the draft audit report;

5. Reviewing, with the management, the quarterly financial statements before submission to the board for approval;

6. Reviewing, with the management, the statement of uses / application of funds raised through an issue (public issue, rights issue, preferential issue, etc.), the statement of funds utilized for purposes other than those stated in the offer document / prospectus / notice and the report submitted by the monitoring agency monitoring the utilization of proceeds of a public or rights issue, and making appropriate recommendations to the board to take up steps in this matter;

7. Reviewing and monitoring the auditor's independence and performance, and effectiveness of audit process;

8. Approval or any subsequent modification of transactions of the listed entity with related parties;

9. Scrutiny of inter-corporate loans and investments;

10. Valuation of undertakings or assets of the listed entity, wherever it is necessary;

11. Evaluation of internal financial controls and risk management systems;

12. Reviewing, with the management, performance of statutory and internal auditors, adequacy of the internal control systems;

13. Reviewing the adequacy of internal audit function, if any, including the structure of the internal audit department, staffing and seniority of the official heading the department, reporting structure coverage and frequency of internal audit;

14. Discussion with internal auditors of any significant findings and follow up there on;

15. Reviewing the findings of any internal investigations by the internal auditors into matters where there is suspected fraud or irregularity or a failure of internal control systems of a material nature and reporting the matter to the board;

16. Discussion with statutory auditors before the audit commences, about the nature and scope of audit as well as post-audit discussion to ascertain any area of concern;

17. to look into the reasons for substantial defaults in the payment to the depositors, debenture holders, shareholders (in case of non-payment of declared dividends) and creditors

18. to review the functioning of the whistle blower mechanism;

19. approval of appointment of chief financial officer after assessing the qualifications, experience and background, etc. of the candidate;

20. Carrying out any other function as is mentioned in the terms of reference of the audit committee.

21. reviewing the utilization of loans and/ or advances from/investment by theholding company in the subsidiary exceeding rupees 100 crore or 10% of the asset size of the subsidiary, whichever is lower including existing loans / advances / investments existing as on the date of coming into force of this provision.

22. consider and comment on rationale, cost-benefits and impact of schemes involving merger, demerger, amalgamation etc., on the listed entity and its shareholders

B. Role of Audit Committee Under SEBI (LODR), 2015

1. management discussion and analysis of financial condition and results of operations;

2. statement of significant related party transactions (as defined by the audit committee), submitted by management;

3. management letters / letters of internal control weaknesses issued by the statutory auditors;

4. internal audit reports relating to internal control weaknesses; and

5. the appointment, removal and terms of remuneration of the chief internal auditor shall be subject to review by the audit committee.

6. statement of deviations:

(a) quarterly statement of deviation(s) including report of monitoring agency, if applicable, submitted to stock exchange(s) in terms of Regulation 32(1).

(b) annual statement of funds utilized for purposes other than those stated in the offer document/prospectus/ notice in terms of Regulation 32(7).

I. Regulations under SEBI Listing Regulations, 2015 related to Frauds

(a) Para 6, Part A of Schedule III

The Company shall disclose within 24 hours of occurrence disclose to the Stock Exchange any fraud or defaults by a listed entity, its promoter, director, key managerial personnel, senior management or subsidiary or arrest of key managerial personnel, senior management, promoter or director whether occurred within India or abroad.

(b) Para 17: Part A of Schedule

Initiation of Forensic audit: In case of initiation of forensic audit,(by whatever name called), the following disclosures shall be made to the stock exchanges by listed entities within 12 hours if initiated by the Company or within 24 hours if initiated by external agency:

(a) The fact of initiation of forensic audit along-with name of entity initiating the audit and reasons for the same, if available;

(b) Final forensic audit report (other than for forensic audit initiated by regulatory / enforcement agencies) on receipt by the listed entity along with comments of the management, if any.

(C) Para 19: Part A of Schedule

Within 24 hours of Action(s) initiated or orders passed by any regulatory, statutory, enforcement authority or judicial body against the listed entity or its directors, key managerial personnel, senior management, promoter or subsidiary, in relation to the listed entity, in respect of the following:

(a) search or seizure; or

(b) re-opening of accounts under section 130 of the Companies Act, 2013; or

(c) investigation under the provisions of Chapter XIV of the Companies Act, 2013;

(d) Para 9: Part B of Schedule: Reg 30(4)

Fraud/defaults etc. by directors (other than key managerial personnel) or employees of listed entity within 24 hours.

(e) Reg 30 (8): Disclosure on web site

The listed entity shall disclose on its website all such events or information which has been disclosed to stock exchange(s) under this regulation, and such disclosures shall be hosted on the website of the listed entity for a minimum period of five years and thereafter as er the archival policy of the listed entity, as disclosed on its website.

(f) Regulation 51 (2) read with Schedule II - Part B

(17) fraud/defaults by promoter or key managerial personnel or director or

employees of listed entity or by listed entity or arrest of key managerial personnel or promoter;

(g) Part B: Compliance Certificate [See Regulation 17(8)]

The chief executive officer and the chief financial officer shall provide as part of the compliance certificate to the board of directors that-

They have indicated to the auditors and the Audit committee

(1) significant changes in internal control over financial reporting during the year;

(2) significant changes in accounting policies during the year and that the same has been disclosed in the notes to the financial statements; and

(3) instances of significant fraud of which they have become aware and the involvement therein, if any, of the management or an employee having a significant role in the listed entity's internal control system over financial reporting.

(h) NBFCs

The NBFCs are required to comply with the requirements provided under Master Direction - Monitoring of Frauds in NBFCs (Reserve Bank) Directions, 2016. Chapter IV of the abovementioned master directions deal with the Reporting of Frauds to Reserve Bank of India.

(I) SEBI (Prohibition of Fraudulent and Unfair Trade Practices Relating to Securities Market) Regulations, 2003

Reg. 2(c) Fraud: includes any act, expression, omission or concealment committed whether in a deceitful manner or not by a person or by any other person with his connivance or by his agent while dealing in securities in order to induce another person or his agent to deal in securities, whether or not there is any wrongful gain or avoidance of any loss, and shall also include —

1. a knowing misrepresentation of the truth or concealment of material fact in order that another person may act to his detriment;
2. a suggestion as to a fact which is not true by one who does not believe it to be true;
3. an active concealment of a fact by a person having knowledge or belief of the fact;
4. a promise made without any intention of performing it;
5. a representation made in a reckless and careless manner whether it be true or false;
6. any such act or omission as any other law specifically declares to be fraudulent,
7. deceptive behavior by a person depriving another of informed consent or full participation,
8. a false statement made without reasonable ground for believing it to be true.
9. the act of an issuer of securities giving out misinformation that affects the market price of the security, resulting in investors being effectively misled even though they did not rely

on the statement itself or anything derived from it other than the market price.

And "fraudulent" shall be construed accordingly;

Reg 3. Prohibition of certain dealings in securities

Reg 4. Prohibition of manipulative, fraudulent and unfair trade practices

J. Independent directors {ID} and the Roles envisaged under Companies Act, 2013

Schedule IV [Section 149(8)] Code for Independent Directors

The Code is a guide to professional conduct for independent directors. Adherence to these standards by independent directors and fulfilment of their responsibilities in a professional and faithful manner will promote confidence of the investment community, particularly minority shareholders, regulators and companies in the institution of independent directors. Guidelines of professional conduct: An independent director shall:

1. uphold ethical standards of integrity and probity;
2. act objectively and constructively while exercising his duties;
3. exercise his responsibilities in a bona fide manner in the interest of the company;

4. devote sufficient time and attention to his professional obligations for informed and balanced decision making;

5. not allow any extraneous considerations that will vitiate his exercise of objective independent judgment in the paramount interest of the company as a whole, while concurring in or dissenting from the collective judgment of the Board in its decision making;

6. not abuse his position to the detriment of the company or its shareholders or for the purpose of gaining direct or indirect personal advantage or advantage for any associated person;

7. refrain from any action that would lead to loss of his independence;

8. where circumstances arise which make an independent director lose his independence, the independent director must immediately inform the Board accordingly;

9. assist the company in implementing the best corporate governance practices.

II. Role and functions:

The independent directors shall:

1. help in bringing an independent judgment to bear on the Board's deliberations especially on issues of

strategy, performance, risk management, resources, key appointments and standards of conduct;

2. bring an objective view in the evaluation of the performance of board and management;

3. scrutinise the performance of management in meeting agreed goals and objectives and monitor the reporting of performance;

4. satisfy themselves on the integrity of financial information and that financial controls and the systems of risk management are robust and defensible;

5. safeguard the interests of all stakeholders, particularly the minority shareholders;

6. balance the conflicting interest of the stakeholders;

7. determine appropriate levels of remuneration of executive directors, key managerial personnel and senior management and have a prime role in appointing and where necessary recommend removal of executive directors, key managerial personnel and senior management;

8. moderate and arbitrate in the interest of the company as a whole, in situations of conflict between management and shareholder's interest.

III. Duties:

The independent directors shall—

1. undertake appropriate induction and regularly update and refresh their skills, knowledge and familiarity with the company;
2. seek appropriate clarification or amplification of information and, where necessary, take and follow appropriate professional advice and opinion of outside experts at the expense of the company;
3. strive to attend all meetings of the Board of Directors and of the Board committees of which he is a member;
4. participate constructively and actively in the committees of the Board in which they are chairpersons or members;
5. strive to attend the general meetings of the company;
6. where they have concerns about the running of the company or a proposed action, ensure that these are addressed by the Board and, to the extent that they are not resolved, insist that their concerns are recorded in the minutes of the Board meeting;
7. keep themselves well informed about the company and the external environment in which it operates;
8. not to unfairly obstruct the functioning of an otherwise proper Board or committee of the Board;

9. pay sufficient attention and ensure that adequate deliberations are held before approving related party transactions and assure themselves that the same are in the interest of the company;
10. ascertain and ensure that the company has an adequate and functional vigil mechanism and to ensure that the interests of a person who uses such mechanism are not prejudicially affected on account of such use;
11. report concerns about unethical behaviour, actual or suspected fraud or violation of the company's code of conduct or ethics policy;
12. act within their authority, assist in protecting the legitimate interests of the company, shareholders and its employees;
13. not disclose confidential information, including commercial secrets, technologies, advertising and sales promotion plans, unpublished price sensitive information, unless such disclosure is expressly approved by the Board or required by law.

Liability

The Companies Act, 2013 restricts and limits the liability of Independent Directors only in respect of acts of omission or commission by a company which had occurred with his knowledge, attributable through board processes, and with his consent or connivance or where he had not acted diligently.

Guidelines to Independent Directors {IDs}

ID should be vigilant and seek to play a larger role in fraud risk management initiatives.

ID should ask the Company to provide them financial ratios of financial statements for the historical period so that he can compare them with the current period's ratios to be able to detect any trend abnormality.

ID may ask for the Company's to develop strong Anti-fraud policies and ensure compliances thereto annually.

ID may insist that the company to have a strong Internal Audit set up especially to audit high value transactions, non-regular transactions, feasibility reports submitted for expansions and diversifications, compliances with purpose of pubic fund raising or funds raising for specific purposes; Analyze and re[ort on Cost-over run projects r activities etc.

Today, regulatory requirements place the accountability for having effective fraud risk management on the board/ senior management. Coupled with the growing focus on ethics and current dynamic business environment, this has also increased the importance of the role of IDs in being effective deterrents to fraud, mismanagement, and lapses in corporate governance.

IDs should review periodically the fraud risk management initiatives in the Company. They should update their knowledge on the changes across the fraud risk landscape, and the best practices/ latest technologies in preventing/ fighting fraud.

IDs should look for special training on fraud risk management, independent screening of high-risk areas and increased visibility on the review and continuous monitoring mechanisms in place in the companies for timely detection of unusual activities.

Chapter IX

Frauds and Punishments in India

Corporate fraud consists of illegal or unethical activities undertaken by an employee or company that are done in a dishonest or illegal manner, and are designed to give an advantage to the perpetrator or company. Some of the Corporate frauds are found to be highly complicated to unearth fast. Often services of forensic experts become necessary to unravel the truth.

Some of the Regulatory Legislations imposing Punishments for Frauds

1. Indian Contract Act 1872

Fraud is defined in Section 17 as under-

Fraud means and includes any of the following acts committed by a party to a contract, or with his connivance, or by his agent, with intent to deceive another party thereto or his agent, or to induce him to enter into the contract:

1. the suggestion, as a fact, of that which is not true, by one who does not believe it to be true;

2. the active concealment of a fact by one having knowledge or belief of the fact;

3. a promise made without any intention of performing it;

4. any other act fitted to deceive;

5. any such act or omission as the law specially declares to be fraudulent.

Explanation— Mere silence as to facts likely to affect the willingness of a person to enter into a contract is not fraud, unless the circumstances of the case are such that, regard being had to them, it is the duty of the person keeping silence to speak, or unless his silence, is, in itself, equivalent to speech.

Punishment for Breaches of Contract

Sec 73. Compensation for loss or damage caused by breach of contract: When a contract has been broken, the party who suffers by such breach is entitled to receive, from the party who has broken the contract, compensation for any loss or damage caused to him thereby, which naturally arose in the usual course of things from such breach, or which the parties knew, when they made the contract, to be likely to result from the breach of it.

Such compensation is not to be given for any remote and indirect loss or damage sustained by reason of the breach.

Compensation for failure to discharge obligation resembling those created by contract.—When the obligation has been incurred and has not been discharged, any person injured by the failure to discharge it is entitled to receive the same compensation from the party in default, as if such person had contracted to discharge it and had broken his contract.

Sec 74. Compensation for breach of contract where penalty stipulated for: When a contract has been broken, if a sum is named in the contract as the amount to be paid in case of such breach, or if the contract contains any other stipulation by way of penalty, the party complaining of the breach is entitled, whether or not actual damage or loss is proved to have been caused thereby, to receive from the party who has broken the contract reasonable compensation not exceeding the amount so named or, as the case may be, the penalty stipulated for.

Explanation.—A stipulation for increased interest from the date of default may be a stipulation by way of penalty.

2. Indian Penal Code 1860. (IPC)

A. Criminal Conspiracy

120A. Definition of criminal conspiracy: When two or more persons agree to do, or cause to be done,—

1. an illegal act, or

2. an act which is not illegal by illegal means, such an agreement is designated a criminal conspiracy:

   Provided that no agreement except an agreement to commit an offence shall amount to a criminal conspiracy unless some act besides the agreement is done by one or more parties to such agreement in pursuance thereof.

   Explanation—It is immaterial whether the illegal act is the ultimate object of such agreement, or is merely incidental to that object.

120B. Punishment of criminal conspiracy: (1) Whoever is a party to a criminal conspiracy to commit an offence punishable with death, imprisonment for life or rigorous imprisonment for a term of two years or upwards, shall, where no express provision is made in this Code for the punishment of such a conspiracy, be punished in the same manner as if he had abetted such offence.

3. Whoever is a party to a criminal conspiracy other than a criminal conspiracy to commit an offence punishable as aforesaid shall be punished with imprisonment of

B. False Evidence and Offences against Public Justice

191. Giving false evidence: Whoever, being legally bound by an oath or by an express provision of law to state the truth, or being bound by law to make a declaration upon any subject, makes any statement which is false, and which he either knows or believes to be false or does not believe to be true, is said to give false evidence.

Explanation1.—A statement is within the meaning of this section, whether it is made verbally or otherwise.

Explanation 2.—A false statement as to the belief of the person attesting is within the meaning of this section, and a person may be guilty of giving false evidence by stating that he believes a thing which he does not believe, as well as by stating that he knows a thing which he does not know.

192. Fabricating false evidence: Whoever causes any circumstance to exist or makes any false entry in any book or record, or electronic record or makes any document or electronic record containing a false statement, intending that such circumstance, false entry or false statement may appear in evidence in a judicial proceeding, or in a proceeding taken by law before a public servant as such, or before an arbitrator, and that such circumstance, false entry or false statement, so appearing in evidence, may cause any person who in such proceeding is to form an opinion upon the evidence, to entertain an erroneous opinion touching any point material to the result of such proceeding is said "to fabricate false evidence"

193. Punishment for false evidence: Whoever intentionally gives false evidence in any of a judicial proceeding, or fabricates false evidence for the purpose of being used in any stage of a judicial proceeding, shall be punished with imprisonment of either description for a term which may extend to seven years, and shall also be liable to fine; and whoever intentionally gives or fabricates false evidence in any other case, shall be punished with imprisonment of either description for a term which may extend to three years, and shall also be liable to fine.

195. Giving or fabricating false evidence with intent to procure conviction of offence punishable with imprisonment for life or imprisonment: Whoever gives or fabricates false evidence intending thereby to cause, or knowing it to be likely that he will thereby cause, any person to be convicted of an offence which by the law for the time being in force in India is not capital, but punishable with imprisonment for life or imprisonment for a term of seven years or upwards, shall be punished as a person convicted of that offence would be liable to be punished.

195A. Threatening any person to give false evidence: Whoever threatens another with any injury to his person, reputation or property or to the person or reputation of any one in whom that person is interested, with intent to cause that person to give false evidence shall be punished with imprisonment of either description for a term which may extend to seven years, or with fine, or with both; and if innocent person is convicted and sentenced in consequence of such false evidence, with death or imprisonment for more than seven years, the person who threatens shall be punished with the same punishment and sentence in the same manner and to the same extent such innocent person is punished and sentenced.

196. Using evidence known to be false: Whoever corruptly uses or attempts to use as true or genuine evidence any evidence which he knows to be false or fabricated, shall be punished in the same manner as if he gave or fabricated false evidence.

197. Issuing or signing false certificate: Whoever issues or signs any certificate required by law to be given or signed, or relating to any fact of which such certificate is by law admissible in evidence, knowing or believing that such certificate is false in any material point, shall be punished in the same manner as if he gave false evidence.

198. Using as true a certificate known to be false: Whoever corruptly uses or attempts to use any such certificate as a true certificate, knowing the same to be false in any material point, shall be punished in the same manner as if he gave false evidence.

199. False statement made in declaration which is by law receivable as evidence: Whoever, in any declaration made or subscribed by him, which declaration any Court of Justice, or any public servant or other person, is bound or authorised by law to receive as evidence of any fact, makes any statement which is false, and which he either knows or believes to be false or does not believe to be true, touching any point material to the object for which the declaration is made or used, shall be punished in the same manner as if he gave false evidence.

200. Using as true such declaration knowing it to be false: Whoever corruptly uses or attempts to use as true any such declaration, knowing the same to be false in any material point, shall be punished in the same manner as if he gave false evidence. Explanation.—A declaration which is inadmissible merely upon the ground of some informality, is a declaration within the meaning of sections 199 and 200.

201. Causing disappearance of evidence of offence, or giving false information to screen offender: Whoever, knowing or having reason to believe that an offence has been committed, causes any evidence of the commission of that offence to disappear, with the intention of screening the offender from legal punishment, or with that intention gives any information respecting the offence which he knows or believes to be false,

if a capital offence.—shall, if the offence which he knows or believes to have been committed is punishable with death be punished with imprisonment of either description for a term which may extend to seven years, and shall also be liable to fine;

if punishable with imprisonment for life.—and if the offence is punishable with imprisonment for life, or with imprisonment which may extend to ten years, shall be punished with imprisonment of either description for a term which may extend to three years, and shall also be liable to fine; if punishable with less than ten years' imprisonment.—and if the offence is punishable with imprisonment for any term not extending to ten years, shall be punished with imprisonment of the description provided for the offence, for a term which may extend to one-fourth part of the longest term of the imprisonment provided for the offence, or with fine, or with both.

202. Intentional omission to give information of offence by person bound to inform: Whoever, knowing or having reason to believe that an offence has been committed, intentionally omits to give any information respecting that offence which he is legally bound to give, shall be punished with imprisonment of either description for a term which may extend to six months, or with fine, or with both.

203. Giving false information respecting an offence committed: Whoever, knowing or having reason to believe that an offence has been committed, gives any information respecting that offence which he knows or believes to be false, shall be punished with imprisonment of either description for a term which may extend to two years, or with fine, or with both.

Explanation.—In sections 201 and 202 and in this section the word "offence" includes any act committed at any place out of India, which, if committed in India, would be punishable under any of the following sections, namely, 302, 304, 382, 392, 393, 394, 395, 396, 397, 398, 399, 402, 435, 436, 449, 450, 457, 458, 459 and 460.

204. Destruction of document to prevent its production as evidence: Whoever secretes or destroys any document and electronic record which he may be lawfully compelled to produce as evidence in a Court of Justice, or in any proceeding lawfully held before a public servant, as such, or obliterates or renders illegible the whole or any part of such document or electronic record with the intention of preventing the same from being produced or used as evidence before such Court or public servant as aforesaid, or after he shall have been lawfully summoned or required to produce the same for that purpose, shall be punished with imprisonment of either description for a term which may extend to two years, or with fine, or with both.

205. False personation for purpose of act or proceeding in suit or prosecution: Whoever falsely personates another, and in such assumed character makes any admission or statement, or confesses judgment, or causes any process to be issued or becomes bail or security, or does any other act in any suit or criminal prosecution, shall be punished with imprisonment of either description for a term which may extend to three years, or with fine, or with both.

206. Fraudulent removal or concealment of property to prevent its seizure as forfeited or in execution: Whoever fraudulently removes, conceals, transfers or delivers to any person any property or any interest therein, intending thereby to prevent that property or interest therein from being taken as a forfeiture or in satisfaction of a fine, under a sentence which has been pronounced, or which he knows to be likely to be pronounced, by a Court of Justice or other competent authority, or from being taken in execution of a decree or order which has been made, or which he knows to be likely to be made by a Court of Justice in a civil suit, shall be punished with imprisonment of either description for a term which may extend to two years or with fine, or with both.

207. Fraudulent claim to property to prevent its seizure as forfeited or in execution: Whoever fraudulently accepts, receives or claims any property or any interest therein, knowing that he has no right or rightful claim to such property or interest, or practices any deception touching any right to any property or any interest therein, intending thereby to prevent that property or interest therein from being taken as a forfeiture or in satisfaction of a fine, under a sentence which has been pronounced, or which he knows to be likely to be pronounced by a Court of Justice or other competent authority, or from being taken in execution of a decree or order which has been made, or which he knows to be likely to be made by a Court of Justice in a civil suit, shall be punished with imprisonment of either description for a term which may extend to two years, or with fine, or with both.

208. Fraudulently suffering decree for sum not due: Whoever fraudulently causes or suffers a decree or order to be passed against him at the suit of any person for a sum not due or for a larger sum than is due to such person or for any property or interest in property to which such person is not entitled, or fraudulently causes or suffers a decree or order to be executed against him after it has been satisfied, or for anything in respect of which it has been satisfied, shall be punished with imprisonment of either description for a term which may extend to two years, or with fine, or with both.

209. Dishonesty making false claim in Court: Whoever fraudulently or dishonestly, or with intent to injure or annoy any person, makes in a Court of Justice any claim which he knows to be false, shall be punished with imprisonment of either description for a term which may extend to two years, and shall also be liable to fine.

210. Fraudulently obtaining decree for sum not due: Whoever fraudulently obtains a decree or order against any person for a sum not due, or for a larger sum than is due or for any property or interest in property to which he is not entitled, or fraudulently causes a decree or order to be executed against any person after it has been satisfied or for anything in respect of which it has been satisfied, or fraudulently suffers or permits any such act to be done in his name, shall be punished with imprisonment of either description for a term which may extend to two years, or with fine, or with both.

211. False charge of offence made with intent to injure: Whoever, with intent to cause injury to any person, institutes or causes to be instituted any criminal proceeding against that person, or falsely charges any person with having committed an offence, knowing that there is no just or lawful ground for such proceeding or charge against that person, shall be punished with imprisonment of either description for a term which may extend to two years, or with fine, or with both;

and if such criminal proceeding be instituted on a false charge of an offence punishable with death, imprisonment for life, or imprisonment for seven years or upwards, shall be punishable with imprisonment of either description for a term which may extend to seven years, and shall also be liable to fine.

212. Harbouring offender: Whenever an offence has been committed, whoever harbours or conceals a person whom he knows or has reason to believe to be the offender, with the intention of screening him from legal punishment, if a capital offence.—shall,

if the offence is punishable with death, be punished with imprisonment of either description for a term which may extend to five years, and shall also be liable to fine;

if punishable with imprisonment for life, or with imprisonment.—and if the offence is punishable with imprisonment for life, or with imprisonment which may extend to ten years, shall be punished with imprisonment of either description for a term which may extend to three years, and shall also be liable to fine; and

if the offence is punishable with imprisonment which may extend to one year, and not to ten years, shall be punished with imprisonment of the description provided for the offence for a term which may extend to one-fourth part of the longest term of imprisonment provided for the offence, or with fine, or with both.

"Offence" in this section includes any act committed at any place out of India, which, if committed in 3 [India], would be punishable under any of the following sections, namely, 302, 304, 382, 392, 393, 394, 395, 396, 397, 398, 399, 402, 435, 436, 449, 450, 457, 458, 459 and 460; and every such act shall, for the purposes of this section, be deemed to be punishable as if the accused person had been guilty of it in 3 [India].]

Exception.—This provision shall not extend to any case in which the harbour or concealment is by the husband or wife of the offender.

213. Taking gift, etc., to screen an offender from punishment: Whoever accepts or attempts to obtain, or agrees to accept, any gratification for himself or any other person, or any restitution of property to himself or any other person, in consideration of his concealing an offence or of his screening any person from legal punishment for any offence, or of his not proceeding against any person for the purpose of bringing him to legal punishment,

if a capital offence.—shall, if the offence is punishable with death, be punished with imprisonment of either description for a term which may extend to seven years, and shall also be liable to fine;

if punishable with imprisonment for life, or with imprisonment.—and if the offence is punishable with 1 [imprisonment for life], or with imprisonment which may extend to ten years, shall be punished with imprisonment of either description for a term which may extend to three years, and shall also be liable to fine; and

if the offence is punishable with imprisonment not extending to ten years, shall be punished with imprisonment of the description provided for the offence for a term which may extend to one fourth part of the longest term of imprisonment provided for the offence, or with fine, or with both.

214. Offering gift or restoration of property in consideration of screening offender: Whoever gives or causes, or offers or agrees to give or cause, any gratification to any person, or restores or causes the restoration of any property to any person, in consideration of that person's concealing an offence, or of his screening any person from legal punishment for any offence, or of his not proceeding against any person for the purpose of bringing him to legal punishment, if a capital offence.—shall,

if the offence is punishable with death, be punished with imprisonment of either description for a term which may extend to seven years, and shall also be liable to fine;

if punishable with imprisonment for life, or with imprisonment.—and if the offence is punishable with 1 imprisonment for life or with imprisonment which may extend to ten years, shall be punished with imprisonment of either description for a term which may extend to three years, and shall also be liable to fine; and

if the offence is punishable with imprisonment not extending to ten years, shall be punished with imprisonment of the description provided for the offence for a term which may extend to one-fourth part of the longest term of imprisonment provided for the offence, or with fine, or with both.

Exception.—The provisions of sections 213 and 214 do not extend to any case in which the offence may lawfully be compounded.

C. Fraud

Fraud is defined as the taking or gaining of property, money, vouchers, or anything of value from another person through deception, lying, or trickery supported by verbal or written documents, causing the victim to place his trust in the perpetrator and willingly hand over something of value from himself to the perpetrator. When fraud is committed against government property or valuable items, it is considered a serious felony.

The following provisions of the Indian Penal Code, 1860 deal with consequences of fraud:

24. Dishonestly: Whoever does anything with the intention of causing wrongful gain to one person or wrongful loss to another person, is said to do that thing "dishonestly"

421. Dishonest or fraudulent removal or concealment of property to prevent distribution among creditors: Any person who fraudulently or dishonestly conceals, removes or delivers or transfer or causes the transfer of any property to another person; or anyone who has deceitfully/ fraudulently, had concealed or had removed or had delivered or had transferred or had caused to be transferred any property, without appropriate consideration; the mentioned concealment or removal or delivery or transfer was done to prevent the distribution of that property, as per the law among the creditors of accused person or the creditors of another person.

- shall be punished for fraud with imprisonment of either description for a term which may extend to two years or fine or both.
- The fraudster shall be punished with imprisonment of either description for a term which may extend to two years, or with fine, or with both
- The act is non-cognizable, bailable, triable by any Magistrate, compoundable by the creditor who is affected but only with the permission of the court.

422. Dishonestly or fraudulently preventing debt being available for creditors: Any person who fraudulently or dishonestly makes omissions or performs an act, whereby the act or omission done by him creates a situation where no amount is made available as per law for the payment of his debts or the debts of another person, shall be-

- Punished for cheating with imprisonment of either description for a term which may extend to two years or fine or both.

This is a charge that can be bailed out.

423. Dishonest or fraudulent execution of deed of transfer containing false statement of consideration: Any person who has fraudulently or dishonestly executed, signed, or became a party to any instrument or deed; the instrument or deed implies to transfer or create a charge upon the concerned property or charge on interest on the involved property; the concerned deed or instrument contains a false statement related to the consideration of such charge or transfer or a false statement related to the person or persons for whose benefit or use the deed is intended to operate

- the punishment for cheating is imprisonment of either description for a term which may extend to two years or fine or both.

This is a bailable offence.

424. Dishonest or fraudulent removal or concealment of property: Any person who has fraudulently or dishonestly removed, or concealed any property of himself or another person; anyone who has fraudulently or dishonestly assisted in the removal or concealment of a property of himself or another person; any individual who has dishonestly or fraudulently given up or released any claim or demand to which he is entitled

- The punishment for cheating is imprisonment of either description for a term which may extend to two years or fine or both.

This is a bailable charge.

D. Cheating

Cheating is when someone deceives another person into believing something that is not true. Cheating has an impact on a person's physique, reputation, and any property that the individual may acquire or own. Cheating can be done by someone in a fiduciary relationship, and it has an impact on the person who has been defrauded. In order to fool the opposing party, a person can cheat by misrepresenting the facts or utilising fake proof. The individual who is fooled considers the deceiving party's representations to be real, which has a negative impact on the person's mental and physical health. Cheating can cause stress, and tension, and have a negative impact on a person's mental health. It can also lead to trust issues, making it difficult for the individual who has been duped to trust someone else again. After being duped, a person may suffer from low self-esteem and financial loss due to the loss of property.

405. Criminal breach of trust: Whoever dishonestly or fraudulently conceals or removes any property of himself or any other person, or dishonestly or fraudulently assists in the concealment or removal thereof, or dishonestly releases any demand or claim to which he is entitled, shall be punished with imprisonment of either description for a term which may extend to two years, or with fine, or with both.

415. Cheating: Whoever, by deceiving any person, fraudulently or dishonestly induces the person so deceived to deliver any property to any person, or to consent that any person shall retain any property, or intentionally induces the person so deceived to do or omit to do anything which he would not do or omit if he were not so deceived, and which act or omission causes or is likely to cause damage or harm to that person in body, mind, reputation or property, is said to "cheat".

Explanation.—A dishonest concealment of facts is a deception within the meaning of this section.

416. Cheating by personation: A person is said to "cheat by personation" if he cheats by pretending to be some other person, or by knowingly substituting one person for or another, or representing that he or any other person is a person other than he or such other person really is.

Explanation.—The offence is committed whether the individual personated is a real or imaginary person.

417. Punishment for cheating: Whoever cheats shall be punished with imprisonment of either description for a term which may extend to one year, or with fine, or with both.

418. Cheating with knowledge that wrongful loss may ensue to person whose interest offender is bound to protect: Whoever cheats with the knowledge that he is likely thereby to cause wrongful loss to a person whose interest in the transaction to which the cheating relates, he was bound, either by law, or by a legal contract, to protect,

shall be punished with imprisonment of either description for a term which may extend to three years, or with fine, or with both.

419. Punishment for cheating by personation: Whoever cheats by personation shall be punished with imprisonment of either description for a term which may extend to three years, or with fine, or with both.

420. Cheating and dishonestly inducing delivery of property: Whoever cheats and thereby dishonestly induces the person deceived to deliver any property to any person, or to make, alter or destroy the whole or any part of a valuable security, or anything which is signed or sealed, and which is capable of being converted into a valuable security,

shall be punished with imprisonment of either description for a term which may extend to seven years, and shall also be liable to fine.

462. Punishment for same offence when committed by person entrusted with custody: Whoever, being entrusted with any closed receptacle which contains or which he believes to contain property, without having authority to open the same, dishonestly, or with intent to commit mischief, breaks open or unfastens that receptacle, shall be punished with imprisonment of either description for a term which may extend to three years, or with fine, or with both.

E. Mischief

425. Mischief: Whoever with intent to cause, or knowing that he is likely to cause, wrongful loss or damage to the public or to any person, causes the destruction of any property, or any such change in any property or in the situation thereof as destroys or diminishes its value or utility, or affects it injuriously, commits "mischief".

Explanation 1.—It is not essential to the offence of mischief that the offender should intend to cause loss or damage to the owner of the property injured or destroyed. It is sufficient if he intends to cause, or knows that he is likely to cause, wrongful loss or damage to any person by injuring any property, whether it belongs to that person or not.

Explanation 2.—Mischief may be committed by an act affecting property belonging to the person who commits the act, or to that person and others jointly.

F. Forgery

463. Forgery: Whoever makes any false document or false electronic record or part of a document or electronic record, with intent to cause damage or injury], to the public or to any person, or to support any claim or title, or to cause any person to part with property, or to enter into any express or implied contract, or with intent to commit fraud or that fraud may be committed, commits forgery.

464. Making a false document: A person is said to make a false document or false electronic record—

First-Who dishonestly or fraudulently—

(a) makes, signs, seals or executes a document or part of a document;

(b) makes or transmits any electronic record or part of any electronic record;

(c) affixes any electronic signature on any electronic record;

(d) makes any mark denoting the execution of a document or the authenticity of the electronic signature,

with the intention of causing, it to be believed that such document or part of document, electronic record or electronic signature was made, signed, sealed, executed, transmitted or affixed by or by the authority of a person by whom or by whose authority he knows that it was not made, signed, sealed, executed or affixed; or

Secondly.—Who without lawful authority, dishonestly or fraudulently, by cancellation or otherwise, alters a document or an electronic record in any material part thereof, after it has been made, executed or affixed with electronic signature either by himself or by any other person, whether such person be living or dead at the time of such alteration;

or

Thirdly.—Who dishonestly or fraudulently causes any person to sign, seal, execute or alter a document or an electronic record or to affix his electronic signature on any electronic record knowing that such person by reason of unsoundness of mind or intoxication cannot, or that by reason of deception practiced upon him, he does not know the contents of the document or electronic record or the nature of the alteration.

Explanation 1.—A man's signature of his own name may amount to forger

Explanation 2.—The making of a false document in the name of a fictious person, intending it to be believed that the document was made by a real person, or in the name of a deceased person, intending it to be believed that the document was made by the person in his lifetime, may amount to forgery.

Explanation 3.—For the purposes of this section, the expression "affixing electronic signature" shall have the meaning assigned to it in clause (d) of sub-section (1) of section 2 of the Information Technology Act, 2000 (21 of 2000).]

465. Punishment for forgery: Whoever commits forgery shall be punished with imprisonment of either description for a term which may extend to two years, or with fine, or with both.

466 . Forgery of record of Court or of public register, etc.: Whoever forges a document or an electronic record, purporting to be a record or proceeding of or in a Court of Justice, or a register of birth, baptism, marriage or burial, or a register kept by a public servant as such, or a certificate or document purporting to be made by a public servant in his official capacity, or an authority to institute or defend a suit, or to take any proceedings therein, or to confess judgment, or a power of attorney,

shall be punished with imprisonment of either description for a term which may extend to seven years, and shall also be liable to fine.

Explanation.—For the purposes of this section, "register" includes any list, data or record of any entries maintained in the electronic form as defined in clause (r) of sub-section (1) of section 2 of the Information Technology Act, 2000 (21 of 2000).]

467. Forgery of valuable security, will, etc.: Whoever forges a document which purports to be a valuable security or a will, or an authority to adopt a son, or which purports to give authority to any person to make or transfer any valuable security, or to receive the principal, interest or dividends thereon, or to receive or deliver any money, movable property, or valuable security, or any document purporting to be an acquittance or receipt acknowledging the payment of money, or an acquittance or receipt for the delivery of any movable property or valuable security, shall be punished with imprisonment for life, or with imprisonment of either description for a term which may extend to ten years, and shall also be liable to fine.

Forgery for purpose of cheating: Whoever commits forgery, intending that the document or electronic record forged shall be used for the purpose of cheating,

shall be punished with imprisonment of either description for a term which may extend to seven years, and shall also be liable to fine.

469. Forgery for purpose of harming reputation: Whoever commits forgery, intending that the document or electronic record forged shall harm the reputation of any party, or knowing that it is likely to be used for that purpose,

shall be punished with imprisonment of either description for a term which may extend to three years, and shall also be liable to fine.

470. Forged document: A false document or electronic record made wholly or in part by forgery is designated "a forged document or electronic record".

471. Using as genuine a forged document or electronic record: Whoever fraudulently or dishonestly uses as genuine any document or electronic record which he knows or has reason to believe to be a forged document or electronic record,

shall be punished in the same manner as if he had forged such document or electronic record.

472. Making or possessing counterfeit seal, etc., with intent to commit forgery punishable under section 467: Whoever makes or counterfeits any seal, plate or other instrument for making an impression, intending that the same shall be used for the purpose of committing any forgery which would be punishable under section 467 of this Code, or, with such intent, has in his possession any such seal, plate or other instrument, knowing the same to be counterfeit,

shall be punished with imprisonment for life, or with imprisonment of either description for a term which may extend to seven years, and shall also be liable to fine.

Making or possessing counterfeit seal, etc., with intent to commit forgery punishable otherwise: Whoever makes or counterfeits any seal, plate or other instrument for making an impression, intending that the same shall be used for the purpose of committing any forgery which would be punishable under any section of this Chapter other than section 467, or, with such intent, has in his possession any such seal, plate or other instrument, knowing the same to be counterfeit,

shall be punished with imprisonment of either description for a term which may extend to seven years, and shall also be liable to fine.

474. Having possession of document described in section 466 or 467, knowing it to be forged and intending to use it genuine: Whoever has in his possession any document or electronic record, knowing the same to be forged and intending that the same shall fraudulently or dishonestly be used as genuine, shall, if the document or electronic record is one of the description mentioned in section 466 of this Code, be punished with imprisonment of either description for a term which may extend to seven years, and shall also be liable to fine; and if the document is one of the description mentioned in section 467, shall be punished with imprisonment for life, or with imprisonment of either description, for a term which may extend to seven years, and shall also be liable to fine.

475. Counterfeiting device or mark used for authenticating documents described in section 467, or possessing counterfeit marked material: Whoever counterfeits upon, or in the substance of, any material, any device or mark used for the purpose of authenticating any document described in section 467 of this Code, intending that such device or mark shall be used for the purpose of giving the appearance of authenticity to any document then forged or thereafter to be forged on such material, or who, with such intent, has in his possession any material upon or in the substance of which any such device or mark has been counterfeited,

shall be punished with imprisonment for life, or with imprisonment of either description for a term which may extend to seven years, and shall also be liable to fine.

476. Counterfeiting device or mark used for authenticating documents other than those described in section 467, or possessing counterfeit marked material:

Whoever counterfeits upon, or in the substance of, any material, any device or mark used for the purpose of authenticating any document or electronic record other than the documents described in section 467 of this Code, intending that such device or mark shall be used for the purpose of giving the appearance of authenticity to any document then forged or thereafter to be forged on such material, or who with such intent, has in his possession any material upon or in the substance of which any such device or mark has been counterfeited,

shall be punished with imprisonment of either description for a term which may extend to seven years, and shall also be liable to fine.

477. Fraudulent cancellation, destruction, etc., of will, authority to adopt, or valuable security: Whoever fraudulently or dishonestly, or with intent to cause damage or injury to the public or to any person, cancels, destroys or defaces, or attempts to cancel, destroy or deface, or secretes or attempts to secrete any document which is or purports to be a will, or an authority to adopt a son, or any valuable security, or commits mischief in respect of such document,

shall be punished with imprisonment for life, or with imprisonment of either description for a term which may extend to seven years, and shall also be liable to fine.

477A. Falsification of accounts: Whoever, being a clerk, officer or servant, or employed or acting in the capacity of a clerk, officer or servant, willfully, and with intent to defraud, destroys, alters, mutilates or falsifies any book, electronic record, paper, writing valuable security or account which belongs to or is in the possession of his employer, or has been received by him for or on behalf of his employer, or willfully, and with intent to defraud, makes or abets the making of any false entry in, or omits or alters or abets the omission or alteration of any material particular from or in. any such book, electronic record, paper, writing valuable security or account, shall be punished with imprisonment of either description for a term which may extend to seven years, or with fine, or with both.

3. Prevention of Corruption Act 2013.

Following are the punishment prescribed for offences under the Act:

Sec. 7. Public servant taking gratification other than legal remuneration in respect of an official act

- shall be punishable with imprisonment which shall be not less than six months but which may extend to five years and shall also be liable to fine.

Sec. 8. Taking gratification, in order, by corrupt or illegal means, to influence public servant

- shall be punishable with imprisonment for a term which shall be not less than six months but which may extend to five years and shall also be liable to fine.

Sec. 9. Taking gratification, for exercise of personal influence with public servant

- shall be punishable with imprisonment for a term which shall be not less than six months but which may extend. to five years and shall also be liable to fine.

Sec. 10. Punishment for abetment by public servant of offences defined in section 8 or 9

- shall be punishable with imprisonment for a term which shall be not less than six months but which may extend to five years and shall also be liable to fine.

Sec. 11. Public servant obtaining valuable thing, without consideration from person concerned in proceeding or business transacted by such public servant

- shall be punishable with imprisonment for a term which shall be not less than six months but which may extend to five years and shall also be liable to fine.

Sec. 12. Punishment for abetment of offences defined in section 7 or 11

- shall be not less than six months but which may extend to five years and shall also be liable to fine.

Sec. 13. Criminal misconduct by a public servant

- shall be punishable with imprisonment for a term which shall be not less than one year but which may extend to seven years and shall also be liable to fine.

Sec. 14. Habitual committing of offence under sections 8, 9 and 12

- shall be punishable with imprisonment for a term which shall be not less than two years but which may extend to seven years and shall also be liable to fine.

Sec. 15. Punishment for attempt

- Whoever attempts to commit an offence referred to in clause (c) or clause (d) of sub-section (1) of section 13 shall be punishable with imprisonment for a term which may extend to three years and with fine.

4. Prevention of Money laundering Act 2012.

Offence of money-laundering {Sec. 3} — Whosoever directly or indirectly attempts to indulge or knowingly assists or knowingly is a party or is actually involved in any process or activity connected with the proceeds of crime including its concealment, possession, acquisition or use and projecting or claiming it as untainted property shall be guilty of offence of money-laundering.

Explanation—For the removal of doubts, it is hereby clarified that—

(i) a person shall be guilty of offence of money-laundering if such person is found to have directly or indirectly attempted to indulge or knowingly assisted or knowingly is a party or is actually involved in one or more of the following processes or activities connected with proceeds of crime, namely—

(a) concealment; or (b) possession; or (c) acquisition; or (d) use; or (e) projecting as untainted property; or (f) claiming as untainted property, in any manner whatsoever;

(ii) the process or activity connected with proceeds of crime is a continuing activity and continues till such time a person is directly or indirectly enjoying the proceeds of crime by its concealment or possession or acquisition or use or projecting it as untainted property or claiming it as untainted property in any manner whatsoever.

Punishment for money-laundering {Sec 4}—Whoever commits the offence of money-laundering shall be punishable with rigorous imprisonment for a term which shall not be less than three years but which may extend to seven years and shall also be liable to fine.

Provided that where the proceeds of crime involved in money-laundering relates to any offence specified under paragraph 2 of Part A of the Schedule, the provisions of this section shall have effect as if for the words "which may extend to seven years", the words "which may extend to ten years" had been substituted.

5. The Companies Act 2013.

447. Punishment for fraud — Any person who is found to be guilty of fraud, involving an amount of at least ten lakh rupees or one per cent of the turnover of the company, whichever is lower, without prejudice to any liability including repayment of any debt under this Act or any other law for the time being in force, shall be punishable with imprisonment for a term which shall not be less than six months but which may extend to ten years and shall also be liable to fine which shall not be less than the amount involved in the fraud, but which may extend to three times the amount involved in the fraud:

Provided that where the fraud in question involves public interest, the term of imprisonment shall not be less than three years.

Where the fraud involves an amount less than ten lakh rupees or one per cent of the turnover of the company, whichever is lower, and does not involve public interest, any person guilty of such fraud shall be punishable with imprisonment for a term which may extend to five years or with fine which may extend to fifty lakh rupees or with both.

Explanation to the Section defines Fraud, Wrongful gain and wrongful loss as under:

(i) **fraud** in relation to affairs of a company or any, body corporate, includes any act, omission, concealment of any fact or abuse of position committed by any person or any other person with the connivance in any manner, with intent to deceive, to gain undue advantage from, or to injure the interests of, the company or its shareholders or its creditors or any other person, whether or not there is any wrongful gain or wrongful loss;

(ii) **wrongful gain** means the gain by unlawful means of property to which the person gaining is not legally entitled.

(iii) **wrongful loss** means the loss by unlawful means of property to which the person losing is legally entitled.

448. Punishment for false statement— Save as otherwise provided in this Act, if in any return, report, certificate, financial statement, prospectus, statement or other document required by, or for, the purposes of any of the provisions of this Act or the rules made thereunder, any person makes a statement—

(a) which is false in any material particulars, knowing it to be false; or

(b) which omits any material fact, knowing it to be material, he shall be liable under section 447.

449. Punishment for false evidence— Save as otherwise providedinthisAct,ifanypersonintentionallygivesfalseevidence—

(a) upon any examination on oath or solemn affirmation, authorised under this Act; or

(b) in any affidavit, deposition or solemn affirmation, in or about the winding up of any company under this Act, or otherwise in or about any matter arising under this Act, he shall be -

punishable with imprisonment for a term which shall not be less than three years but which may extend to seven years and with fine which may extend to ten lakh rupees.

450. Punishment where no specific penalty or punishment is provided— If a company or any officer of a company or any other person contravenes any of the provisions of this Act or the rules made thereunder, or any condition, limitation or restriction subject to which any approval, sanction, consent, confirmation, recognition, direction or exemption in relation to any matter has been accorded, given or granted, and for which no penalty or punishment is provided elsewhere in this Act, shall be-

punishable with penalty which may extend to ten thousand rupees, and where the contravention is continuing one, with a further penalty which may extend to one thousand rupees for every day after the first during which the contravention continues, subject to a maximum of two lakh rupees and

every officer of the company who is in default shall be liable to a penalty of ten thousand rupees, and in case of continuing contravention, with a further penalty of one thousand rupees each day after the first during which the contravention continues, subject to a maximum of fifty thousand rupees. .

451. Punishment in case of repeated default within a period of three years— Where a company or an officer of a company commits an offence punishable either with fine or with imprisonment and where the same offence is committed for the second or subsequent occasions, within a period of three years, then -

that company and every officer thereof who is in default shall be punishable with twice the amount of fine for such offence in addition to any imprisonment provided for that offence.

Section 212. Investigation into affairs of Company by Serious Fraud Investigation Office.

(2) Where any case has been assigned by the Central Government to the Serious Fraud Investigation Office for investigation under this Act, no other investigating agency of Central Government or any State Government shall proceed with investigation in such case in respect of any offence under this Act and in case any such investigation has already been initiated, it shall not be proceeded further with and the concerned agency shall transfer the relevant documents and records in respect of such offences under this Act to Serious Fraud Investigation Office.

(5) The company and its officers and employees, who are or have been in employment of the company shall be responsible to provide all information, explanation, documents and assistance to the Investigating Officer as he may require for conduct of the investigation,

(6) Notwithstanding anything contained in the Code of Criminal Procedure, 1973, offence covered under Section

447 of this Act shall be cognizable and no person accused under those sections shall be on bail or on his own bond unless-

(i) the Public Prosecutor has been given an opportunity to oppose the application for such release; and

(ii) where the public prosecutor opposed the application, the Court is satisfied that there are reasonable grounds for believing that he is not guilty of such offence and that he is not likely to commit any offence while on bail:

Provided that a person, who is under the age of sixteen years or is a woman or is sick or infirm, may be released on bail, if the Special Court so directs:

Provided that Special Court shall not take cognizance of any offence referred to in this sub-section except upon a complaint in writing made by-

(a) the Director, Special Fraud Investigation; or

(b) any officer of the Central Government authorised, by a general or special order in writing in this behalf by that Government.

(8) If any officer below the rank of Assistant Director of SFIO authorised in this behalf by the Central Government by general or special order, has on the basis of material information in his possession reason to believe in writing that any person has been guilty of any offence punishable under sections referred to in sub-section (6), he may arrest

such person and shall, as soon as may be, inform him of the grounds for such arrest.

6. Information Technology Act 2008.

Sec. 43 Penalty and Compensation for damage to computer, computer system, etc.

If any person without permission of the owner or any other person who is in-charge of a computer, computer system or computer network –

(a) accesses or secures access to such computer, computer system or computer network or computer resource

(b) downloads, copies or extracts any data, computer data base or information from such computer, computer system or computer network including information or data held or stored in any removable storage medium

(c) introduces or causes to be introduced any computer contaminant or computer virus into any computer, computer system or computer network

(d) damages or causes to be damaged any computer, computer system or computer network, data, computer data base or any other programmes residing in such computer, computer system or computer network

(e) disrupts or causes disruption of any computer, computer system or computer network

(f) denies or causes the denial of access to any person authorised to access any computer, computer system or computer network by any means

(g) provides any assistance to any person to facilitate access to a computer, computer system or computer network in contravention of the provisions of this Act, rules or regulations made thereunder

(h) charges the services availed of by a person to the account of another person by tampering with or manipulating any computer, computer system, or computer network

(i) destroys, deletes or alters any information residing in a computer resource or diminishes its value or utility or affects it injuriously by any means

(j) Steals, conceals, destroys or alters or causes any person to steal, conceal, destroy or alter any computer source code used for a computer resource with an intention to cause damage, he **shall be liable** to pay damages by way of compensation not exceeding one crore rupees to the person so affected.

43A. Compensation for failure to protect data

Where a body corporate, possessing, dealing or handling any sensitive personal data or information in a computer resource which it owns, controls or operates, is negligent in implementing and maintaining reasonable security practices and procedures and thereby causes wrongful loss or wrongful gain to any person,

such body corporate **shall be liable** to pay damages by way of compensation, not exceeding five crore rupees, to the person so affected.

44. Penalty for failure to furnish information, return, etc.

If any person who is required under this Act or any rules or regulations made thereunder to -

(a) furnish any document, return or report to the Controller or the Certifying Authority, fails to furnish the same,

he shall be liable to a penalty not exceeding one lakh and fifty thousand rupees for each such failure;

(b) file any return or furnish any information, books or other documents within the time specified therefor in the regulations, fails to file return or furnish the same within the time specified therefore in the regulations,

he shall be liable to a penalty not exceeding five thousand rupees for every day during which such failure continues:

(c) maintain books of account or records, fails to maintain the same,

he **shall be liable** to a penalty not exceeding ten thousand rupees for every day during which the failure continues.

45. Residuary Penalty Whoever contravenes any rules or regulations made under this Act, for the contravention of which no penalty has been separately provided,

shall **be liable to pay** a compensation not exceeding twenty-five thousand rupees to the person affected by such contravention or a penalty not exceeding twenty-five thousand rupees.

65. Tampering with Computer Source Documents Whoever knowingly or intentionally conceals, destroys or alters or intentionally or knowingly causes another to conceal, destroy or alter any computer source code used for a computer, computer programme, computer system or computer network, when the computer source code is required to be kept or maintained by law for the time being in force,

shall **be punishable** with imprisonment up to three years, or with fine which may extend up to two lakh rupees, or with both.

66. Computer Related Offences If any person, dishonestly, or fraudulently, does any act referred to in section 43, he

shall **be punishable** with imprisonment for a term which may extend to two three years or with fine which may extend to five lakh rupees or with both.

66 A. Punishment for sending offensive messages through communication service, etc. Any person who sends, by means of a computer resource or a communication device, -

(a) any information that is grossly offensive or has menacing character; or

(b) any information which he knows to be false, but for the purpose of causing annoyance, inconvenience, danger, obstruction, insult, injury, criminal intimidation, enmity, hatred, or ill will, persistently makes by making use of such computer resource or a communication device,

(c) any electronic mail or electronic mail message for the purpose of causing annoyance or inconvenience or to deceive or to mislead the addressee or recipient about the origin of such messages

shall **be punishable** with imprisonment for a term which may extend to two three years and with fine.

66B. Punishment for dishonestly receiving stolen computer resource or communication device Whoever dishonestly receives or retains any stolen computer resource or communication device knowing or having reason to believe the same to be stolen computer resource or communication device,

shall **be punished with** imprisonment of either description for a term which may extend to three years or with fine which may extend to rupees one lakh or with both.

66C. Punishment for identity theft Whoever, fraudulently or dishonestly make use of the electronic signature, password or any other unique identification feature of any other person, shall **be punished with** imprisonment of either description for a term which may extend to three years and shall also be liable to fine which may extend to rupees one lakh.

66D. Punishment for cheating by personation by using computer resource

Whoever, by means of any communication device or computer resource cheats by personation,

shall **be punished with** imprisonment of either description for a term which may extend to three years and shall also be liable to fine which may extend to one lakh rupees.

66E. Punishment for violation of privacy Whoever, intentionally or knowingly captures, publishes or transmits the image of a private area of any person without his or her consent, under circumstances violating the privacy of that person,

shall be **punished with** imprisonment which may extend to three years or with fine not exceeding two lakh rupees, or with both

66F. Punishment for cyber terrorism

(1) Whoever-

(A) with intent to threaten the unity, integrity, security or sovereignty of India or to strike terror in the people or any section of the people by –

(i) denying or cause the denial of access to any person authorized to access computer resource; or

(ii) attempting to penetrate or access a computer resource without authorisation or exceeding authorized access; or

(iii) introducing or causing to introduce any Computer Contaminant. and by means of such conduct causes or is likely to cause death or injuries to persons or damage to or destruction of property or disrupts or knowing that it is likely to cause damage or disruption of supplies or services essential to the life of the community or adversely affect the critical information infrastructure specified under section 70, or

(B) knowingly or intentionally penetrates or accesses a computer resource without authorisation or exceeding authorized access, and by means of such conduct obtains access to information, data or computer database that is restricted for reasons of the security of the State or foreign relations; or any restricted information, data or computer database, with reasons to believe that such information, data or computer database so obtained may be used to cause or likely to cause injury to the interests of the sovereignty and integrity of India, the security of the State, friendly relations with foreign States, public order, decency or morality, or in relation to contempt of court, defamation or incitement to an offence, or to the advantage of any foreign nation, group of individuals or otherwise, commits the offence of cyber terrorism.

(2) Whoever commits or conspires to commit cyber terrorism **shall be punishable** with imprisonment which may extend to imprisonment for life'.

67C. Preservation and Retention of information by intermediaries (1) Intermediary shall preserve and retain such information as may be specified for such duration and in such manner and format as the Central Government may prescribe.

(2) Any intermediary who intentionally or knowingly contravenes the provisions of sub section (1)

shall be punished with an imprisonment for a term which may extend to three years and shall also be liable to fine.

68. Failure/refusal to comply with orders The Controller may, by order, direct a Certifying Authority or any employee of such Authority to take such measures or cease carrying on such activities as specified in the order if those are necessary to ensure compliance with the provisions of this Act, rules or any regulations made thereunder. Any person who fails to comply with any such order shall be guilty of an offence.

Penalty for contravention - Imprisonment up to 2 years, or/and with fine up to ₹100,000

69. Failure/refusal to decrypt data if the Controller is satisfied that it is necessary or expedient so to do in the interest of the sovereignty or integrity of India, the security of the State, friendly relations with foreign States or public order or for preventing incitement to the commission of any cognizable offence, for reasons to be recorded in writing, by order, direct any agency of the Government to intercept any information transmitted through any computer resource. The subscriber or any person in charge of the computer resource shall, when called upon by any agency which has been directed, must extend all facilities and technical assistance to decrypt the information. The subscriber or any person who fails to assist the agency referred is deemed to have committed a crime.

Penalty for contravention - Imprisonment up to **seven years and possible fine.**

70. Securing access or attempting to secure access to a protected system The appropriate Government may, by notification in the Official Gazette, declare that any computer, computer system or computer network to be a protected system. The appropriate Government may by order in writing, authorise the persons who are authorised to access protected systems. If a person who secures access or attempts to secure access to a protected system, then he is committing an offence.

Penalty for contravention - Imprisonment up to ten years, or/and with fine.

71. Penalty for misrepresentation Whoever makes any misrepresentation to, or suppresses any material fact from, the Controller or the Certifying Authority for obtaining any license or Electronic Signature Certificate, as the case may be, shall be **punished with** imprisonment for a term which may extend to two years, or with fine which may extend to one lakh rupees, or with both.

72. A Punishment for Disclosure of information in breach of lawful contract Save as otherwise provided in this Act or any other law for the time being in force, any person including an intermediary who, while providing services under the terms of lawful contract, has secured access to any material containing personal information about another person, with the intent to cause or knowing that he is likely to cause wrongful loss or wrongful gain discloses, without the consent of the person concerned, or in breach of a lawful contract, such material to any other person

shall be punished with imprisonment for a term which may extend to three years, or with a fine which may extend to five lakh rupees, or with both.

73. Penalty for publishing electronic Signature Certificate false in certain particulars (1) No person shall publish an Electronic Signature Certificate or otherwise make it available to any other person with the knowledge that

(a) the Certifying Authority listed in the certificate has not issued it; or

(b) the subscriber listed in the certificate has not accepted it; or

(c) the certificate has been revoked or suspended, unless such publication is for the purpose of verifying a digital signature created prior to such suspension or revocation

(2) Any person who contravenes the provisions of sub-section (1) **shall be punished** with imprisonment for a term which may extend to two years, or with fine which may extend to one lakh rupees, or with both.

74. Publication for fraudulent purpose Whoever knowingly creates, publishes or otherwise makes available an Electronic Signature Certificate for any fraudulent or unlawful purpose **shall be punished** with imprisonment for a term which may extend to two years, or with fine which may extend to one lakh rupees, or with both

76. Confiscation Any computer, computer system, floppies, compact disks, tape drives or any other accessories related thereto, in respect of which any provision of this Act, rules, orders or regulations made there under has been or is being contravened, shall be liable to confiscation:

7. SEBI Act, 1992

Reg. 15G - Penalty for insider trading.

If any insider who,—

(i) either on his own behalf or on behalf of any other person, deals in securities of a body corporate listed on any stock exchange on the basis of any unpublished price-sensitive information; or

(ii) communicates any unpublished price-sensitive information to any person, with or without his request for such information except as required in the ordinary course of business or under any law; or

(iii) counsels, or procures for any other person to deal in any securities of any, body corporate on the basis of unpublished price-sensitive information,

shall be liable to a penalty which shall not be less than ten lakh rupees but which may extend to twenty-five crore rupees or three times the amount of profits made out of insider trading, whichever is higher.

15H. Penalty for non-disclosure of acquisition of shares and takeovers.

If any person, who is required under this Act or any rules or regulations made thereunder, fails to,—

(i) disclose the aggregate of his shareholding in the body corporate before he acquires any shares of that body corporate; or

(ii) make a public announcement to acquire shares at a minimum price; or

(iii) make a public offer by sending letter of offer to the shareholders of the concerned company; or

(iv) make payment of consideration to the shareholders who sold their shares pursuant to letter of offer, he **shall be liable** to a penalty which shall not be less than ten lakh rupees but which may extend to twenty-five crore rupees or three times the amount of profits made out of such failure, whichever is higher.

15HA. Penalty for fraudulent and unfair trade practices.

If any person indulges in fraudulent and unfair trade practices relating to securities, he shall be liable to a penalty which shall not be less than five lakh rupees but which may extend to twenty-five crore rupees or three times the amount of profits made out of such practices, whichever is higher.

15HAA. Penalty for alteration, destruction, etc., of records and failure to protect the electronic database of Board.

shall be liable to a penalty which shall not be less than one lakh rupees but which may extend to ten crore rupees or three times the amount of profits made out of such act, whichever is higher.

1. Securities and Exchange Board of India (Prohibition of Fraudulent and Unfair Trade Practices relating to Securities Market) Regulations, 2003

Section 2(c): c) "fraud" includes any act, expression, omission or concealment committed whether in a deceitful manner or not by a person or by any other person with his connivance or by his agent while dealing in securities in order to induce another person or his agent to deal in securities, whether or not there is any wrongful gain or avoidance of any loss, and shall also include —

1. a knowing misrepresentation of the truth or concealment of material fact in order that another person may act to his detriment;
2. a suggestion as to a fact which is not true by one who does not believe it to be true;
3. an active concealment of a fact by a person having knowledge or belief of the fact;
4. a promise made without any intention of performing it;
5. a representation made in a reckless and careless manner whether it be true or false;
6. any such act or omission as any other law specifically declares to be fraudulent,
7. deceptive behavior by a person depriving another of informed consent or full participation,
8. a false statement made without reasonable ground for believing it to be true.
9. the act of an issuer of securities giving out misinformation that affects the market price of the security, resulting in investors being effectively misled even though they did not rely on the statement itself or anything derived from it other than the market price.

Section 3. Prohibition of certain dealings in securities.

Section 4. Prohibition of manipulative, fraudulent and unfair trade practices

Section 11. (1) The Board may, without prejudice to the provisions contained in sub-sections (1), (2), (2A) and (3) of section 11 and section 11B of the Act, by an order, for reasons to be recorded in writing, in the interests of investors and securities market, issue or take any of the following actions or directions, either pending investigation or enquiry or on completion of such investigation or enquiry, namely:

(a) suspend the trading of the security found to be or prima facie found to be involved in fraudulent and unfair trade practice in a recognized stock exchange;

(b) restrain persons from accessing the securities market and prohibit any person associated with securities market to buy, sell or deal in securities;

(c) suspend any office – bearer of any stock exchange or self-regulatory organization from holding such position;

(d) impound and retain the proceeds or securities in respect of any transaction which Is in violation or prima facie in violation of these regulations;

(e) direct an intermediary or any person associated with the securities market in any manner not to dispose of or alienate an asset forming part of a fraudulent and unfair transaction;

(f) require the person concerned to call upon any of its officers, other employees or representatives to refrain from dealing in securities in any particular manner;

(g) prohibit the person concerned from disposing of any of the securities acquired in contravention of these regulations;

(h) direct the person concerned to dispose of any such securities acquired in Contravention of these regulations, in such manner as the Board may deem fit, for restoring the status quo ante;

(2) Any final order passed under sub-regulation (1) shall be put on the website of the Board.

9. Prosecutions and Punishments under Income Tax Act, 1961.

Section 132(3) in case of search and seizure

The section empowers the tax authorities to initiate search proceedings at the premises of the taxpayer, after serving an order on the owner or the person who is in immediate possession or control thereof that he shall not remove, part with or otherwise deal with it, except with the previous permission of such officer.

Section 275A provides for prosecution for contravention of any of the provisions by the taxpayers.

The punishment is rigorous imprisonment of up to a period of 2 years and shall also be liable for fine.

Failure to afford necessary facility to authorised officer to inspect books of account or other documents as is required under section 132(1)(iib)

shall be punishable with rigorous imprisonment of up to a period of 2 years and shall also be liable to fine.

Fraudulent Removal, concealment, transfer or delivery of property to thwart tax recovery

If the taxpayer fraudulently removes, conceals, transfers or delivers to any person, any property or any interest therein, intending thereby to prevent that property or interest therein from being attached for recovery of tax, then prosecution proceedings can be initiated under **section 276.** - rigorous imprisonment for a term which may extend to two years and shall also be liable for fine.

Failure to pay/ensure payment of TDS or Division Distribution Tax to the credit of the Government

shall be punishable with rigorous imprisonment which shall not be less than 3 months but which may extend to 7 years and with fine.

Failure to pay the tax collected under the provisions of section 206C

If a person wilfully attempts in any manner whatsoever to evade any tax, penalty or interest chargeable or imposable, or under reports his income, under this Act, he shall, without prejudice to any penalty that may be imposable on him under any other provision of this Act, be punishable u/s **276(C)**

(i) in a case where the amount sought to be evaded or tax on under-reported income exceeds twenty-five hundred thousand rupees, with rigorous imprisonment for a term which shall not be less than six months but which may extend to seven years and with fine;

(ii) in any other case, with rigorous imprisonment for a term which shall not be less than three months but which may extend to two years and with fine.

Section 276C(2) of Income Tax Act If a person wilfully attempts in any manner whatsoever to evade the payment of any tax, penalty or interest under this Act, he shall, without prejudice to any penalty that may be imposable on him under any other provision of this Act, be punishable with rigorous imprisonment for a term which shall not be less than three months but which may extend to two years and shall, in the discretion of the court, also be liable to fine.

Willful failure to produce accounts and documents under section 142(1) or to comply with a direction issued under section 142(2A)

Section 276D provides for prosecution in the case of willful failure by the taxpayer to produce accounts and documents under section 142(1) or to comply with a direction issued under section 142(2A). As per section 276D, if a person willfully fails to produce accounts and documents as required in any notice issued under section 142(1) or willfully fails to comply with a direction issued to him under section 142(2A), he shall be punishable with rigorous imprisonment for a term which may extend to one year and with fine

Section 277. False statement in verification or delivery of false account, etc.

If a person makes a statement in any verification under this Act or under any rule made thereunder, or delivers an account or statement which is false, and which he either knows or believes to be false, or does not believe to be true, he shall be punishable,—

(i) in a case where the amount of tax, which would have been evaded if the statement or account had been accepted as true, exceeds twenty-five hundred thousand rupees, with rigorous imprisonment for a term which shall not be less than six months but which may extend to seven years and with fine;

(ii) in any other case, with rigorous imprisonment for a term which shall not be less than three months but which may extend to 3 two years and with fine.

Section 277 A. Falsification of books of account or document, etc., to enable any other person to evade any tax, penalty or interest chargeable/leviable under the Act

If any person (hereafter in this section referred to as the first person) willfully and with intent to enable any other person (hereafter in this section referred to as the second person) to evade any tax or interest or penalty chargeable and imposable under this Act, makes or causes to be made any entry or statement which is false and which the first person either knows to be false or does not believe to be true, in any books of account or other document relevant to or useful in any proceedings against the first person or the second person, under this Act, the first person shall be punishable with rigorous imprisonment for a term which shall not be less than three months but which may extend to three years and with fine.

Section 278. Abetment to make a false return, etc.

If a person abets or induces in any manner another person to make and deliver an account or a statement or declaration relating to [1] any income or any fringe benefits chargeable to tax which is false and which he either knows to be false or does not believe to be true or to commit an offence under sub-section (1) of section 276C, he shall be punishable,—

(i) in a case where the amount of tax, penalty or interest which would have been evaded, if the declaration, account or statement had been accepted as true, or which is willfully attempted to be evaded, exceeds [2] twenty-five hundred thousand rupees, with rigorous imprisonment for a term which shall not be less than six months but which may extend to seven years and with fine;

(ii) in any other case, with rigorous imprisonment for a term which shall not be less than three months but which may extend to [3] two years and with fine.

Second and subsequent offences under sections 276B, 276C(1), 276CC, 277 or 278

shall be punishable with imprisonment for a period which shall not be less than 6 months but which may extend to 7 years and with fine

Section 278 B. Punishment in case of offence by a company

- every person who, at the time the offence was committed was in charge of and was responsible to the company for the conduct of the business of the company as well as the company shall be deemed to be guilty of the offence and shall be liable to be proceeded against and punished accordingly.

10. Insolvency and Bankruptcy Code, 2016.

Offences committed by the officer of the corporate debtor or the corporate debtor and the subsequent penalties

Section	Offence	Punishment
68	willfully concealed any property or any debt, fraudulently removed any part of the property, of the value of ten thousand or more, or willfully concealed, destroyed or made a false entry in, or altered any document relating to the property of the corporate debtor or its affairs, or At any time after the insolvency commencement date, taken in pawn or pledge, or otherwise received the property knowing it to be so secured, transferred or disposed of	• **Imprisonment** Min. 3 years, Max. 5 years. • **Fine** Min. One Lakh Max. One crore Or • **Both**

69	Entering into transactions defrauding creditors or removing any part of the property of the corporate debtor within two months before the date of any unsatisfied judgment, decree or order for payment of money obtained against the corporate debtor.	• **Imprisonment–** Min. three years Max.five years • **Fine –** Min. one lakh Max. one crore • **Both**
70(1)	On or after the insolvency commencement date, does not disclose or deliver all or part of the property or, any books or papers to the resolution professional which he is required to be delivered, or fails to provide any information regarding the accounts of the corporate debtor or	• **Imprisonment-** Min. 3 Years Max.5 Years • **Fine** – Min. one Lakh Max. one Crore • **Both**

71	On and after the insolvency commencement date, destroys, mutilates, alters or falsifies any books, papers or securities, or makes or is in the knowledge of making of any false or fraudulent entry in the accounts with the intention to defraud any person.	• **Imprisonment**– Min. three Years Max. five Years • **Fine** –Min. one Lakh Max. one Crore • **Both**
72	Makes any material and willful omission in any statement relating to the affairs of the corporate debtor.	• **Imprisonment**– Min. three Years Max. five Years • **Fine** – Min. one Lakh Max. one Crore • **Both**
73	Before or after the insolvency commencement date, makes a false representation or commits any fraud for the purpose of obtaining the consent of the creditors to an agreement with reference to the affairs of the corporate debtor.	• **Imprisonment**- Min. one Year Max. five Years • **Fine** – Min. one Lakh Max. one Crore • **Both**

74 (C)	violates or willfully permits contravention of the provisions of section 14 of the code or under if Sec. 74(3) if he contravenes any of the terms of such resolution plan or abets such contravention.	• **Imprisonment**– Min. three Years Max.five Years • **Fine** –Min. one Lakh Max. three Lakh • **Both**
77	a corporate debtor provides information which is false in material particulars, in the application under section 10 knowing it to be false and omits any material fact, knowing it to be material	• **Imprisonment** - Min. three Years Max. five Years • **Fine** –Min. one Lakh Max. one Crore • **Both**
186(a)	If the bankrupt knowingly makes a false representation or willfully omits or conceals any material information while making an application for bankruptcy by a debtor	• **Imprisonment** - Max. 6 months • **Fine** –Max. 5 lakh • **Both**
186(b)	If the bankrupt fraudulently has failed to provide or deliberately withheld the production of, destroyed, falsified or altered, his books of accounts, financial information and other records under his custody or control.	• **Imprisonment** - Max. one year • **Fine** –Max. 5 lakh • **Both**

186(c)	If the bankrupt has contravened the restrictions under section 140 or the provisions of section 141 (Disqualification of bankrupt and Restrictions)	• **Imprisonment** - Max. 6 months • **Fine** –Max. 5 lakh • **Both**
186(d)	If the bankrupt has failed to deliver the possession of any property comprised in the estate of the bankrupt under his possession or control, which he is required to deliver under section 156	• **Imprisonment** - Max. 6 months • **Fine** –Max. 5 lakh • **Both**
186(e)	If the bankrupt has failed to account, without any reasonable cause or satisfactory explanation, for any loss incurred of any substantial part of his property comprised in the estate of the bankrupt from the date which is twelve months before the filing of the bankruptcy application.	• **Imprisonment** - Max. 2 years • **Fine** –If loss is quantifiable– up to three times of the value of the loss, If loss is not quantifiable– which may extend to five lakh rupees, • **Both**
186(f)	If the bankrupt has absconded or attempts to abscond after the bankruptcy commencement date	• **Imprisonment** - Max. 1 year • **Fine** –Max. 5 lakh • **Both**

11. Reserve Bank of India (Frauds classification and reporting by commercial banks and select FIs) directions, 2016.

8.10 Staff Accountability

8.10.1 As in the case of accounts categorised as NPAs, banks must initiate and complete a staff accountability exercise within six months from the date of classification as a Fraud. Wherever felt necessary or warranted, the role of sanctioning official(s) may also be covered under this exercise. The completion of the staff accountability exercise for frauds and the action taken shall be placed before the SCBF and intimated to the RBI through the FMR Update Application supplied to them.

8.10.2 Banks may bifurcate all fraud cases into vigilance and non-vigilance. Only vigilance cases should be referred to the investigative authorities. Non-vigilance cases may be investigated and dealt with at the bank level within a period of six months. It is emphasised that banks should strive to complete the staff accountability exercise within six months as clearing the air on the staff members concerned in a shorter time frame is appropriate and desirable.

8.10.3 In cases involving very senior executives of the bank, the Board / ACB/ SCBF may initiate the process of fixing staff accountability. It is clarified that very senior executives include the EDs and MD & CEOs of banks.

8.10.4 Staff accountability should not be held up on account of the case being filed with law enforcement agencies. Both the criminal and domestic enquiry should be conducted simultaneously.

8.11 Filing Complaints with Law Enforcement Agencies

8.11.1 Banks are required to lodge the complaint with the law enforcement agencies immediately on detection of fraud. There should ideally not be any delay in filing of the complaints with the law enforcement agencies since delays may result in the loss of relevant 'relied upon' documents, non-availability of witnesses, absconding of borrowers and also the money trail getting cold in addition to asset stripping by the fraudulent borrower.

8.11.2 It is observed that banks do not have a focal point for filing CBI / Police complaints. This results in a non-uniform approach to complaint filing by banks and the investigative agency has to deal with dispersed levels of authorities in banks. This is among the most important reasons for delay in conversion of complaints to FIRs. It is, therefore, enjoined on banks to establish a nodal point / officer for filing all complaints with the CBI on behalf of the bank and serve as the single point for coordination and redressal of infirmities in the complaints.

8.11.3 The complaint lodged by the bank with the law enforcement agencies should be drafted properly and invariably be vetted by a legal officer. It is also observed that banks sometimes file complaints with CBI / Police on the grounds of cheating, misappropriation of funds, diversion of funds etc., by borrowers without classifying the accounts as fraud and/or reporting the accounts as fraud to RBI. Since such grounds automatically constitute the basis for classifying an account as a fraudulent one, banks should invariably classify such accounts as frauds and report the same to RBI.

8.12 Penal measures for fraudulent borrowers

8.12.1 In general, the penal provisions as applicable to willful defaulters would apply to the fraudulent borrower including the promoter director(s) and other whole - time directors of the company insofar as raising of funds from the banking system or from the capital markets by companies with which they are associated is concerned, etc. In particular, borrowers who have defaulted and have also committed a fraud in the account would be debarred from availing bank finance from Scheduled Commercial Banks, Development Financial Institutions, Government owned NBFCs, Investment Institutions, etc., for a period of five years from the date of full payment of the defrauded amount.

After this period, it is for individual institutions to take a call on whether to lend to such a borrower.

The penal provisions would apply to non-whole time - directors (like nominee directors and independent directors) only in rarest of cases based on conclusive proof of their complicity.

8.12.2 No restructuring or grant of additional facilities may be made in the case of RFA or fraud accounts. However, in cases of fraud/malfeasance where the existing promoters are replaced by new promoters and the borrower company is totally delinked from such erstwhile promoters/ management, banks and JLF may take a view on restructuring of such accounts based on their viability, without prejudice to the continuance of criminal action against the erstwhile promoters/management.

8.12.3 No compromise settlement involving a fraudulent borrower is allowed unless the conditions stipulate that the criminal complaint will be continued.

8.12.4 In addition to above borrower - fraudsters, third parties such as builders, warehouse/cold storage owners, motor vehicle/tractor dealers, travel agents, etc. and professionals such as architects, valuers, chartered accountants, advocates, etc. are also to be held accountable if they have played a vital role in credit sanction/disbursement or facilitated the perpetration of frauds. Banks are advised to report to Indian Banks Association (IBA) the details of such third parties involved in frauds.

8.12.5 Before reporting to IBA, banks have to satisfy themselves of the involvement of third parties concerned and also provide them with an opportunity of being heard. In this regard the banks should follow normal procedures and the processes followed should be suitably recorded. On the basis of such information, IBA would, in turn, prepare caution lists of such third parties for circulation among the banks.

Chapter X

Some of the Corporate Failures/Frauds in India

{Not in any order}

Frauds of huge and unparalleled magnitude that are coming to public knowledge speaks volumes for the poor ethics and corporate governance in the corporate sector. The lack of consciousness and poor moral values of the Owners of businesses and everyone associated with them are the factors leading to this situation. No amount of tightening of the legislations seem to instill any fear in the minds of such persons.

It may be seen from only some of the corporate frauds illustrated in the following pages of this Chapter, how the negative aspects of human qualities viz., Greed, Ego, Arrogance, Selfishness, poor upbringing, lack of morality etc., have played havoc in the corporate sector in particular and the economy in general.

A. Factors Responsible for failure of companies

Profitability issues	Disastrous acquisition strategies;	Massive Debts	Poor management
Overpowering promoters	Lack of Strategy,	Money laundering	Fleeing the country;
Severe competition	Fabrication of Books and Financial Statements	Diversion of Funds	Failed Corporate Governance
Compromised Auditors	Lack of independence of Auditors	Improper/Weak Board Structure	Failure of Independent Directors to discharge their statutory role
Use of Front companies	Overambitious Growth Plans	Environmental matters	Unquestioned Related Party dealings
Non-adherence with Accounting/ Auditing Standards	Mass scale bribery and corruption	Market collapse	Ponzi Schemes
Failed business model	Poor/unstable top management	criminal breach of trust, cheating, misappropriation and forgery for diversion of public money;	Collusion with bankers

Political interference	Embezzlement	Misconduct	Criminal conspiracy
Imprudent lending practices	Evergreening of loans	Gross under provisioning of NPAs	Over invoicing by vendors
Accounting manipulations	Overstatement of profits	Non - disclosure of Related Parties, subsidiaries, associates, joint ventures	Questionable role of Credit Rating Agencies
Invoicing without shipments;	Fraud by directors	Cheating the banks	criminal misconduct by promoters, unknown officials of lenders
Assignment of dues to ARC without security	Loans utilized for non-sanctioned purposes	Most transactions only with limited buyers, sellers, sister concerns; subsidiaries. No genuine business transactions.	Non-disclosure of true & fair information
Collective misconduct by the Key Managerial Persons	Payment of dividend from fake profits etc.		

B. Overview of Fraudulent Practices in Troubled Corporates in India

1. The Kingfisher Airlines

Established in **2003.** Owner, United Breweries Group/Vijay Mallya.

At its peak, had a fleet of 69 aircraft -mostly A320 family planes. Orders placed for Airbus and Boeing Aircrafts for intercontinental services.

The airlines never turned a profit. Debt grew deeper.

Yet in 2007, failing Air Deccan was acquired and merged mainly to get around the Indian aviation rule which did not allow the airline in existence for less than five years to fly internationally.

On October 20 2012, the airline's license was suspended by the DGCA.

It limped on in a state of bankruptcy until finally, on March 2nd 2016, the consortium of banks moved to recover dues.

Mallya was declared willful defaulter.

Mallya owes a Rs 9,000 crore from 17 Indian banks and is accused of fraud and money laundering cases in the country.

Enforcement Director registered money laundering case on the basis of a CBI probe into an alleged wilful default of Rs.900 crore loan in conspiracy with IDBI Bank officials.

Lack of strategy; lack of management;

However, Mallya fled to the UK in 2017 to escape all creditors. Despite an extradition effort by the Indian government to return him to the country, he remains at large, branded a 'fugitive economic offender'.

Jet Airways –

Founded in 1992. Was the country's largest and longest-serving private airline with several firsts to its credit and became a preferred airline to many.

Downfall -

Competition from low - cost airlines adding to losses

Acquired Sahara airlines unwisely for Rs 1450 cr.

Operations ceased in 2019.

Lenders approached NCLT for bankruptcy proceedings with debt of Rs 8500 cr and total liabilities of around Rs.25000 crores

In September 2019, the Enforcement Directorate questioned Naresh Goyal for investigating charges of foreign exchange violation against him. He was detained and questioned for money laundering by the ED in 2020.

The company indulged in multiple fraudulent practices of -

- overstating commission paid to a Dubai related party based in Dubai for years. This resulted in significant overstatement of expenses and underreporting of profits.

- diversion of funds by giving loans of around Rs.3353 Crores
- accounting of invoices of fake on Jet miles

After multiple bidding over 18 months, Jet was purchased by Kalrock, part of the Fritsch Group, in 2020, who is non - experienced in the airlines business.

Naresh Goyal was arrested eptember 1, 2023 in the Rs 538 crore Canara Bank fraud case. Ahead of his arrest, he was questioned by the Enforcement Directorate as he was heading to the Serious Fraud Investigation Office (SFIO) for questioning. After remaining in the custody of the agency till September 14, he was sent to judicial custody. His lawyers have move the Bombay High Court on the plea against his arrest and remand orders as "unwarranted, arbitrary and illegal.

2. Satyam Computer Services Ltd

Commencement – 1987. Promoter Ramalinga Raju and his brother. BSE listing 1991.

Company bagged multiple awards. Raju was awarded Ernest and Youngest Entrepreneur in 2007. By the end of 2008, global revenue crossed 2 billion.

Downfall

Self-confession by Raju of committing fraud Rs 7000 crores Through fabrication of financial statements, bank statements, to mislead the government, markets and customers.

The scam exposed loopholes in the corporate governance akin to 2009 Enron scandal.

The auditors - PWC were found guilty.

The CBI took charge of the case. Raju brothers and the auditors were sentenced to prison and were charged a huge sum as a penalty.

The company was taken over by Tech Mahindra.

3. Bhushan Steel Ltd {BPSL}

Incorporated 1999. Promoter: Sanjay Singal.

ED alleged that Bhushan Steel defrauded 33 banks and financial institutions of several thousand crores in seven years by money laundering.

The bank funds were used for creating assets (including equity investment in Bhushan Power & Steel Limited and properties in Delhi and London).

Sanjay Singal, CMD was arrested on November 22, 2019. Apart from attachment of some of the assets (Rs 4229.54cr), the ED initiated investigation under PMLA against Bhushan Steel and others for criminal conspiracy with unknown public servants of banks and others to cheat banks, financial institutions.

The firm was used by Sanjay Singal to fraudulently divert huge amount of bank funds through companies, shell companies and entities.

The ED stated that forgery was also committed causing wrongful loss to the lending banks and corresponding wrongful gain to themselves.

The company was eventually auctioned off to JSW Bhushan Power & Steel Limited who offered an Rs. 19,350 crore repayment proposal. The banks lost out on 60% of their loan amount.

4. Essar Steel

Ruias set up the Company in 1969.

Essar's ambitious growth plans, failed due to delay in environmental approvals and non-availability of natural gas.

By 2015, the company was saddled with financial creditor dues exceeding Rs 49,000 crore.

In June 2017, Essar was named among the list of 12 stressed accounts submitted by RBI that would have to undergo insolvency action under the IBC.

Essar Steel was put up for auction and later acquired jointly by Arcelor Mittal and Japan's Nippon Steel. The company was renamed ArcelorMittal Nippon Steel India (AM/NS India).

5. Dewan Housing Finance Ltd. {DHFL} – Non-banking company

DHFL was established in 1984.

First ever fraud housing finance company.,

Kapil Wadhwan, the promoter syphoned of funds and alleged money laundering activities.

Per January 2019 allegations Rs. 31,000 crores loans taken by DHFL in the names of shell companies were diverted for personal gains of promoters.

Rs 14,282 crore from funds of slum development rehabilitation were also diverted.

DHFL secured reconfirmation of high safety rating by Agencies.

Sold businesses to pay their debt and In 2019 even defaulted in its bond payments and Rs 900 crore worth of interest payments.

Bond downgrading caused a fall in the stock prices by over 97%.

RBI ordered superseding the board of DHFL citing corporate governance failure.

On 27 January 2020, Kapil Wadhawan was arrested under the Prevention of Money Laundering Act (PMLA). The arrest was related to providing loans to the organized criminal enterprise of Dawood Ibrahim.

The ED has linked Yes Bank for various fraud and transactions amounting to RS 3700 crores as debentures in DHFL.

On 24 March 2021, CBI filed a new suit against DHFL and its promoters Kapil Wadhawan and Dheeraj Wadhawan, wherein the later were accused of syphoning off the welfare subsidy fund of Pradhan Mantri Awas Yojana by creating 260,000 fake home loan accounts under the same scheme under the guise of a non-existent branch. The suit says, fake loans were granted worth ₹14,046 crore of which ₹11,755.79 crore were routed to shell corporations and citing these loans, subsidy amounts were claimed under Pradhan Mantri Awas Yojana.

Meanwhile, the RBI had approved the DHFL takeover by the Piramal Group -Piramal Capital and Housing Finance Limited reportedly for Rs 14,700 crore..

NFRA, in April 2023, charged that K Varghese & Co (the Audit Firm), not only accepted a legally invalid appointment but also flouted the provisions of the Chartered Accountants Act, which requires ensuring a valid appointment as per the norms.

The regulator also investigated the auditors' compliance with the applicable Standards on Auditing (SAs) in the performance of the branch audit of DHFL.

It was revealed that the auditors had not complied laws under Standards on Auditing, and had not maintained proper audit documentation and displayed flawed understanding and interpretations of the various stipulations in the law and standards in an unprofessional manner that established their professional misconduct.

In four separate orders, NFRA levied a fine of Rs 1 lakh each on auditors - - Mathew Samuel, Sam Varghese, Harish Kumar T K and M Baskaran. The auditors are partners of audit firm K Varghese & Co.

Besides, all of them were restrained for a period of one year from undertaking any audit in respect of financial statements or internal audit of the functions and activities of any company or body corporate during the ban period.

How fraud was committed:

- Granting of loans to related parties of promoters
- Loans granted to parties, who were not credit worthy or were unknown having same addresses in obscure locations
- Evergreening of bad loans
- Creation of around 6 lacs dummy accounts at one branch, using name of borrowers who had already repaid loans. These accounts were used to grant loans which were used to siphon funds to promoter companies. These loans ultimately turned out to be non-recoverable
- Utilisation of borrowed funds for personal purposes, such as acquiring personal properties, yachts etc.

- Consequently, huge amounts were shown as recoverable in the balance sheet, which were not recoverable

6. Lanco Infratech

Founded in 1986

Promoters - Two members of Lok Sabha.

Company had unmatched growth in initial years and won large construction contracts.

The company diversified into areas like power generation, transportation, solar energy, coal mining, etc.

Repeated charges of corrupt practices, caused the company into financial trouble.

Debt of over Rs 50,000 crore.

In July 2013 the company filed for corporate debt restructuring.

RBI pushed the Company before NCLT. In late 2017 the company faced insolvency proceedings before NCLT and the Board of Directors was suspended.

The lenders were wary of accepting resolution proposals that involve significant haircuts of upwards of 75% of the debt amount.

In 2018 liquidation of Lanco Infratech was ordered.

7. Tirupati Infrastructure Projects

The consortium of banks granted a term loan of ₹ 300 crore to the company between 2009 and 2014 for the construction of Hotel Radisson Blu at Paschim Vihar, New Delhi, along with commercial spaces.

The company had started showing stress in 2012, and after several efforts to salvage the account, it turned into a non-performing asset (NPA) in 2014.

It alleged that the company, its promoters, and its directors, with dishonest intentions, have caused wrongful loss to lending banks and wrongful gain to themselves by employing fraudulent and suspicious transactions, mainly by diversion and siphoning off the income generated from the project.

The CBI registered an FIR against the company on May 25, 2022, for allegedly causing a loss to the tune of Rs 289.15 crore, to a consortium of public sector banks led by the Bank of India by illegally diverting loan funds which it had taken for a high-end hotel project.

The Bank of India has alleged that the cumulative loss suffered by banks has spiraled over Rs 979 crore as on December 13, 2021, owing to accumulating dues.

The Bank of India alleged that the company entered into a sale agreement with third parties without the consent of the lending banks and falsified statements, pointed out by the forensic auditor appointed by the banks.

CBI stated that the Company had also sold several commercial/retail/office spaces of the said hotel-cum-commercial building to various parties without intimating the lender banks, and funds obtained from these buyers were diverted/siphoned off

The CMD of the company Jag Mohan Garg was arrested in July 2023.

8. Yash Jewellery Private Limited

Yash Jewelry was established in 2007 in collaboration with Andin International Inc., New York, which had 40 per cent equity.

In 2008 Pramod Goenka {brother of the infamous Vinod Goenka of DB Reality} the Promoter, purchased the stake of Andin International in 2008. In April 2023, CBI booked Pramod Goenka, and his company Yash Jewelry for an alleged cheating which caused a loss of over Rs 405 crore to SBI after the account was declared NPA in 2014.

It was alleged that accused Pramod Goenka and two others entered into criminal conspiracy to cheat the bank after inducing it to sanction loans of Rs 235 crore, which they siphoned off, causing a loss of Rs 405.58 crore.

Pramod Goenka, holding shares of DB Realty, is reported missing reportedly kidnapped by an African gang in Maputo, Mozambique. since February 2018.

9. Amtek Auto Limited {AAL}

The company owned by Arvind Dham was once the most prominent and profitable auto ancillary company. AAL started to expand at a rate they could not handle when the automobile industry was opened up in the 1990s. The company embarked on frenetic and aggressive 22 acquisitions via debt funding. RBI ordered the Company to be referred to NCLT.

In November 2022, the SFIO told the Supreme Court that loans close to Rs 22,000 crore involving Amtek Auto and its group companies, are under its scanner.

It was observed by the RP that the companies had –

(A) given loans and advances to related parties,

(B) transferred debit balances to capital work in progress,

(C) manipulated the books and executed other fraudulent transactions with related parties at the cost of stakeholders.

The SFIO said pursuant to the commencement of investigation, a total of nine look out circulars (LOCs) have been opened against the promoters and associates of AAL which has the effect of preventing them from leaving the country.

The SFIO said a petition under Section 241 and Section 242 of the Companies Act, 2013 for disgorgement of assets of the directors and promoters of AAL and three other group companies has already been filed before the competent tribunal having jurisdiction.

10. Videocon Industries Limited {Videocon}

Videocon is an Indian multinational conglomerate, headquartered in Mumbai· The company was founded in 1979, by Venugopal Dhoot. The group had 17 manufacturing sites in India and plants in Mainland China, Poland, Italy and Mexico. It was the third largest picture tube manufacturer in the world· valued at US$5.5 billion.

Once the Company was the third largest picture tube manufacturer in the world valued at US$5.5 billion.

The company stopped trading and entered corporate insolvency proceeding in June 2018.

It is claimed that Chanda Kochhar approved a high-valued loan for Dhoot's company, Videocon after he agreed to make investments in renewable business of Kochhar's husband. In the alleged loan fraud, ICICI bank sanctioned a loan of Rs 1,875 crore to Videocon group between 2009 and 2011. These loans were later claimed as non-performing assets which led to a loss of Rs 1730 crore to the bank.

In June 2021, NCLT approved Vedanta Group's bid to take over Videocon, paving way for the new ownership.

Dhoot was fined Rs 5 crore by Sebi, besides failing to declare his ownership of Supreme Energy and the fact that QTAPL and CFL were related parties in connection with certain transactions. The order was issued following Sebi's probe into certain "quid pro quo" arrangements between Venugopal Dhoot and Chanda Kochhar, former MD and CEO of ICICI Bank Ltd., in exchange for providing certain credit facilities to ICICI Bank and certain entities associated with the Videocon group as reported in media reports in March 2018.

According to CBI allegations, ICICI Bank extended facilities of Rs 3,250 crore to companies belonging to the Videocon Group in violation of the Banking Regulation Act, RBI norms, and the bank's credit policy.On 4 October 2018, Chanda Kochhar, the ex MD and CEO of ICICI Bank had to step down from her position following allegations of corruption in sanctioning loans to Videocon. It was alleged that Venugopal Dhoot, the promoter of Videocon had fraudulently transferred part of the loan received from ICICI Bank to the Kochhars' business enterprise.

Dhoot was arrested by the CBI in connection with the ICICI Bank-Videocon loan scam in December 2022 but granted interim bail In January 2023 by the Bombay High Court on the grounds that his arrest was not in compliance with the law

10A. Alok Industries

This ISO 9001:2000 certified company was established in 1986 by Surendra Bhagirathmal Jiwrajka. and had an ISO 9001:2000 certification. It created global sized capacities and expanded its markets across the global territories. The main business involved weaving, knitting, processing, home textiles, ready -made garments and polyester yarns. It exports 26% of its products to over 90 countries in the USA,

Alok Industries, reportedly, made mistake of not using the existing plant facilities for expansion, instead of opening new plants. What Alok didn't watch out for was the possibility of a fall in demand in the industry. These factors saw Alok's asset turnover worsen in addition to low demand they also fell prey to cut-throat competition.

Another one of Alok's mistakes was entering the real estate market in 2007. Consistent losses and increasing debt further worsened Alok's position. Reliance and JM Financial Asset Reconstruction Company won the bid for the company with a plan of Rs. 5000 crores in March 2019.

11. Sahara India Pariwar Scam

Sahara India Parivar, the once one of the most diversified corporate houses, declined fast when it indulged into many non-profiting businesses and also engaged itself into many unfair practices to defraud the stakeholders.

Since 2009, when the Sahara Group's activities first came under the radar of SEBI leading up to the arrest of Sahara India Pariwar founder Subrato Roy in 2014, both parties have been engaged in an aggressive regulatory conflict. SEBI alleged that Sahara India Real Estate Corp Ltd (SIRECL) and Sahara Housing Investment Corp Ltd (SHICL), which issued Optional Fully Convertible Debentures (OFCD), illegally collected investor money. SEBI went on to order Sahara to issue a full refund to its investors, which was challenged by Sahara before the Securities Appellate Tribunal (SAT).

When the SAT upheld SEBI's order, Sahara moved to the Supreme Court in August 2012. On 26 February 2014, the Supreme Court ordered the detention of Roy for failing to appear before it in connection with dispute with SEBI. and is now out on parole since May 2016. Sahara was allowed to sell a part of its assets in India to raise part of the money in question and deposit Rs 10000 crore with SEBI. As of 31 January 2019, Sahara still had to pay ₹10,621 crore to meet its total liability.

Roy was released on parole in 2017 following two years in prison for non-payment of dues

SEBI said outstanding liability of the Parivar's two companies and Roy stand at Ra 62,600 crore including interest in November 2020.

12. Cafe Coffee day {CCD}

V. G. Siddhartha started the café chain in 1996 when he incorporated Coffee Day Global, which is the parent of the Coffee Day chain. The first CCD outlet was set up on July 11, 1996, at Brigade Road, Bangalore, Karnataka. It rapidly expanded to other cities in India, with more than 1,000 cafés open across the nation by 2011.

On 29 July 2019, Siddhartha went missing, and his body was found in the Nethravathi river backwaters two days later. A letter, assumed to be written by Siddhartha addressing the board of directors and staff, was made public in which he takes responsibility for not creating a profitable business model.

In March 2020, Coffee Day Enterprises Limited announced that it has reached an agreement to sell Global Village Technology Park, a 90-acre tech park on the outskirts of Bengaluru, for a total consideration of ₹2,700 crore for repaying the debt of Cafe Coffee Day's associate firms and their promoters. In July 2023, IndusInd Bank filed a bankruptcy petition against Cafe Coffee Day.

13. Kwality products

The CBI has registered the case against Kwality Ltd and its directors Sanjay Dhingra, Siddhant Gupta, Arun Srivastava besides other unidentified persons accusing that they had cheated the Bank of India-led consortium comprising BOI to the tune of about Rs.1400.62 crore.

The company was one of the country's most popular dairy product makers.

They allegedly cheated the banks by way of "diversion of bank funds, sham transactions with related parties, fabricated documents/receipts, falsified books of accounts" and created false assets and liabilities etc.

A Bench of the National Company Law Tribunal (NCLT) in January 2021 has ordered the liquidation of debt-ridden dairy and allied products firm Kwality Limited, after the Committee of Creditors (CoC) rejected the resolution plan submitted by Haldiram Snacks, the sole bidder for Rs 142 crore. The NCLT passed the liquidation order on in January 2021.

The company, which was founded in 1992, owes over Rs 1,900 crore to its lenders, and was admitted into insolvency in December 2018 on a petition moved by Punjab National Bank (PNB) and global private equity firm KKR.

14. Amrapali Builders

The Amrapali case has been the most infamous case of real estate fraud in recent times, with over 42,000 homebuyers left in the lurch, without a means to fight against a prominent builder.

In July 2019, the Supreme Court cancelled the registration of the Amrapali Group, directed the state-owned National Building Construction Corporation (NBCC) to complete the unfinished projects, and instructed the Enforcement Directorate to charge the builders with money laundering and fraud.

It has also exposed the role of state government bodies and banks that were complicit in duping innocent homebuyers.

Diversion of funds

The Supreme Court stated the laid down plan through which Amrapali trapped innocent customers — generating money and investing it not to complete projects, but to increase the directors' "own personal assets".

It was also said that the group had not prepared any accounts from 2015 to 2018, and that all the money earned during that period was "diverted".

The court noted that Amrapali's directors diverted the money by creating "dummy companies, realising professional fees, creating bogus bills, selling flats at undervalue price, payment of excessive brokerage, etc".

The money Amrapali had obtained from banks was diverted to create "personal assets of directors, creation of assets in closely held companies by the directors along with their partners and relatives, for personal expenses of directors, to give advances without carrying interest for several years".

The Supreme Court has also noted that there was "total non-monitoring by the bankers", and identified a trail of bogus companies created by the Amrapali Group to divert funds. Close to 50 companies, some of which were also in the real estate segment such as La Residential, lent unaccounted money to Amrapali, which was never paid back. The forensic report has noted that most of these companies had either no acting directors or members connected to the Amrapali Group.

Collusion by govt authorities

An important facet of the verdict is how the forensic report helped the court unearth the trail which proved that the Noida Authority and Greater Noida Authority worked in connivance with the Amrapali Group to dupe homebuyers.

The investigation began with the fact that Amrapali was due to pay a colossal amount of Rs 5,500 crore to the two authorities. Meagre instalments were paid from 2010 to 2013, but "defaults continued to exist in the nature of premium money, lease money and also compensation to farmers whose land was acquired".

The court noted that the authorities "very well knew" that there were defaults, but allotted further land to the Amrapali Group "without insisting on payment of dues", and also allowed it to sub-lease plots executed by builders, allowing Amrapali to earn revenue without making payment to the state bodies.

Terming this as a "clear breach of public trust", the Supreme Court stated that "the officials of the authorities acted clearly in collusion with the builders and overlooked the interest of the authorities and homebuyers".

Role of banks in shielding Amrapali

There existed a perception that it wasn't just homebuyers but also banks that were duped by Amrapali. However, the verdict paints a completely different picture.

The Supreme Court quoted the forensic audit report as noting that the "Bank of Baroda, Syndicate Bank, Bank of India, Corporation Bank did not monitor utilisation of funds and acted as a mute spectator to diversion which was almost happening evidently in all banking transactions".

Giving an example, the court stated that in the case of Amrapali Zodiac Developers, Bank of Baroda had advanced an amount which "was diverted immediately on receipt".

The court stated that the bankers' "inaction" resulted in such a fraud.

The audit report submitted to Supreme Court reveals that around Rs 3,500 crore of homebuyers' money was diverted by the Amrapali top brass. According to the auditors, the money was spent on houses, luxury cars and weddings among others and also invested in shares and mutual funds.

In October 2018, Supreme Court Judges stated that the statutory auditors of the Amrapali Group were "hand in glove" with the group's top echelon.

The Central Bureau of Investigation (CBI) has booked Anil Sharma, the former CMD of the insolvent Amrapali group along with eight others for the murder of former secretary of Balika Vidyapeeth, Sharad Chandra in Bihar nine years ago. The CBI which took over the investigation of the case on the orders of the Patna High Court said the motive behind the murder was to take over the land and assets belonging to the educational institution.

15. C G Consumers {Earlier Crompton Greaves Ltd}

In June 2021, the CBI carried out searches at six locations after registering a fresh case of fraud of Rs 2,435 crore in Yes Bank and other consortium banks against former

CG Power and Industrial Solutions chairman Gautam Thapar who is already under probe in more such cases, officials said.

Thapar faces multiple CBI FIRs for alleged bank fraud and corruption. The present case is based on a complaint from the State Bank of India on behalf of the consortium of 11 other lender banks, including Yes Bank.

Besides Thapar, the CBI has also booked CG Power and Industrial Solutions, erstwhile Crompton Greaves Ltd, and the then executives, including chief executive officer and managing director K N Neelkanth, executive director and CFO Madhav Acharya, director B Hariharan, non-executive director Omkar Goswami and CFO Venkatesh Ramamoorthy.

It was alleged that the said accused had cheated SBI and other consortium member banks, including Bank of Maharashtra, Axis bank, Yes Bank, Corporation Bank, Barclays Bank, IndusInd Bank etc..

It is alleged in the FIR that they between 2015 and 2019 allegedly cheated the banks by way of diversion of bank funds and sham transactions with related parties.

CBI stated they also allegedly misrepresented and falsified account books, entries, vouchers and financial statements providing false, incorrect or misleading information to secure credit which they siphoned off by diverting them to other companies

16. Avantha Group vs, YES Bank

In 2007, after the demise of LM Thapar, Gautam Thapar consolidated all his inheritance under one banner: Avantha Group. It had exposure to sectors such as paper, pulp, power, industrial solutions, consumer electricals, food processing, chemicals, farm forestry and information technology-enabled service (ITeS), among others.

Gautam's global pursuits like Sabah Forest Industries, Malaysia's largest pulp and paper mill went wrong and other acquisitions were by Debt route. Avantha group's foray into the capital-intensive power business didn't see success and it further added to the debt burden. The group kept on pumping money into the power ventures even when it was fast losing its ability to service existing debt.

Instability in top management was a problem.

Hiving off and sale of the profitable Crompton Greaves Consumer Electricals, was a blunder

The CBI has alleged that the accused have indulged in a criminal conspiracy, criminal breach of trust, cheating, and forgery for diversion of public money to the tune of Rs 466.15 crore.

A forensic audit has revealed misappropriation and diversion of funds. Soon after, Yes Bank filed a complaint with the CBI.

The accused have been charged with criminal conspiracy, cheating, criminal breach of trust and forgery. The account has been reported as fraud to the Reserve Bank of India (RBI) on February 9, 2021,

17. Mackstar Group and Rana Kapoor

The Enforcement Directorate (ED) in January 2021 arrested YES Bank founder Rana Kapoor in another money laundering case related to Mackstar Group and PMC Bank. Kapoor is the third person to be arrested in the case. The ED had arrested Mehul Thakur and Madangopal Chaturvedi in connection with the case. It conducted raids at 10 premises, including residence of former underworld don Bhai Thakur and offices of Viva Group, controlled by the Thakur family.

In this case, the ED has alleged that YES Bank had sanctioned a Rs 200 crore-loan to Mackstar Group which was siphoned off by Kapoor, Thakur and Housing Development Infrastructure Ltd (HDIL) promoters Sarang Wadhawan and Rakesh Wadhawan, who also held stake in Mackstar Group. The Wadhawans are the key accused in the Punjab and Maharashtra Co-operative (PMC) Bank scam case.

The ED alleged that the Wadhawans took the loan from YES Bank without knowledge of the other stakeholders of Mackstar Group. The loan was taken for repair and refurbishment of a newly constructed building of Mackstar Group.

In September 2022 while setting aside insolvency proceedings against Mack Star NCLAT observed that out of Rs 147.6 crore - sanctioned by Yes Bank in Mack Star's name for the purpose of renovating 'Kaledonia' a two-year-old building constructed at a cost of Rs 100 crore - more than 99 per cent of the amount was routed back to Yes Bank either on the same day or within a very short period.

18. Cox & King

Founded in the mid-18th century to supply British troops as they plundered the subcontinent, Cox & Kings stayed on after independence and, under the Kerkars' dynastic stewardship, became one of India's leading travel companies. It embodied the glamour and excess that accompanied the rise of India's new economic elite. At its peak in 2018, it had offices in 27 countries from Japan to the US, and claimed to have seven million customers for services that included foreign exchange and conference events, as well as holidays and tours.

A case pertains to a loan of Rs 3,642 crore taken by Cox & Kings from Yes Bank. The money was never returned. The ED claims the loan sanction from Yes Bank was driven by the then CMD Rana Kapoor by bypassing standard norms.

Charges of financial misappropriation have swirled around the company for some years.

In the Yes Bank case, over five years (2015-19), as many as 15 fictitious customers, including a subsidiary named Ezeego, were set up by Cox & Kings for taking the loans, according to investigators. ED found these fictitious high-value debtors in the books of accounts and also another 147 sets of non-existent customers.

Cox & Kings, ED found, had diverted Rs 1,100 crore to another stressed company with which it has no business relationship. The transfer was done without the approval of the Cox & Kings board.

A senior ED official earlier told MoneyControl Khandelwal and Jain purchased various immovable properties from cash diverted from Cox & Kings. Investigations showed Rs 150 crore were diverted from Ezeego to RedKite Capital, promoted by the family members of Khandelwal and Jain.

In another incident, according to ED, Cox & Kings sold one of its subsidiaries, Holiday Break Education Limited, UK (HBEL), for Rs 4,387 crore and instead of discharging the liability of the bank, the company siphoned off a majority of the cash. An estimated $15.34 million was transferred to Kuber Investment Mauritius, which was controlled by Kerkar.

Cox & Kings is also being probed by Kolkata Police for allegedly collecting Rs 40 crore from customers under the pretext of conducting global tours.

Peter Kerkar, the owner, in his complaint, alleged that top executives of Cox & Kings, in connivance with officials of a number of banks, swindled cash from the company. He named Khandelwal, Jain and other officials.

In October 2020, the Enforcement Directorate made two arrests while Cox & Kings, that became embroiled in a scandal over thousands of crores of missing money and was pushed into bankruptcy. The arrest of the CFO Anil Khandelwal, and its internal auditor Naresh Jain were on charges of money laundering.

ED said Cox & Kings manipulated balance sheets of its overseas subsidiaries to seek loans from banks. The scam is estimated at a little over Rs 20,000 crore and involves many banks across India that gave loans to the company but never got them back.

Cox & Kings owes Axis Bank Rs 1,030 crore, IndusInd Bank Rs 239 crore and Kotak Mahindra Bank Rs 174 crore.

An ED official is reported to have told that among other things, the agency is probing how so many banks offered loans to Cox & Kings and what collaterals were offered by the promoters. They are exploring the possibilities of involvement of some of the top officials of the banks in the scam.

Indian Bank alleged that the accused company in pursuance of criminal conspiracy hatched with unknown bank officials had approached the erstwhile Allahabad Bank (now merged with Indian bank) in May 2019, with a request for subscription of the commercial paper of the company, which the bank subscribed for a face value amounting to Rs 50 crore.

"Cox & Kings fraudulently and dishonestly misrepresented financial statements, accounts and concealed the facts, and subsequently diverted the proceeds of the commercial papers.

The aforesaid facts disclosed commission of cognizable offence punishable under Sections 120-B read with 420 of the Indian Penal Code, and Section 7 of Prevention of Corruption Act.

19. Punjab National Bank {PNB} - Nirav Modi {2009}

PNB was the first major banking fraud reported in the country, involving a massive amount of around Rs. 15000 crores. Fraud was committed by Nirav Modi and Mehul Choksi, (through Gitanjali Gems, a listed company owned by him). Both were in the business of importing rough diamonds and exporting polished diamonds.

Over a period, both had built retail chains of diamond business in India and at famous international destinations. Nirav was, particularly, PR and showmanship savvy.

At that time no one questioned the source of his funding. It was only after a few years, that this unprecedented fraud came to light, which shocked the nation as never before.

He was defrauding PNB and other bankers by opening LCs of large amounts without any underlying transactions (paper money in essence), with the connivance of a few junior level banking officials. He exploited an elementary deficiency in the IT systems of non-reconciliation of LCs opened with the underlying transactions. LCs opened were not recorded in the RTGS system as was the requirement applicable to all banks.

Hence, existence of such LCs was not known till the time the fraud was unearthed.

Amounts involved are estimated to be around Rs 16000 crores (including dues of Mehul Choksi). Here again, there were multiple red flags, which were ignored by banks management and regulators, which could have unearthed the fraud much earlier. Periodic inspection reports of RBI, highlighting this deficiency, which were placed before the board, were not actioned, RBI also issued red alert to all banks several times, instructing banks to set right these system deficiencies (mainly RTGS and non-reconciliation). But these also went unattended.

Nirav and Mehul managed to fly out of India and currently India is trying hard in international courts to bring them back to India. In December 2022 it was reported that the fugitive Indian diamond trader lost his appeal to take his fight against extradition before the UK Supreme Court. He is currently behind bars at Wandsworth prison in London, has no legal options left in the UK now.

20. Gitanjali Group {Mehul Chokshi} and PNB Fraud case

In March 2018, a special PMLA court issued non-bailable arrest warrants (NBWs) against Choksi, and his nephews Nirav Modi for suspected collusion with two employees of Punjab National Bank (PNB). A designated PMLA authority held that 41 properties worth about Rs 1,210 crore, attached by the Enforcement Directorate (ED) in the name of Mehul Choksi and his associated firms, are money laundering assets and ordered that their attachment should continue. The central probe agency provisionally attached several properties in many cities and towns under the PMLA. in connection with the about US$2 billion alleged fraud at a Mumbai-based branch of the PNB.

On 7 January 2018, Choksi left India to the Caribbean nation of Antigua and Barbuda. A few days later, the PNB scam was disclosed. On 15 January, he took the oath of citizenship of Antigua and Barbuda, where he applied for the citizenship in November 2017 under the country's Citizenship by Investment program. However, Indian authorities argue that he has not renounced his Indian citizenship. On 17 June, his lawyer informed the Bombay High Court that he left India for medical check-up and not to avoid prosecution in the case. Ever since, CBI has been trying to extradite him back to India.

On 23 May 2021, Choksi went missing in Antigua and Barbuda. Several Indian agencies were in touch with the Dominican government using diplomatic channels urging that he is an Indian citizen and that he had an Interpol Red Corner notice and he should be handed over to the Indian authorities. In early June 2021, Choksi filed an affidavit in the High Court of Dominica claiming there was no arrest warrant against him when he left India in January 2018 seeking medical treatment in the USA. He also stated that he has no intentions of absconding from attending the court and that he doesn't intend to leave Dominica.

In March 2023, Choksi won a court victory in Antigua preventing the Attorney General of Antigua and Barbuda from striking out his claim that there was a constitutional violation arising from the failure to adequately investigate his claims of being victim of inhuman treatment and torture.

21. Aircel Maxis - IDBI Scam

Aircel filed for bankruptcy in March 2018 after reaching a consensus with lenders and shareholders. Founded way back in 1999, Aircel was the sixth largest mobile service provider in India with a subscriber base more than 84 million. The company was founded by C Sivasankaran and it was taken over by Malaysian telecom company Maxis Communications. We take a look at three key reasons behind Aircel's bankruptcy.

The CBI filed a FIR against Maran that alleged that he received Rs 549 crore for favouring Aircel in various deals that were owned by Maxis. The amount was allegedly received by a company owned by Dayanidhi Maran's brother, Kalanidhi Maran. Kalanidhi Maran controls the Sun TV Network.

Aircel stated that it was facing troubled times in highly financially stressed industry. It has suffered significant negative business and reputational impact due to unsustainable debt and increased losses. The company had debt of over Rs 15,000 crore as of December-17 2017. Aircel was unable to reach consensus with respect to the restructuring of its debt and funding.

The case, which is being probed by the CBI and ED, relates to alleged irregularities in the grant of Foreign Investment Promotion Board (FIPB) approval in the Aircel Maxis deal. In July 2018, CBI filed a fresh chargesheet in the Aircel-Maxis case, listing former Finance Minister P Chidambaram, his son and 17 others as an accused in the long running case. A Delhi Court granted regular bail to P Chidambaram and his son.

The case pertains to loans of Rs 322 crore and Rs 523 crore given to the companies of C. Sivasankaran, who was in the Centre of Aircel Maxis probe for alleging that then Telecom Minister Dayanidhi Maran had put pressure on him to sell his company to a Malaysian telecom tycoon, a case in which Maran brothers have been discharged by a special court. The loans later turned non-performing assets or NPAs.

CBI has registered case against – the promoter of Aircel, his son and companies controlled by him - Axcel Sunshine Ltd and Finland-based WinWinD - for allegedly defaulting on loans worth Rs 600 crore taken from IDBI bank.

The CBI has also booked top officials of two public sector banks, a former CMD of IDBI Bank. The agency has named 15 bank officials who worked at senior levels at IDBI Bank in 2010 and 2014 when loans were sanctioned to the companies controlled by Sivasankaran in its FIR registered on a complaint from the Central Vigilance Commission.

22. Religare Finvest Limited {RFL}

RFL's erstwhile promoters, Malvinder and Shivinder Mohan Singh, laundered Rs 2,100 crore along with a co-accused in the fraud case, the Enforcement Directorate (ED) alleged in a charge sheet filed before a local court in January 02020. The agency said the brothers and co-accused Sunil Godhwani, MD used 19 shell companies to launder the funds.

The arrests took place within hours of each other. The brothers were charged with criminal breach of trust, conspiracy, and cheating. Delhi police said that they were arrested under section 409 (criminal breach of trust by a public servant, banker, merchant or agent) and section 420 (cheating) of the Indian Penal Code. Both brothers have denied the charges·

Their former company, Religare Finvest, reported the Singhs' crimes to the EOW, alleging embezzlement.

REL said its wholly-owned subsidiary Religare Finvest Ltd (RFL) completed a One-Time Settlement (OTS) with 16 lenders in March 2023 by making a full and final payment of ₹400 crore. Since January 2018, when the new management took over, RFL has repaid over ₹9,000 crore to its lenders from its collections and with the support of REL.

The settlement is the last milestone in the closure of legacy issues emanating from the misconduct of the erstwhile promoters.

This settlement paves the way for restarting business and focusing on building a niche in the MSME lending space.

23. PMC Bank

Founded in 1984, PMC Bank has 137 branches across seven states, 81 of these in Maharashtra. Its customers include small businesses, housing societies and institutions.

According to an FIR filed in the case, HDIL promoters allegedly colluded with the bank management to draw loans from the bank's Bhandup branch. The bank officials did not classify these loans as non-performing advances, despite non-payment.

Reports estimate the bank's overall exposure to the HDIL group at around Rs 6,500 crore, or over 73 per cent of all of the bank's advances — and all of this is not being serviced.

The bank also allegedly created fictitious accounts of companies which borrowed small sums of money, and created fake reports to hide from regulatory supervision.

In 2018-19, the bank had reported a net profit of Rs 99.69 crore in its annual report.

The bank showed 3.76 per cent (or Rs 315 crore) of advances (Rs 8,383 crore) as gross non-performing assets (NPAs), which was good performance as compared to public-sector banks.

However, it transpired that the bank presented false financial reports to hide the bad loan mess and the alleged collusion with HDIL and other companies

The bank's former chairman Waryam Singh, managing director Joy Thomas and other senior officials, along with

HDIL's executive chairman Rakesh Kumar Wadhawan and his son Sarang, have been named in the FIR and arrested.

The Enforcement Directorate probe in the PMC Bank scam has revealed that majority of loans borrowed from the cooperative bank by HDIL and group companies were used to settle other loans of the group companies. The Supreme Court refused to entertain the bail plea filed on health grounds by jailed businessman Rakesh Wadhawan, accused of money laundering in the multi-crore rupees.

24. YES Bank and Rana Kapoor

On 8 March 2020, the Enforcement Directorate (ED) registered a case against Kapoor under the Prevention of Money Laundering Act (PMLA) and he was arrested.

The Central Bureau of Investigation (CBI) also charged Kapoor and his family members in a bribery and money-laundering case linked to Yes Bank.

According to the ED, Kapoor, his family members, and others, got benefits worth ₹43 billion (US$540 million) through companies controlled by his family as kickbacks for sanctioning huge loans through Yes Bank. He is also accused of receiving bribes for going easy on loans given to a few big corporate groups that had turned into non-performing assets.

The CBI and ED arrested Kapoor in another case which is the outcome of their investigations in DHFL Mumbai case of fraud and embezzlement of over $3 Billion, in which Kapoor was alleged to have received over $100 million in kickbacks over bogus loans extended by Yes Bank to DHFL and the kickbacks were used to purchase expensive properties in Delhi and Mumbai in the name of Kapoor's wife and daughter.

In May 2020, ED filed a charge sheet and named 7 individuals and 5 companies Individuals of Rana Kapoor, Wadhawans.

Currently Kapoor is held at Taloja Jail, Maharashtra. Kapoor's bail application in the Prevention of Money Laundering case filed on the grounds that he is keeping poor health and is at the risk of contracting COVID-19, was rejected by Mumbai Court. The Supreme Court in Aug 2023, refused to entertain bail plea of Yes Bank founder in a money-laundering case against him. The apex court noted that this case rocked the entire financial system.

25. Tata-Mistry fallout

Cyrus Mistry was a director of Tata Sons Ltd. since 2006. The majority of shareholding was held by trusts of the Tata family. This was to ensure that the control remains with the family. The Board frequently disagreed with the decisions of Mistry and ousted him during one such meeting. Mistry alleged that there was dominant control by the nominee directors of the trust, including Ratan Tata, who were the "shadow directors" of Tata Sons Ltd.

Mistry said that he was never provided with a free hand by the promoters to manage the company and that the promoters were stubborn regarding their own projects. He also alleged that there was no independence in the working of the independent directors. Nusli Wadia, who was an independent director was also fired for standing up for Cyrus Mistry to maintain his chairmanship in group companies. This shows the clear abuse of power by the promoters.

26. ILFS

ILFS fraud was one of the large corporate frauds in India and triggered a showdown in the economy, as the company was a key vehicle for infrastructure development of the country. Fraud occurred, in spite of marquee shareholders like LIC, SBI etc., being the largest shareholders, having representatives on board. ILFS had the largest debt exposure of around Rs. 91000 crores (including Rs, 20000 crores invested by PF and pension funds),

Fraud was perpetrated mainly by:

Diversion of borrowed funds to related entities of some of members of top management team; Imprudent lending to parties who were not credit worth for ulterior motives; Evergreening of loans by routing money from one group company to another through an unrelated party; Over invoicing of project costs by vendors, accounting of fake expenses etc., and difference being routed back to related entities of some of members of top management team; Overstatement of profits by non-provisioning of loans, accounting of fake expense, inappropriate recognition of project revenue etc.

The company had unprecedented number of subsidiaries and group companies, (346) which were used to route above transactions

- Non -disclosure of some of these companies as related parties
- Non-disclosure some of subsidiaries, associates, joint ventures

Most of the mutual funds, insurance companies and PF gratuity funds had invested large sums in its debt issuance, due to the high credit rating of the company. It was a case of negligence by reputed credit rating agencies that rating was not downgraded in spite of clear signs of financial stress in the company. Rating was downgraded abruptly to lowest level from the highest only after the company defaulted in its repayment obligations.

The entity was run for years by the same top management team, who were treating ILFS as personal property. Their subordinates and even Board were so overawed by their overpowering persona that no one dared to challenge their decisions. Fraud was going on for years, but could not be detected till the damage was done.

Like Satyam, the government suspended the board and appointed eminent experts to the board chaired by reputed and seasoned banker, Uday Kotak. Currently the company is under resolution process and some of its infrastructure has been sold. However, progress has been slow. Hence, the extent and timing of recovery is uncertain.

The CBI in June 2023 carried out search operations at office of IL&FS Energy Development Company Ltd (IEDCL) and residential premises of its directors in connection with a loan fraud case and recovered incriminating documents and other articles. The IEDCL and its directors were booked by the CBI for cheating the Punjab National Bank to the tune of Rs 100.03 crore.

The CBI registered a corruption case against IL&FS Transportation Network Ltd (ITNL), its former directors and incumbent CFO on a complaint filed by state-run Canara Bank.

The Central Bureau of Investigation (CBI) has registered a corruption case in the IL&FS matter. The case has been registered against ITNL, a step-down subsidiary of the beleaguered NBFC, and its erstwhile directors. Dilip Bhatia who has been named as an accused is the incumbent CFO of ITNL.

The CBI has filed an FIR against IL&FS Transportation Network Limited (ITNL) and its then directors for allegedly causing a loss of more than Rs 6,524 crore to a 19-bank consortium led by Canara Bank, officials said on Friday.

In its FIR, the Central Bureau of Investigation (CBI) has booked Mumbai-based ITNL and its directors and then CFO for alleged criminal conspiracy and cheating.

The company had unprecedented number of subsidiaries and group companies, (346) which were used to route above transactions

27. JVG Group

From being a small-time contractor earning less than Rs 2500 a month, Vijay Kumar Sharma went on to run a group, which on paper had an annual turnover of Rs 1000 crore, in just seven years. Known for his lavish lifestyle - his farmhouse in Delhi, his fleet of expensive cars and the helicopter he had taken on lease to tap deposits from small towns in north India were talked about quite often

In October 1997, the RBI banned all NBFCs of the JVG Group of companies - JVG Finance, JVG Leasing and JVG Securities - from accepting deposits from the public. This was after an investigation revealed that these companies had been accepting deposits in excess of their stipulated limits.

Soon after, JVG downed the shutters of several of its offices in small towns of Maharashtra, Uttar Pradesh and Bihar, claiming it had detected huge irregularities in the operations. The closing of the offices created a panic among the depositors of more than Rs 1000 crore and strong voices were raised against the group in the media. The agents (or the field-workers), who raised deposits from investors on behalf of JVG, were extremely worried. They said they could not go back to their local offices without collecting the dues fearing the wrath of the investors.

The situation seemed rather bleak with rumors of the JVG group being in deep financial crisis. At this point, JVG Chairman claimed that a majority of the certificates were fake and hence they would not be paid back. For many depositors who had invested as little as Rs 500 and who could not even dream of taking the dispute to court. Analysts remarked that the investors and agents had themselves to blame for the loss - because the activities of the JVG Group had always been looked at with suspicion by the industry

In September 2016 upholding the orders of a trial court, additional district and sessions judge sentenced Vijay Kumar Sharma to two years of imprisonment, while disposing of 16 appeals for cheating lakhs of investors. A fine of Rs 2,000 for each case was also imposed on him.

28. Winsome Diamonds Group

Jatin Mehta a Gujarat-based diamond merchant and owner of Winsome Diamonds owes more than Rs 6,500 crores to a consortium of banks – with the biggest hit being the Delhi-based Punjab National Bank with a loss of more than Rs 1,700 crore Running in parallel to the Nirav-Modi Case, Jatin Mehta too was a high profile diamond merchant who fled the country after the credits went sour, while the state-run banks bore the brunt of massive losses.

In the early years of the decade Jatin Mehta was a known face in the banking world who took buyer's credit to purchase gold and turned it around into diamond-studded jewelry which was exported to 13 clients in Dubai. Being a reliable creditor, his firms – Winsome, Su-Raj & Forever Diamonds – enjoyed high credit and their limits kept getting extended.

Unfortunately for the banks of India, in November 2012, Mehta said he could not pay back, saying that the group's customers in the Gulf region – UAE Jewelers' were hit by derivatives and commodities trading losses of $1 billion, thus were unable to pay him. Subsequently, before the development of loans, Mehta, who is believed to have obtained citizenship of ST Kitts and Nevis, resigned from his firms and left the country in 2016.

By early 2014, bankers took the case to the CBI, who along with Mumbai police raided Winsome's directors and offices. For three years, the agency investigated the case without making any arrests. Of the banks which took the hit, Punjab National Bank suffered the most significant loss – more than Rs 1,700 crore – while other banks exposed to the scam included Central Bank of India (Rs 699.54 crore) and IDBI (Rs 388 crore).

In July 2022 the high court in London has issued a worldwide freezing order against fugitive diamond merchant Jatin Mehta, his wife and two sons. The Metha's face allegations of committing a $1 billion fraud through complex transactions. Over a dozen banks in India are owed more than Rs 5,000 crore by the Mehtas who have been comfortably living in London after acquiring citizenship of St Kitts and Nevis, a tax haven, and a country with no extradition arrangement with India.

PNB allegedly discovered the scam in 2013 that round tripping, and white smuggling of goods was being carried out. In essence, simply the underlying invoices were processed in the winsome office in Mumbai, but no shipment of goods was made. At least three of Mehta's UAE-based suppliers were listed on the block global insurance policy and then were taken off the block insurance policy shortly before they defaulted on the amount owed to Winsome/ Forever. Most of these UAE companies were allegedly one-room fronts that did not have the required staff or facilities to store diamonds and jewelry. These revelations allegedly pointed towards the conclusion that the UAE companies were set up with the express purpose of diverting money taken from the banks.

29. ABG Shipyard

Once considered a powerhouse in shipbuilding with an order book of Rs 16,600 crore, Gujarat's ABG Shipyard is now under probe for fraud. On a complaint by State Bank of India, the CBI recently booked ABG Shipyard, its directors, and ABG International Pvt Limited for allegedly causing losses of Rs 22,842 crore to a consortium of 28 banks.

Between 2012 and 2017, ABG Shipyard Ltd (ABG SL), a Gujarat-based firm, purportedly defrauded banks of Rs 22,842 crore total.

According to CBI sources, ABG SL took loans from these banks and then diverted them. It allegedly made investments in overseas subsidiaries from the loan amounts, bought assets in the names of affiliated companies, and also transferred money to several related parties. It is also alleged that the company, whose account became a Non-Performing Asset (NPA) in 2013, violated terms of its arrangement for

Corporate Debt Restructuring (CDR) — a relief mechanism in which lender banks either reduce the interest rates on the loans or increase the tenure of the repayment.

The SBI identified the fraud in January 2019, but filed a complaint only in November that year. A fresh, more comprehensive complaint was filed in August 2020, but the CBI finally registered a case only on 7 February 2021, and booked ABG SL and ABG International Private Ltd.

The investigative agency has also booked ABG's former CMD, former ED and three Directors. Searches conducted lead to recovery of incriminating documents.

The case has raised a storm of questions: How did the fraud go undetected for so long? How was the money diverted? How did the fraud come to light? What led to the delay in registration of the FIR by CBI?

According to CBI, ABG Shipyard and its directors are accused of cheating 28 banks to the tune of 23,000 crore. The account turned non-performing assets (NPAs) in 2013.

A forensic audit carried out by Ernst and Young in 2019 revealed that the funds were diverted to other related companies, said the CBI, adding that loans were allegedly used for investments through overseas subsidiaries.

A separate money laundering investigation has also been started against them by the Enforcement Directorate (ED).

30. Sterling Biotech {SBL}

SBL is a Vadodara-based pharmaceutical company that has been in the news for a while now. The company has been in the news for its alleged involvement in a Rs 8,100-crore bank fraud case. The Sandesara brothers – Nitin and Chetan – along with the latter's wife were declared fugitives under Section 4 of the Fugitive Economic Offenders Act. More than Rs 20 crore worth of assets were attached. The company has a debt in excess of Rs 15,000 crore

ED Claimed that Sandesara brothers scam is much bigger than the fraud committed by PNB scam accused Nirav Modi. ED investigation revealed that SBL Group and its main promoters cheated Indian banks to the tune of over Rs 14,500 crore.

The ED registered a case after the CBI lodged an FIR in October 2017 on account of cheating and bank fraud to the tune of Rs. 5383 crores against the said company and its promoters.

During the investigation, it was revealed that overseas companies of Sandesara Group had availed a loan of around Rs 9000 crore from foreign branches of Indian banks - Andhra, UCO, SBI, Allahabad and BOI.

It was also revealed that loans obtained were diverted for non-mandated purposes, layered and laundered through a web of multiple domestic as well as offshore entities.

In June 2019 the ED had attached properties worth Rs 9778 crore of SBL Group.

Sandesara brothers, declared fugitive economic offenders by a Delhi court on September 2020. The three brothers as the company owners were declared fugitives under the Fugitive Economic Offenders Act in relation to Rs 8,100 crore bank fraud case.

The ED alleged that the pharmaceutical group and its promoters laundered funds obtained through bank loans by "incorporating" shell or dummy companies, conducting circular transactions to artificially inflate turnover of flagship companies, claiming higher depreciations on non-existing machinery, artificial share trading with the use of shell companies and layering and laundering of proceeds of crime within India and abroad through the web of shell companies.

31. GTL Group

Started by Manoj Tirodkar and Global Holding Corporation Pvt Ltd (GHC) in 1987, GTL is engaged in the business of providing telecom network deployment services, operations and maintenance services to telecom operators in India and international markets.

The Central Bank of India registered in January 2023 an FIR against the telecom infrastructure major, unidentified directors, public officials and vendors under IPC sections related to criminal conspiracy, cheating and provisions of the Prevention of Corruption Act, after the company fraudulently obtained loans from a bank consortium of around 24 lenders and subsequently siphoned off majority of the loan amount in conspiracy with vendors and some bank officials, among others.

According to the FIR, enquiries revealed that GTL Limited was extending advances to vendors year on year without supply of material, goods, and eventually these advances were provisioned.

To facilitate the fraud, the perpetrators allegedly created various vendor companies in connivance with GTL Ltd, the CBI said. Among the banks, ICICI Bank has an exposure of Rs 650 crore to GTL Ltd, Bank of India Rs 467 crore and Canara Bank has Rs 412 crore.

"Various vendor companies were created and operated with the mala fide intention of siphoning off the bank short term funds and other credit facilities in connivance with borrower i.e., GTL Limited," the FIR alleged.

The Economic Offences unit of the agency has found that Reserve Bank of India (RBI) had warned IDBI Bank on April 1, 2016 to "red flag" the account and conduct a forensic audit, but in its response submitted two months later, the bank stated on behalf of the entire consortium lenders not to classify the account as 'Red Flags' and also not to appoint a forensic auditor as it may delay the dues settlement.

The RBI reiterated its directive following which a forensic audit was instituted on July 30, 2016.

The CBI has alleged that an amount of Rs 1,213.97 crore (86.84 per cent) is outstanding against four companies - Acuity Trading Pvt Ltd, Lenity Trading Pvt Ltd, Venerate Trading Pvt Ltd and Vinamara Multitrading Pvt Ltd - which were given huge advances for supply of material from financial year 2009-10 to 2011-12, but supply orders were completed. "Eventually, Rs 1,213.97 crore was left outstanding towards these four vendors which was gradually provisioned till 2017-18," the FIR alleged.

The CBI found that advances were given despite their meagre net worth and their recent incorporation. "The enquiry further revealed that all these vendor companies were incorporated within a short span of less than three months. And the Memorandum of Association (MoA) of these vendors of GTL Limited is exactly the same. There are same corrections in all the MoA's which clearly establishes that all the MoA's have been drafted by the same agency/source," the FIR alleged.

During the enquiry of some of these vendors entities were examined.

The CBI has registered a case in August 2023 against GTL unknown public servants and unknown others in connection with an alleged fraud of Rs 4,063 crore involving a consortium of 19 banks and financial institutions on charges of criminal conspiracy, cheating and criminal misconduct.

The officials of 13 banks are under the agency's scanner for allegedly assigning Rs 3,224 crore dues of the company to an asset reconstruction company (ARC) for Rs 1,867 crore without attempting to secure their loans from collateral securities, the FIR alleged.

32. Rotomac Scandal

The Central Bureau of Investigation (CBI) has filed in September 2020 a case against pen manufacturer Rotomac Global Pvt Ltd and its promoter Vikram Kothari, his wife and son for allegedly cheating Bank of India of Rs 806 crores.

This is the third CBI case against the Rotomac group, run by Kanpur based Kotharis, for cheating banks.

In February 2018, CBI filed its first case against Rotomac and Vikram Kothari for allegedly cheating a consortium of seven banks including Bank of Baroda, Indian Overseas Bank, Union Bank of India, Allahabad Bank, Bank of Maharashtra and Oriental Bank of Commerce and Bank of India for allegedly defrauding them of Rs 3,695 crore.

It was alleged that Kothari got loans disbursed based on foreign letters of credit (FLCs) on the pretext of making payments to his buyers and suppliers in places like Dubai, Sharjah and Hong Kong but they didn't exist.

The Kotharis allegedly provided incomplete documents or photocopies of bills of loading to the banks on the pretext that original papers were sent to the importer.

The banks had alleged that Rotomac did not attach the packing list, mandatory insurance copies of goods, certificate of origin of goods, or the inspection certificate from third parties while submitting documents to it. When bank officials visited Rotomac's suppliers and buyers abroad, they found that the import/export business was allegedly running through shell companies.

Later, a second case was registered in February 2020 against the company for allegedly cheating Allahabad Bank of Rs 36 crore.

In the latest FIR, CBI has alleged that the company took loans over a period of time from Bank of India for which there is outstanding of Rs 806 crore.

It has been alleged that company diverted most of the funds taken from the bank.

With three cases registered by CBI, total amount pertaining to bank fraud involving Kanpur based Kotharis comes to around Rs 4,500 crore.

Meanwhile, banks are trying to recover dues by selling properties under SARFAESI, (The Securitisation and Reconstruction of Financial Assets and Enforcement of Security Interest Act), and filing suits at debt recovery tribunals. BoB also filed an insolvency petition against the company and the case was admitted by the National Company Law Tribunal (NCLT) in October, 2017

33. Reliance Capital

Total Debts Rs 20,379.71 crore as on December 31, 2020.

In June 2019 Price Waterhouse & Co, an affiliate of PricewaterhouseCoopers, had resigned as the auditor of two entities of the Anil Ambani-led Reliance Group — Reliance Capital and its Reliance Home Finance unit — alleging diversion of funds and fraud. The audit firm that also informed the Ministry of Corporate Affairs (MCA) about the reasons behind its departure. The auditor had alleged that as part of ongoing audit for the financial year 2018-19, it did not receive satisfactory answers pertaining to certain observations and transactions.

In January 2021, the State Bank of India has informed the Delhi High Court that it has classified three bank accounts of Anil Ambani's - Reliance Communication, Reliance Telecom and Reliance Infratel - as fraud. The High Court has asked the State Bank of India to maintain status quo on the accounts of Anil Ambani's firms

Shortly after it superseded the board of the Anil Ambani NBFC for defaulting on payments to creditors amid serious governance concerns, the RBI on December 02, 2021 filed an application for initiation of CIRP against Reliance Capital Ltd., under Section 227 read with clause (zk) of sub-section (2) of Section 239 of the Insolvency and Bankruptcy Code (IBC), 2016 read with Rules 5 and 6 of the Insolvency and Bankruptcy (Insolvency and Liquidation Proceedings of Financial Service Providers and Application to Adjudication Authority) Rules, 2019 ("FSP Insolvency Rules") at the Mumbai Bench of the Hon'ble National Company Law Tribunal.

34. Reliance Home Finance

In a letter dated 18 April 2019, audit firm PwC highlighted certain observations and sought response from the company's top brass and audit committee. The auditor highlighted that the amount of loans disbursed by RHFL under GPC loans have increased exponentially from Rs900 crore as on 31 March 2018 to around Rs7,900 crore as on 31 March 2019.

PwC also highlighted that the net-worth of borrowers were negative and they had limited or no revenue and profit.

The market regulator launched its own investigation where it found several irregularities in loan disbursal process and collusion between top officials to siphon off money from RHFL. The investigation revealed that several of these borrowers were group companies of RHFL.

Another forensic audit was conducted by the consortium of lenders of RHFL, led by Bank of Baroda.

The forensic auditor has observed that an amount of Rs14,577 crore was disbursed by RHFL to numerous entities as GPC loans, of which Rs12,487 crore was disbursed to 47 potentially indirectly linked entities (PILE).

Another report highlighted that there were 150 loan cases falling under the category of PILEs between FY16-17 and FY18-19. Of these, 100 loan cases amounting to Rs 8,884 crore were still outstanding in the books of RHFL.

"To sum up, all the aforesaid Noticees have played their respective roles in unison duly aided and abetted by other Noticees through a collusive nexus, to translate a preordained scheme into action resulting in siphoning off of huge amounts of funds from RHFL's accounts, a major portion of which had to be declared NPA soon after their sanctions," the Sebi order by WTM SK Mohanty states.

In February 2022 Capital markets regulator, the Securities and Exchange Board of India, has restrained Anil Ambani from the securities market until further orders for alleged fraudulent activities related to Reliance Home Finance Ltd (RHFL).

In a 100-page interim order, SEBI whole time member, SK Mohanty, also restrained Anil Ambani and three others from "associating themselves with any intermediary registered with SEBI , any listed public company or acting directors/ promoters of any public company which intends to raise money from the public".

SEBI said its investigation brought to light as to how Anil Ambani, the Promoter/Chairman and the person under whose control and influence the Company has acted), has conducted himself in exceeding his remit by sanctioning loans in gross deviations of norms (internal as well as regulatory)

"Looking at the conduct and propensity of the Company to indulge in such activities of diversion of funds and misrepresentation of books of accounts, falsification of financial statements resulting into non-disclosure of true & fair information to the public at large, and also considering the collective misconduct exhibited by the Key Managerial Persons of the company, there is an urgent need that the company should be prevented from pursuing such despicable activities which are visibly in violation of securities laws," it said in the order.

35. Reliance Communication

Reliance Communication was forced to shut down its wireless business in 2017 due to its decreasing revenue and debt. Anil Ambani's net worth was $45 billion in 2007 and he used to have a 66 percent share in Reliance Telecommunications.

Reliance Communication used to have a 17 percent market share in 2010, but in 2016, its market share was declined to 10 percent. Besides, the debt of the company has been increased by many folds during the same period.

Reliance Communication had already announced financial bankruptcy; however, the main question comes here what exactly went wrong with Reliance Communication.

It is worth mentioning that debt, price wars, and declining profit affected the entire telecom sector. Similarly, the business of Reliance Communication has been affected, which is why the telco announced bankruptcy.

In June 2021 Reliance Jio has recently filed a petition against the Reliance Communication tower unit in the bankruptcy court. The telecom operator wants disclosures of the audit reports of Reliance Infratel, as its accounts were addressed as fraudulent by some of the company's lenders.

36. Deccan Chronicle Scam {DCHL}

On June 13, 20123 the Enforcement Directorate (ED) arrested T Venkattram Reddy, the former chairman and promoter of the Deccan Chronicle Holdings Private Limited (DCHL) in a money laundering case. The ED has also arrested DCHL's former director P K Iyer and auditor Mani Oomen. According to the ED, the arrested persons were allegedly involved in money laundering adding that they defrauded the banks by submitting forged documents.

The arrests happened after the three were questioned by the ED earlier on Tuesday. The case originates from another investigation conducted by the Central Bureau of Investigation (CBI) into bank fraud and loan non-payment.

Taking to Twitter, the E D added that it has attached movable and immovable properties valued at Rs 386.17 crore belonging to DCHL and its promoters and directors in connection with the case.

According to a press release issued by ED, the probe agency alleged that Deccan Chronicle Holdings Ltd obtained 111 credit facilities in the amount of Rs 9,805 crore from 16 public and private banks under the guise of working capital/ business expansion.

"However, these loans were taken by DCHL on the basis of fabricated books of accounts and the company did not disclose its correct loan liabilities to the banks. DCHL and their promoters/directors understated the financial charges and overstated advertising revenues to consistently defraud the banks for obtaining new loans," the press release stated.

The ED further listed the ways in which the loan funds were diverted and siphoned off by the DCHL promoters.

"In complete violation of the loan terms & conditions, DCHL utilised 73 per cent of the loan amounts only for the cyclical repayment of existing loans. Eventually, the loans turned into non-performing assets and DCHL defaulted on principal loans of around ₹3,000 crore and caused a total loss of ₹8,180 crore to the banks and other financial creditors," ED stated.

ED further accused the arrested persons of diverting funds to subsidiaries and affiliated organisations, including investment in the Indian Premier League (IPL). T. Venkattram Reddy purchased a private plane, while P. K. Iyer purchased a fleet of high-end cars valued at more than Rs. 30 crores. Payments to charitable trusts that were withheld and illegally returned to M/s DCHL's promoters in cash. Declaring and distributing dividends on the basis of fake profits. The promoters, who controlled up to two-thirds of the company, collected approximately Rs. 143 crores among themselves. "Diversion of Rs. 253 crores for share repurchase in order to boost stock prices and paint a financially rosy picture," ED alleged.

Notably, DCHL was the initial owner of the now-defunct IPL franchise Deccan Chargers and publishes the English daily Deccan Chronicle.

37. The Brightcom Group {BGL}

is a digital marketing company founded in 2000 and headquartered in Hyderabad, India with offices in US, Argentina, Brazil, Chile, Uruguay, Mexico, UK, France, Germany, Sweden, Ukraine, Serbia, Israel, China, India, and Australia, and with representatives or partners in Poland, and Italy. It ranked 400th in the Fortune India 500 list in 2020.

Perhaps for the first time, SEBI has gone after the same entity twice.

"This has been done considering the scale and gravity of manipulation," SEBI said in an order dated August 22, 2023.

The regulator's exasperation comes from the fact that the company has not only committed accounting fraud but a separate investigation revealed that it also fabricated bank account statements pertaining to its preferential allotment of shares.

In its latest order, SEBI breaks down how BGL raised money through a preferential issue from entities that were directly or indirectly connected to it. Here's how it went:

1. During FY21 and FY22, BGL issued warrants/shares on a preferential basis four times and raised Rs 867.78 crore from a total of 82 allottees.

2. For 22 entities who were allotted 25.76 crore equity shares for Rs 245.24 crore, the company received only Rs 52.51 crore. The remaining amount of Rs 192.73 crore was either not received by the company or routed back to the same entities through multiple layering of transactions involving subsidiaries and conduits.

3. Among these 22 entities, which were non-promoter entities, four were subsequently categorised as promoter entities.

4. In March 2022, the company's promoter and CMD Suresh Kumar Reddy was inducted as a partner in these four LLPs. Consequently, these four LLPs were re-classified as promoter and promoter group entities.

5. These LLPs were allotted 14.50 crore shares, approximately 30 percent of the total shares allotted on a preferential basis during FY21 and FY22. Of the total consideration of Rs 111.65 crore, the company received only Rs 1.41 crore.

6. SEBI sought receipts from BGL for all transactions with these LLPs and independently asked the banks, too. It found several mismatches.

   For instance, receipts submitted by the company indicated that it received Rs 38.50 crore from Sarita Commosales. However, the bank account statements showed that the company had received only Rs 4.10 crore from Sarita.

7. Further, the SEBI's investigation prima facie revealed that Sarita received a total of Rs 4.07 crore from BGL itself, which reached Sarita through circuitous transactions involving BGL's subsidiaries. The same was done in the case of Kalpana Commosales, too.

8. Despite being re-classified as promoter entities, the lock-in period for shares held by these four LLPs was vacated before the expiry of three years. As per regulations, the shares allotted on a preferential basis to the promoters or promoter group entities are subject to a three-year lock-in period and those allotted to others are subject to a one-year lock-in period.

9. SEBI says that it prima facie appears Suresh Kumar Reddy devised a scheme to bypass the three-year lock-in prescribed under the ICDR Regulations. Through the above method, the shareholding of the promoter group increased from 4.12 percent as of December 31, 2021, to 18.47 percent as of March 31, 2022.

10. Similarly, SEBI has unraveled several more circuitous transactions with other allottees named Varun Damani, Kishan Prakash and Ponna Bhuvaneswari, among others.

In the case of preferential allotment to ace investor Shankar Sharma, Brightcom Group claimed that it has received total consideration of Rs 56.65 crore, of which bank statements show only Rs 39.98 crore, including Rs 14.19 crore which could not be verified.

Veteran investor Shankar Sharma is among the 23 entities who have been prohibited from selling Brightcom Group's shares, according to an interim order released by the market regulator.

38. Union Carbide Disaster

The Bhopal disaster or Bhopal gas tragedy was a chemical accident on the night of 3rd. December 1984 at the Union Carbide India Limited (UCIL) pesticide plant in Bhopal, Madhya Pradesh. Considered the world's worst industrial disaster, over 500,000 people in the small towns around the plant were exposed to the highly toxic gas methyl isocyanate (MIC). Estimates vary on the death toll, with the official number of immediate deaths being 2,259. In 2008, the Government of Madhya Pradesh paid compensation to the family members of 3,787 victims killed in the gas release, and to 574,366 injured victims. A government affidavit in 2006 stated that the leak caused 558,125 injuries, including 38,478 temporary partial injuries and approximately 3,900 severely and permanently disabling injuries.[4] Others estimate that 8,000 died within two weeks, and another 8,000 or more have since died from gas-related diseases.

The owner of the factory, UCIL, was majority owned by the Union Carbide Corporation (UCC) of the United States, with Indian government-controlled banks and the Indian public holding a 49.1 percent stake. In 1989, UCC paid $470 million (equivalent to $907 million in 2021) to settle litigation stemming from the disaster. In 1994, UCC sold its stake in UCIL to Eveready Industries India Limited (EIIL), which subsequently merged with McLeod Russel (India) Ltd. Eveready ended clean-up on the site in 1998, when it terminated its 99-year lease and turned over control of the site to the state government of Madhya Pradesh. Dow Chemical Company purchased UCC in 2001, seventeen years after the disaster.

Civil and criminal cases filed in the United States against UCC and Warren Anderson, chief executive officer of the UCC at the time of the disaster, were dismissed and redirected to Indian courts on multiple occasions between 1986 and 2012, as the US courts focused on UCIL being a standalone entity of India. Civil and criminal cases were also filed in the District Court of Bhopal, India, involving UCC, UCIL, and Anderson. In June 2010, seven Indian nationals who were UCIL employees in 1984, including the former UCIL chairman Keshub Mahindra, were convicted in Bhopal of causing death by negligence and sentenced to two years' imprisonment and a fine of about $2,000 each, the maximum punishment allowed by Indian law. All were released on bail shortly after the verdict. An eighth former employee was also convicted, but died before the judgement was passed.

39. Supertech

The Supreme Court in August 2021 ordered the demolition of Supertech's twin residential towers built in Noida after holding that the project was executed in violation of laws and involved an "unholy nexus" with the Noida Authority. The court held that the construction violated the minimum distance requirement and had been built illegally without taking the consent of the individual flat owners as required under the UP Apartment, Act.

In October 2021 the Uttar Pradesh government suspended three NOIDA officers over their role in illegal construction of Supertech's two 40-storey towers. A special investigation team (SIT) probing the matter has found 26 officials of the NOIDA guilty in the case of which 20 have retired, two have died and four are still serving, the statement read.

On the basis of the SIT's report, the UP government directed that an FIR be lodged with the state vigilance commission against officials of the NOIDA, four directors and two architects of Supretech Limited involved in the case,

Real estate developer Supertech Ltd on March 2022 was declared bankrupt by the NCLT a move that could have a bearing on more than 10,000 home buyers of the firm. Acting on a petition filed by the Union Bank of India for non-payment of around Rs 432 crore worth dues, the bankruptcy court ordered the initiation of insolvency proceedings against real estate firm Supertech Ltd.

In June 2023, the ED arrested Supertech's chairman RK Arora in connection with a money laundering case. according to the FIRs, the company "defrauded" the general public. According to the ED, the probe found that the funds were collected by Supertech from homebuyers and also took project-specific term loans from banks/financial institutions for the purpose of construction of projects/flats and misappropriated. The ED also said that the real estate firm also "defaulted" on its payments to the banks/financial institutions and around Rs 1,500 crore of such loans have become NPA.

40. Byju's-Edtech

In December 2022 The National Commission for Protection of Child Rights (NCPCR) alleged that Byju's is calling phone numbers of children and their parents, and threatening them that their future will be ruined if they don't buy their courses.

They are targeting first-generation learners. It has also been mentioned in the news report that some customers have also claimed that they were exploited and deceived, and had put their savings and futures in jeopardy," the NCPCR had said in a statement.

In April 2023, the Enforcement Directorate conducted searches and seizures at three premises in Bengaluru, including its CEO and founder Byju Raveendran's properties.

The operation was carried after a complaint was lodged against CEO and his company 'Think & Learn Private Limited" under the provisions of the FEMA. It was alleged that FDI to the tune of Rs 28,000 crore during the period from 2011 to 2023 was received; remitted Rs 9,754 crore to various foreign jurisdictions during the period in the name of overseas direct investment and the company booked around Rs 944 crore as advertisement and marketing expenses, including the amount remitted to foreign jurisdictions.

The ED further said the company has not prepared its audited financial statements since FY21 and hence genuineness of the figures provided by the company is being cross-examined and tallied with banks.

In June 2023 Deloitte and three board members of Byju's have severed ties with it amid the edtech company's escalating legal battle with its lenders and its plummeting valuation in the eyes of some investors.

Deloitte, which was slated to audit Byju's until 2025, has quit with "immediate effect" mid-term, due to "long-delayed" financial statements by the company, according to the auditing firm's resignation letter filed to the regulator.

Byju's in a statement said it has appointed BDO as its new auditor. Deloitte said there was a "significant impact" on its ability to perform the audit according to necessary standards and that it has "not received any communication on the resolution of the audit report modifications" for 2020-21.

In August 2023 it is revealed that Byju exposed some students' names, phone numbers, addresses and email IDs; loan details such as payouts, links to scanned documents and transactional information related to some students. Byju's explained that it was exposed some students' names, phone numbers, addresses and email IDs. The exposed data also included loan details such as payouts, links to scanned documents and transactional information related to some students' due to a mis figured Apache Kafka Server and that the problem is fixed. Byju's confirmed to TechCrunch it had fixed the security lapse but claimed "no data or information was exposed or compromised" during the week that the servers were exposed.

41. NSE Co-Location Scam

Things started going south in 2015 when a Singapore-based whistle-blower alleged that a Delhi-based member on the NSE was accessing privileged price information by linking to servers and getting access to least crowded servers. This later came to be known as the co-location scam. The whistleblower also explained the flaws in the co-location systems and alleged that several NSE employees were colluding with these traders.

The SEBI investigation revealed that between 2011 2014, a handful of traders managed to get secured preferential access to o NSE's trading servers—via its colocation facilities. This where a trader's servers are placed in the stock exchange's data Centre. The access included facilities like early logins, and split - second access to the data feed in the exchange, resulting in huge gains by the trader. According to tax officials, these traders made gains to the tune of Rs 50,000 crore.

Some traders even got multiple IP addresses in dissemination servers and secondary servers for accessing the data, resulting in market manipulation. One such broker was OPG securities. With the help of NSE officials OPG

Securities had allegedly abused the server architecture of the NSE and with the help of Chanakya software it would get speed advantage and also get connected to the backup servers which had zero load. It would help OPG Securities to get better and fast access to the market feed compared to other brokers which then helped it make massive financial gains

SEBI has banned OPG Securities from the market for five years and asked it to cough up Rs 15.57 crore.

Ravi Narain, CEO & MD between 2010-2013 and Chitra 2013 to 2016 till her removal. Both said they were unfamiliar with the technology and that they were not involved in day-to-day operations of the colocation facility. Despite a three-year-long investigation, SEBI in February 2021on;y slapped a fine of Rs 25 lakh on Chitra and Narain. It also imposed a fine of Rupees One crore on NSE.

Chitra was raided by Tax Officials. She has been under CBI lens. SEBI also directed the NSE to forfeit the excess leave encashment of Rs 1.54 crore and the deferred bonus of Rs 2.83 crore, of Ramkrishna, which was retained by the exchange and deposit the money to its Investor Protection Fund Trust.

Himalayan Yogi' case

In February 2022, the said that for the past 20 years, she had been allowing an unidentified 'Himalayan yogi' to advise her on important decisions. The case was investigated by the CBI.

She leaked key business information pertaining to day-to-day operations. She was arrested by the CBI on 7th March 2022.

While ending this Chapter it may be appropriate to reproduce a Press Trust of India's Report taken from the extract of RBI's Annual Report on Fraud in India.

RBI Annual Report

(PTI - May 30, 2023}

The number of frauds in the banking sector went up to 13,530 in 2022-23 year-on-year, but the amount involved nearly halved at Rs 30,252 crore.

Frauds occurred predominantly in the category of digital payments (card/internet), in terms of number. However, in terms of value, frauds have been reported primarily in the loan portfolio (advances category).

A total of 9,097 frauds had taken place in 2021-22 involving Rs 59,819 crore. In 2020-21, the number of frauds was 7,338 and amount involved was Rs 1,32,389 crore.

"An assessment of bank group-wise fraud cases over the last three years indicates that while private sector banks reported maximum number of frauds, public sector banks continued to contribute maximum to the fraud amount during 2022-23.

Data are in respect of frauds of Rs 1 lakh and above reported during the three years.

The report said there was a 55 per cent decline in the amount involved in the total frauds reported during 2021-22 over 2020-21.

Further, proportionately, the decline in the total amount involved in frauds continued during 2022-23, with a reduction of 49 per cent over 2021-22.

"While small value card/internet frauds contributed maximum to the number of frauds reported by the private sector banks, the frauds in public sector banks were mainly in loan portfolio.

Frauds reported in a year could have occurred several years prior to the year of reporting.

The central bank also said an analysis of the vintage of frauds reported during 2021-22 and 2022-23 shows a significant time-lag between the date of occurrence of a fraud and its detection.

The amount involved in frauds that occurred in previous financial years formed 93.7 per cent of the frauds reported in 2021-22 in terms of value.

Similarly, 94.5 per cent of the frauds reported in 2022-23 by value occurred in previous financial years.

During 2022-23, while public sector banks reported 3,405 frauds involving Rs 21,125 crore, private banks reported 8,932 cases involving Rs 8,727 crore. The rest were from foreign banks, financial institutions, small finance banks, and payment banks.

As per the data, 95 per cent or Rs 28,792 crore of the total Rs 30,252 crore was reported in cases related to loans (advances).

The central bank said amounts involved reported do not reflect the amount of loss incurred. Depending on recoveries, the loss incurred gets reduced. Further, the entire amount involved is not necessarily diverted.

The RBI said it would be taking more steps to check fraud in the banking sector.

Frauds of Rs. 496,803 crores were reported by banks in the last five financial years. An average of Rs. 272 crores of fraud were reported by banks in India every day. The total number of fraud cases reported in the last five years was 37,882. Small consolation is that despite increase in the number, there has been a decline in the value of fraud in recent financial years.

Fortune India

"The number of financial frauds rose to 5,406 in the first six months of the financial year 2022-23 compared with 4,069 in the corresponding period a year ago

At ₹18,746 crore, loan-related frauds clocked the biggest share in the first half of FY23, as per RBI data. "Based on the date of occurrence of frauds, advances-related frauds formed the biggest category prior to 2019-20. Subsequently, however, in terms of number of frauds, the modus operandi shifted to card or internet-based transactions," the RBI says, adding that cash frauds are also on the rise.

The number of fraud cases reported by private lenders outnumbered those by public sector banks (PSBs) for the second consecutive year in 2021-22. In terms of the amount involved, however, the share of PSBs was 66.7% in 2021-22, as compared with 59.4% in the previous year.

With the exponential growth of digital payments and expanding digitalization of the financial ecosystem, cyber security risks for financial institutions are also increasing, the central bank says".

Fortune India

Causes for collapses as emerged

Accounting Frauds; Demand Draft Frauds; Bill Discounting Fraud; Letters of Credit Fraud; Skimming of Crad Information Fraud; Gorged or Fraudulent Documents Fraud; Forgery/ Altered Cheques Fraud; Fraudulent Loan Applications; Fraudulent Loans; ATM Frauds; Money Laundering; Electronic Transfer Fraud; forgery, cheating and criminal conspiracy, gross violation of RBI guidelines

Chapter XI

Some of The Global Corporate Failures/Frauds Collapses in Brief

Name/Country/ Year	**Brief History and Reasons for Collapse**
Edsel-Ford USA/1959	In 1958, Ford's newest vehicle, launched on "E-Day," flailed, flopped, and imploded. Ford kept the Edsel under wraps as a new kind of futuristic, experimental car. One fateful day in 1958, the Edsel was revealed…and immediately faceplanted. This car of the future was blah by anyone's standards. By November 1959, when Ford finally mercy-killed the Edsel, it had lost an estimated $250 million–nearly $2 billion in today's dollars. Edsel is now synonymous with a **marketing business failure**
Allied Crude Vegetable Oil Refining Corp USA/1963	Commodities trader Tino De Angelis defrauded clients, including the Bank of America into thinking he was trading vegetable oil. He got loans and made money using the oil as collateral. He showed inspectors tankers of water, with a bit of oil on the surface. When the **fraud** was exposed, the business collapsed.

Name/Country/ Year	Brief History and Reasons for Collapse
Carrian Group Hongkong/1983	The Group was known for rapid expansion in the 1980s, which ended in collapse amidst a major **corruption and fraud scandal.** In January 1980, the group, purchased Gammon House in Central District, for HK$998 million and in April 1980 it announced the sale of Gammon House for HK$1.68 billion and thereby creating developed public interest in Carrian. In the same year, Carrian capitalized on its notoriety by acquiring a publicly listed Hong Kong company, renaming it Carrian Investments Ltd., and using it as a vehicle to raise funds from the financial markets. Its rapid expansion has led to rumors over the source of its capital speculating the capital came from Imelda Marcos, Gosbank, and a lumber corporation in Borneo **Accounting fraud**. Auditor was **murdered**, an adviser committed **suicide.** The largest **collapse** in Hong Kong history.
Texaco USA/1987	Went for **bankruptcy** after legal battle with Pennzoil. It was later resurrected and taken over by Chevron.
Tucker 48 USA/1988	The rise and fall of the Tucker Corporation remains an enigma of U.S. automotive history. The 1948 Tucker automobile was heralded as the car of tomorrow, and by performance standards, the car was years ahead of its time. Francis Ford Coppola's 1988 movie Tucker: The Man and His Dream brought to life the difficulties Preston Tucker faced as he tried to

Name/Country/ Year	Brief History and Reasons for Collapse
	start producing a car years' ahead of its time. The movie is captivating because it attributes the collapse of the Tucker Corporation to public choice theory. Despite the movie's portrayal of an alliance between the automobile industry and the S.E.C. to bring down the Tucker Company, historians have found no evidence of a conspiracy. Rather, the collapse of the Tucker Corporation can be attributed to two problems. First**, lack of financial planning** and refusal to utilize conventional loans scared away venture capital. Second, the S.E.C.'s determination that preselling car features was illegal left the Tucker Corporation financially **bankrupt**
Qiuntex Australia/1989	An Australian financial services company founded in 1975 as Takeovers, Equities & Management Securities (TEAM). The first signs of collapse showed in October 1989, when the American subsidiary filed for Chapter 11 bankruptcy protection after Qintex failed to provide financing for a debt payment. The Australian Stock Exchange suspended Qintex's stock shortly after when the company failed to respond to questions of its financial health. A month later, in November 1989, Qintex Ltd went into receivership with debts of over A$1.9 billion. The collapse happened just six weeks after the company lost a bid to acquire MGM/ UA studios for A$1.5 billion.

Name/Country/ Year	Brief History and Reasons for Collapse
	Its collapse was prompted by what was later seen as an **excessive amount of debt** in the business. It was in 1991 that bank-appointed receivers created Seven Network Limited in order to bundle together the company's assets. The CEO was found to have received **fees improperly** using his position. Company collapsed.
Polly Peck International (PPI) UK/ 1990	**PPI** was a small British textile company which expanded rapidly in the 1980s and became a constituent of the FTSE 100 Index before collapsing in 1991 with **debts** of £1.3bn, eventually leading to the flight of its CEO, Asil Nadir to Northern Cyprus in 1993. 5. Polly Peck was one of several corporate scandals that led to the reform of UK company law, resulting in the early versions of the UK Corporate Governance Code. On 26 August 2010 Nadir returned to the UK to try to clear his name. Prosecutors alleged that he **stole** more than £150m from Polly Peck and he faced trial on 13 specimen charges totaling £34m. Nadir was found guilty on 10 counts of theft totaling £29m. On 23 August 2012 at the Old Bailey he was sentenced to **10 years in prison.**

Name/Country/ Year	Brief History and Reasons for Collapse
Bank of Credit & Commerce International UK/1991	BCCI was a major international bank founded in 1972 by Agha Hassan Abedi, a Pakistani financier. BCCI also acquired parallel banks through acquisitions. By 1980, BCCI was reported to have assets of over $4 billion with over 150 branches in 46 countries. BCCI expanded rapidly and by 1991 it had 420 offices around the world and a presence in 70 countries.
	BCCI came under the scrutiny of numerous financial regulators and intelligence agencies in the 1980s due to concerns that it was **poorly regulated.** Reality was not reflected in BCCI's accounts because the **losses were concealed** in a Cayman Islands subsidiary. As the losses mounted Abedi resorted to more and more desperate ways of keeping the bank afloat. The bank only kept going by **fraudulent accounting and massive misappropriations of depositors' funds**. Investigations and the inquiry report in June 1991 by Price Waterhouse at the behest of Bank of England revealed that BCCI was involved in **massive money laundering and other financial crimes, and illegally gained controlling interest** in a major American bank. The report indicated massive **manipulation of non-performing loans, fictitious transactions and charges, unrecorded deposit liabilities, fictitious profits and concealment of losses.** BCCIs assets were ultimately liquidated, and a pool was established to reimburse depositors who had lost their funds when the bank shut down.

Name/Country/ Year	Brief History and Reasons for Collapse
Pan Am World Airways USA/1991	Pan Am was the principal and largest international air carrier and unofficial overseas flag carrier for much of the 20th century. It was the first airline to fly worldwide and pioneered numerous innovations of the modern airline industry, such as jumbo jets and computerized reservation systems. Until its dissolution in 1991, Pan Am "epitomized the luxury and glamour of intercontinental travel. **Reasons for demise in 1991** Arrogance of founder Juan Terry Trippe in conducting business and who never planned for a qualified, long-term successor. Poor management, deregulation, unions, apathy etc., Surges in oil prices and decreased demand for flights. Following a hijacking in 1986 and the terrorist bombing in Lockerbie Scotland, Pan Am went out of business.
Maxwell Communications Corporation and Mirror Group Newspaper UK/1991	Maxwell Communications established in 1964 was a leading British media company. It was listed on the London Stock Exchange and was a constituent of the FTSE 100 Index. The company acquired Macmillan Publishers, a large US publisher, in 1988 and Science Research Associates and the Official Airline Guide later that year.

Name/Country/ Year	Brief History and Reasons for Collapse
	By the end of the 1980s the Maxwell Empire, comprising more than 400 companies was loosely organized into three clusters. All the three holding companies were also directly and indirectly linked to dozens of other family-controlled enterprises. In 1991 the global empire of publishing and other businesses collapsed amidst scandal about shocking **financial maneuvers.** Investigations revealed that Maxwell's group companies owed £2.8 billion to its bankers. Maxwell's untimely death triggered a **flood of instability** with banks frantically calling in their massive loans. Thousands of employees of the Mirror Group had paid into pension funds totaling many millions of pounds, which Maxwell had 'borrowed' in a desperate attempt to prop up the ailing Maxwell Communication. The Company **went into administration**. Its properties were sold to various media companies. The London based Maxwell Communication Corporation - parent of the giant U.S. book publisher Macmillan also filed the Chapter 11 bankruptcy petition in New York, in part, because bulk of its revenue and operating profit was generated in the United States. Flaws in Corporate Governance **Domineering CEO Maxwell; personal control over movement of funds; relegation of ethical and professional standards; Ineffective Board; Lack of Transparency of financial activities; Flaws in the Audit.**

Name/Country/ Year	**Brief History and Reasons for Collapse**
Barings Bank UK/1995	An employee in Singapore, Nick Leeson, traded futures, **signed off on his own accounts** and became increasingly indebted. The London directors were subsequently **disqualified, as being unfit to run a company** in Re Barings plc . The bank collapsed in 1995 after suffering losses of £827 million (£1.7 billion in 2021) resulting from fraudulent investments, primarily in futures contracts, conducted by its employee Nick Leeson. The Bank of England attempted an unsuccessful weekend bailout,] and employees around the world did not receive their bonuses. Barings was declared insolvent on 26 February 1995, and administrators began managing the finances of Barings Group and its subsidiaries. The bank's assets were subsequently acquired by the Dutch ING Groep, forming ING Barings. This subsidiary was later sold to ABN Amro in 2001.
Bre-X Minerals Ltd Canada/1998	Bre-X was a Canadian gold mining company that infamously defrauded investors by falsifying gold samples and misstating its available gold reserves. From a peak valuation of over $6 billion Canadian dollars (CAD), Bre-X's shares collapsed and the company soon **filed for bankruptcy**. Among the many victims of the Bre-X scandal were Canadian pension funds

Name/Country/ Year	Brief History and Reasons for Collapse
	such as the Ontario Teachers Pension Plan and the Quebec Public Sector Pension Fund, which faced combined losses of over $150 million CAD. Bre-X was a group of companies in Canada. Bre-X Minerals Ltd., was involved in a major **gold mining scandal** when it reported it was sitting on an enormous gold deposit Busang at Indonesia. Bre-X bought the Busang site in March 1993 and in October 1995 announced significant amounts of gold had been discovered, sending its stock price soaring. Originally a penny stock, its stock price reached a peak at CAD$286.50 (split adjusted) in May 1996 on the Toronto Stock Exchange (TSE), with a total capitalization of over CAD $6 billion. Bre-X Minerals collapsed in 1997 after the **gold samples were found to be fraudulent**. Bre-X collapsed and its shares became worthless in one of the biggest stock scandals in Canadian history, and the biggest mining scandal of all time.
Livent Canada/1998	Livent was a theatre production company founded in 1989. The company initially found success with its productions winning the Tony Award for Best Revival of a Musical (1995). In 1998, Livent announced the discovery of **"accounting irregularities".** Revised financial statements showed previously undisclosed losses, and the company filed for **bankruptcy protection.**

Name/Country/ Year	Brief History and Reasons for Collapse
	As a result, the company's stock price plummeted, and its assets were eventually sold off in 1999. The company's collapse led to **criminal and civil litigation**. An Ontario court found that Drabinsky and Gottlieb had systematically doctored Livent's financial statements, and **sentenced them to jail** terms of several years for fraud and forgery. A judgment was also obtained against **Deloitte & Touche in respect of Deloitte's negligence in conducting the audit** for 1997 fiscal year. In 2014 $85.6-milllion lawsuit judgment was pronounced against Deloitte.
Flowtex Germany/ 2000	FlowTex operated a Ponzi scheme in which non-existing construction equipment was sold to investors in order to immediately be leased back by FlowTex. This required an exponentially growing number of investors to afford the lease payments. The fraud was the largest corporate scandal in German history and caused financial damages of about 4.9bn DM (≈€3.3bn).
	What started as a legal business with a viable model soon turned into **large-scale fraud**; in reality, FlowTex had only produced 181 machines that were **sold multiple times**, with the certificates and identification plates **manipulated** according to the scam. At one point, the same machine was paraded at various different fake construction sites to

Name/Country/ Year	Brief History and Reasons for Collapse
	potential investors during the same inspection. Over a period of ten years or so, they secured loans worth more than two billion Euros for non-existent drilling systems and the scam is widely tipped as Germany's **largest ever prosecuted case of white-collar crime.**
Pets.com USA/2000	When Pets.com was launched in 1998, Amazon was involved in the first round of venture funding due to its potential. In 999, the e-commerce giant had a 54 percent stake in the company. Reasons for demise in 2000 A victim of the **dot-com bubble.** **Most spending** *on* warehouses and shipment **infrastructures** **Lack of solid business plan** even after take - over of competitor Petstore.com. Despite brand recognition, Pets.com's liquidation was completed.
Polaroid USA/2000	Polaroid, once a household name synonymous with instant photography, has become a cautionary tale of a company that **failed to adapt and innovate** in the face of changing technology. This **lack of vision** would contribute greatly to its downfall, among other factors. It was a combination of **improper conduct at the top, controversies,** and failure to adapt to changing times that caused the **bankruptcy** of Polaroid. Polaroid was a victim of patent violations and poor company policy.

Name/Country/ Year	Brief History and Reasons for Collapse
	The business principles that kept them successful since founding in 1937 started to fail right around the year 2000.
Bethlehem Steel Corporation USA/2000	This was an American Steel making company. Until its closure in 2003 it was one of the world's largest steel producing and shipbuilding companies. At the height of its success and productivity, the company was a symbol of American manufacturing leadership in the world, and its decline and ultimate liquidation in the late 20th century is similarly cited as an example of America's **diminished manufacturing leadership**. Multiple factors contributed to the decline and failure of Bethlehem Steel. **First**, the **market was changing.** Materials like aluminium and plastic were beginning to replace steel. Starting in the 1960s, the corporation faced increasing competition from foreign mills and mini-mills within the US. In the late 1970s, a number of disasters forced the shutdown and caused costly cleanup efforts of several facilities. **Finally,** a **recession** in the early 1980s and shrinking profits continued to propel the decline.
Commodore Computers USA/2000	Commodore was an American manufacturer of home computers and electronics. The company, which was founded by Jack Tramiel and Manfred Kapp, was a major player during the burgeoning PC market of the 70s, 80s, and early 90s. Commodore **failed to keep pace with advancements in personal computing**, which opened the door for IBM and Apple. This lack of innovation was no doubt caused by the

Name/Country/ Year	Brief History and Reasons for Collapse
	appointment of a CEO who cut research and development funds to almost nothing.
Cinar Canada/2001	Micheline Charest and Ronald Weinberg, the co-founders of this animation studio, were accused of **transferring over $120 million** to the Bahamas without the approval of its board of directors. The company was later sold in 2004 to a consortium that includes Nelvana founder Michael Hirsch and was subsequently renamed Cookie Jar Group. Cookie Jar in turn was acquired in 2012 by what is now called WildBrain. In 2016, **Weinberg was sentenced** to 8 years and 11 months in prison, and is currently on parole.
HIH Insurance Australia/2001	This was Australia's second largest and renowned insurance company which went into the provisional liquidation on 15th March 2001. Total losses were estimated up to A$5.3 billion. The members of HIH **management were charged as culprits, which led to their imprisonment**. According to the reports of an appointed provisional liquidator, HIH had lost more than $800 million over six months to 31st of December 2000. The company falls under various shortcomings including the **failure to rapid expansion, extensive and complex reinsurance arrangements, an unsupervised delegation of authority, underpricing, false reports, reserve issues, self-dealing, fraud and irresponsible management**. This caused the demise of HIH insurance company, which was considered as one of the biggest corporate Collapse in Australia.

Name/Country/ Year	Brief History and Reasons for Collapse
Pacific Gas & Electric Company USA/2001	After a **change in regulation** in California, PG&E determined it was unable to continue delivering power, and despite the California Public Utilities Commission's efforts, it went into **bankruptcy,** leaving homes without energy. The company hoped to come out of bankruptcy by June 30, 2020, and was successful. when U.S. Bankruptcy Judge Dennis Montali issued the final approval of the plan for PG&E to exit bankruptcy.
Swissair Switzerland/2001	Factors behind collapse Like other airlines that flew to the United States, Swissair's operations and profitability were disrupted in the wake of the September 11, 2001 attacks. **Failure of the Board of Directors**, which included politicians as members, to oversee the actions of the Chief Operating Officer since 1996 and a board member since 1993 who became later board president who left behind a **convoluted corporate structure and financial commitments.** which would only come to light when Mario Corti was trying to save the airline. The judiciary is continuing to examine why Swissair acquired counselling that supported the Hunter Strategy, and why Swissair continued to make certain **payments despite nearing insolvency.** Questions have also been raised about federal aid given to Swissair and the politicians involved.

Name/Country/ Year	Brief History and Reasons for Collapse
	The highly **competitive nature** of the market during the business's final years also precipitated its demise: like subsidiary Sabena, Swissair fell victim to the competition of budget airlines such as Ryanair and EasyJet. The Swiss financial community's reputation for good business sense was already seriously damaged by the Swissair disaster. The following causes are widely recognized as crucial factors: The management **underestimated the dangers and difficulties in acquisitions** and investments of partially ailing airlines. The indebtedness created by an uncompromising and too little adapted to the realities of implementation, "Hunter strategy" and the **lack of monitoring by the Board.** An orderly transfer of operations at Crossair was denied by the **failure to reach a bridging loan** and the delayed transfer of the share purchase price. Increasing **competition from low-cost carriers** such as Ryanair and EasyJet, caused Swissair to lose passenger revenues. A full merger with Sabena was impossible due to Swissair's **financial crisis.** A McDonnell-Douglas MD-11, operating **Flight 111, crash**ed in 1998 killing everyone on board, and lowering customer confidence.

Name/Country/ Year	Brief History and Reasons for Collapse
Enron USA/2001	Enron scandal **an accounting scandal** involving Enron Corporation. Upon being publicized in October 2001, the company declared **bankruptcy and its accounting firm, Arthur Andersen –was effectively dissolved.** Enron was cited as the biggest audit failure. When Jeffrey Skilling was hired, Kenneth, the founder developed a staff of executives that – by the use of accounting loopholes, special purpose entities, and **poor financial reporting** – were able to hide billions of dollars in debt from failed deals and projects. Chief Financial Officer Andrew Fastow and other executives **misled Enron's board of directors and audit committee on high-risk accounting practices and pressured Arthur Andersen to ignore the issues.** Shareholders filed a \$40 billion lawsuit after the company's stock price, which achieved a high of US\$90.75 per share in mid-2000, plummeted to less than \$1 by the end of November 2001. The U.S. Securities and Exchange Commission (SEC) began an investigation, and rival Houston competitor Dynegy offered to purchase the company at a very low price. The deal failed, and on December 2, 2001, Enron filed for bankruptcy under Chapter 11 of the United States Bankruptcy Code. Enron's \$63.4 billion in assets made it the largest corporate bankruptcy in U.S. history until the WorldCom scandal the following year.

Name/Country/ Year	Brief History and Reasons for Collapse
	Many executives at Enron were **indicted** for a variety of charges and some were later **sentenced** to prison, including Lay and Skilling. Arthur Andersen was found guilty of **illegally destroying documents** relevant to the SEC investigation, which voided its license to audit public companies and effectively closed the firm. By the time the ruling was overturned at the U.S. Supreme Court, Arthur Andersen had lost the majority of its customers and had ceased operating. Enron employees and shareholders received limited returns in lawsuits, despite losing billions in pensions and stock prices. As a consequence of the scandal, new regulations and legislation were enacted to expand the accuracy of financial reporting for public companies. One piece of legislation, the Sarbanes–Oxley Act, increased penalties for destroying, altering, or fabricating records in federal investigations or for attempting to defraud shareholders. The act also increased the accountability of auditing firms to remain unbiased and independent of their clients.
Flooz.com USA/2001	Flooz.com blew through up to $50 million dollars trying to convince new Internet users that money online would work like frequent flier miles or gift cards. Part of that money went to a notoriously **bad ad campaign** featuring Whoopi Goldberg (before she was cool again). And the name? Flooz is derived from the Arabic word for money. In August, 2001 the company folded their chairs and went home.

Name/Country/ Year	Brief History and Reasons for Collapse
One-Tel Australia/2001	At the time of its collapse, it was the fourth largest telecommunications company in Australia with more than two million customers and operations in eight countries. Analyses of quantitative and qualitative data from diverse sources suggest that One-Tel's collapse is a classic case of **failed expectations, strategic mistakes, wrong pricing policy, and unbridled growth.**
	The company's meteoric rise and fall was associated with serious **deficiencies in its corporate governance including weaknesses in internal control, financial reporting, audit quality, board's scrutiny of management, management communication with the board, and poor executive pay-to-performance link.** Thus, the collaps**e of** One-Tel has several important lessons on the role of corporate governance in preventing corporate collapse.
Arther Andersen USA/2002	Arthur Andersen -part of Big-5, was engaged in auditing, tax advising, consulting and other professional services to large corporations. The firm collapsed by mid-2002, as details of its questionable accounting practices for energy company Enron and telecommunications company WorldCom. The scandals were a factor in the enactment of the Sarbanes-Oxley Act of 2002. A US court convicted Andersen of **obstruction of justice by shredding documents** relating to the Enron scandal.

Name/Country/ Year	**Brief History and Reasons for Collapse**
WorldCom USA/2002	WorldCom was in **financial trouble and used questionable accounting techniques to hide its losses** from investors and others. The company filed for **bankruptcy** because of the scandal, and several key figures were punished, including its CEO and CFO. WorldCom emerged from bankruptcy, restructured, and was purchased by Verizon.
Adelphia Communications Corporation USA/2002	This was an American cable television company founded by brothers Gus and John Rigas. The company became one of the most successful in the United States and reached over two million subscribers in 1998. In addition to cable television, Adelphia later started providing high-speed internet, phone services and voice messaging for businesses. Despite its success, in 2002 the company filed for **bankruptcy amid an internal corruption scandal.** An investigation was launched and later revealed that some members of the Rigas family used $2.3 billion to **illegitimately purchase personal luxuries.** A trial for the case was launched and saw John Rigas being **sentenced to 15 years** in prison, while his son Timothy Rigas received a sentence of 20 years. John Rigas was released in 2016 as a result of health issues.

Name/Country/ Year	Brief History and Reasons for Collapse
Compaq Computer USA/2002	An American information technology company founded in 1982 that developed, sold, and supported computers and related products and services. They provided some of the first IBM PC compatible computers and were the first company to reverse engineer the IBM personal computer. Reasons for failure: Compaq **divested some of its parts** that it didn't want to. Face **increasing competition** from Intel and Intel produced motherboards and chipsets which were used by Compaq but the overall price for the PC was less as offered by Intel along with CPU components proving the same quality at a much lower price. **DOT.com bubble** where internet companies brought PCs but once their businesses failed and Compaq lost a lot of big customers. In 2002 the company was acquired by HP for 25 billion dollars
MG Rover Group UK/2003	After **diminishing demand,** and getting a £6.5m loan from the UK government in April 2005, the company went into **administration.** After the loss of 30,000 jobs, Nanjing Automobile Group bought the company's assets.

Name/Country/ Year	**Brief History and Reasons for Collapse**
Parmalat Italy/2003	In 2003, multinational Italian dairy and food corporation Parmalat collapsed with a €14 billion ($20bn; £13bn) **hole in its accounts**, in what remains Europe's biggest bankruptcy. The Parmalat **bankruptcy** greatly affected football team AC Parma, in which Parmalat was the major shareholder. When it said a **4-billion-euro** bank account held by a Cayman Islands unit **did not exist**, forcing management to seek **bankruptcy protection and triggering a criminal fraud probe**. Despite the company's investment-grade credit rating, concerns had swirled for months over Parmalat's failure to explain why it did not use cash shown on its balance sheet to cut debt. There have been two main trials into Parmalat's collapse, one in Italy's financial capital Milan and the other in Parma, close to the group's headquarters. In Milan, Tanzi, the **founder. was sentenced to 10 years** in prison for **market rigging and obstructing market regulators.** He is appealing against the ruling. In Parma, a trial began in March 2008 and focuses on allegations of fraudulent **bankruptcy** and **criminal conspiracy** within Parmalat.

Name/Country/ Year	**Brief History and Reasons for Collapse**
	A streamlined version of the dairy group, stripped of loss-making foreign units, relisted on Milan's bourse on October 6, 2005. The shares opened at 3.15 euros, giving it a value of some 5 billion euros - - or almost three times its capitalization before the collapse - - as investors bet on revenue from damages suits and on potential takeover bids. Parmalat's collapse sparked **litigation worldwide** against dozens of banks, including Bank of America Corp and Citigroup Inc, by current Parmalat management and by investors. Parmalat has recouped more than 2 billion euros from settlements with banks including Morgan Stanley and the former Merrill Lynch, now part of Bank of America.
Hit Factory USA/2003	Deep in New York, in the heart of Hell's Kitchen, The Hit Factory was one the world's most recognized recording Studios. Started by Edward Germano in 1975, it saw everyone from Tony Bennett to U2 record amazing tracks. After Germano's death in 2003, his wife Janice took over operations. Citing the "digital age," she closed the doors and **sold the building, moving the operations** to an existing Hit Factory in Miami. Troy Germano, Edward's son, later acknowledged publicly that his mother **simply closed it out of greed.** She wanted to move to Miami and thought she could make good money on the building's sale. It is now a luxury condominium complex, with prices starting at $1 million.

Name/Country/ Year	Brief History and Reasons for Collapse
Refco USA/2005	After becoming a public company in August 2005, it was revealed that Phillip R. Bennett, the company's CEO and chairman, had **concealed $430m of bad debts**. Its underwriters were Credit Suisse First Boston, Goldman Sachs, and Bank of America Corp.
	The law requires that such financial connections between corporation and its own top officers be shown as what is known as a **related party transaction in various financial statements.** As a result, Refco said, "its financial statements, as of, and for the periods ended, Feb. 28, 2002, Feb. 28, 2003, Feb. 28, 2004, Feb. 28, 2005, and May 31, 2005, taken as a whole, for each of Refco Inc., Refco Group Ltd. LLC and Refco Finance Inc. should no longer be relied upon leading to a number of investigations. **Bennett was arrested and charged with one count of securities fraud** for using U.S. mail, interstate commerce, and securities exchanges to lie to investors. Refco shares were trading for more than $28 per share, and as of October 19, they had dropped (on the pink sheets) to $0.80 per share. The company entered **Chapter 11** and Bennett was sentenced to 16 years in prison.
Chiquita Brands International Sàrl Switzerland/2007	A producer and distributor of bananas and other produce. Chiquita was the leading distributor of bananas in the United States. In November 2001, Chiquita filed for Chapter 11 bankruptcy protection in order to restructure the company. The group had to face several charges such as:

Name/Country/ Year	Brief History and Reasons for Collapse
	Monopolistic Practices by refusing to supply certain customers and by charging dissimilar prices for equivalent transactions. (1976} **Payments to foreign Terrorist Groups**. On 14 March 2007, Chiquita Brands was fined $25 million as part of a settlement with the United States Justice Department for having ties to Colombian paramilitary groups. On 7 December 2007, the 29th Specialized District Attorney's Office in Medellín, Colombia subpoenaed the Chiquita board to answer questions "concerning charges for conspiracy to commit an aggravated crime and financing illegal armed groups". In 2016, Judges allowed Colombians to sue former Chiquita Brand International executives for the company's **funding of the outlawed right-wing paramilitary organization** that murdered their family members. n 2018, A recurrent issue in agricultural large-scale production are **workers' rights violations**, in which Chiquita has been involved as well. Besides the above, Chiquita was repeatedly pulled up in **Environmental violation** issues in some European countries.

Name/Country/ Year	Brief History and Reasons for Collapse
Bayou Hedge Fund Group Israel/2006	The group of companies and hedge funds were founded and headed by Samuel Israel III. Approximately $450m was raised by the group from investors, who were **defrauded** from nearly the start with funds being **misappropriated for personal use**. After poor returns in 1998, the investors were lied to about the fund's returns, and a **fake accounting firm was set up to provide misleading audited results.** In 2005, Samuel Israel III and CFO Daniel Marino pleaded guilty to multiple charges including conspiracy and fraud. **Marino was convicted of fraud and sentenced to 20 years in prison. Israel was sentenced to 20 years prison and ordered to forfeit $300 millio**
IndyMac USA/2008	IndyMac invested heavily in Alt-A mortgages and reverse mortgages. After many of these **loans failed** and couldn't be sold during the U.S. subprime mortgage crisis the company had to file for **Chapter 7 bankruptcy.** The primary causes of IndyMac's failure were largely associated with its **business strategy** of originating and securitizing Alt-A loans on a large scale. This strategy resulted in rapid growth and a **high concentration of risky assets**. During 2006, IndyMac originated over $90 billion of mortgages.

Name/Country/ Year	Brief History and Reasons for Collapse
	When home prices declined in the latter half of 2007 and the secondary mortgage market collapsed, IndyMac was forced to hold $10.7 billion of loans it could not sell in the secondary market. Its reduced liquidity was further exacerbated in late June 2008 when account holders withdrew $1.55 billion or about 7.5% of IndyMac's deposits. While the run was a contributing factor in the timing of IndyMac's demise, the underlying cause of the failure was the **unsafe and unsound manner in which the thrift was operated.**
Lehman Brothers USA.2008	filed for **bankruptcy** on September 15, 2008. Hundreds of employees, mostly dressed in business suits, left the bank's offices one by one with boxes in their hands. At the time of its collapse, Lehman was the fourth-largest investment bank in the United States with 25,000 employees worldwide. It had $639 billion in assets and $613 billion in liabilities. The bank became **a symbol of the excesses of the 2007-08 Financial Crisis, engulfed by the subprime meltdown that swept through** financial markets and cost an estimated $10 trillion in lost economic output. Lehman's bankruptcy had four underlying causes: **Risk**: The bank had taken on too much risk without a corresponding ability to raise cash quickly. Cash flow problem is what led to its bankruptcy.

Name/Country/ Year	Brief History and Reasons for Collapse
	Culture: Management rewarded excessive risk-taking as they wanted to stay ahead of competitors and they also thought the company was too smart to fail. **Overconfidence**: The firm relied on complicated financial products based on quick real estate growth just as the real estate market began to decline. Management thought it would make more money owning these assets but its timing couldn't have been worse, as real estate prices were falling. **Regulator inaction**: The Securities and Exchange Commission and other regulators didn't take action. As early as 2007, the SEC knew Lehman Brothers was taking on too much risk, but the agency never required Lehman to do anything about it. It also did not publicly disclose to rating agencies that the bank had exceeded risk limits.
AIG USA/2008	AIG is an American multinational finance and insurance corporation with operations in more than 80 countries and jurisdictions. The company operates through three core businesses: general insurance, life & retirement, and a standalone technology-enabled subsidiary. On May 1, 2005, **investigations conducted by outside counsel at the request of AIG's Audit Committee and the consultation with AIG's independent auditors,**

Name/Country/ Year	Brief History and Reasons for Collapse
	PricewaterhouseCoopers LLP resulted in AIG's decision to restate its financial statements for the years ended December 31, 2003, 2002, 2001 and 2000, the quarters ended March 31, June 30 and September 30, 2004, and 2003 and the quarter ended December 31, 2003. On November 9, 2005, the company was said to have delayed its third-quarter earnings report because it had to restate earlier financial results, to **correct accounting errors**. During the financial crisis of 2007–2008, the Federal Reserve bailed the company out for $180 billion and assumed controlling ownership stake, with the Financial Crisis Inquiry Commission correlating AIG's failure with the mass sales of unhedged insurance. AIG repaid $205 billion to the United States government in 2012.
Washington Mutual {WMU} USA/2008	WMU once was the largest failed bank in US history. Five main reasons why WaMu failed. **First**, it did a lot of business in California, where the housing market did worse than in other parts of the country. **Second,** its rapid branch expansion, which resulted in poor branch locations in too many markets, and too many subprime mortgages to unqualified buyers. **Third,** the collapse of the secondary market for mortgage-backed securities in August 2007.

Name/Country/ Year	Brief History and Reasons for Collapse
	Fourth, was the Lehman Brothers bankruptcy on September 15, 2008. WaMu depositors panicked and withdrew $16.7 billion out of their savings and checking accounts over the next 10 days, over 11 percent of WaMu's total deposits. **Fifth** reason was its moderate size. It was not big enough to be "too big to fail," and as a result, the US Treasury or the Federal Reserve wouldn't bail it out like they did Bear Stearns or American International Group.
Royal Bank of Scotland Group (RBS) UK/2008	Following the takeover of ABN-Amro, and the collapse of Lehman Brothers, RBS found itself **insolvent** as the international credit market seized up. 58% of the shares were bought by the UK government. The bank collapsed for the following reasons- **significant weaknesses in RBS's capital position**, as a result of management decisions and permitted by an inadequate global regulatory capital framework **over-reliance on risky short-term wholesale funding,** which was permitted by an inadequate approach to the regulation of liquidity **concerns and uncertainties about RBS's underlying asset quality** because of little fundamental analysis by the FSA

Name/Country/ Year	Brief History and Reasons for Collapse
	substantial losses in credit trading activities, which eroded market confidence and both the bank and the regulator underestimated how bad the losses were the **ABN Amro acquisition took place with "inadequate due diligence**" underlying **deficiencies in RBS management, governance and culture** which made it prone to make poor decisions"
ABN - Amro Netherlands/2008	ABN Amro was involved in a **hostile takeover** by a consortium of banks led by **Royal Bank of Scotland (RBS) in** 2007**.** The deal was **very expensive** and **risky** for RBS, and it **coincided** with the **global financial crisis** of 2008**.** As a result, RBS faced **huge losses** and had to be **bailed out** by the UK government, while ABN Amro was **split up** and **sold off** to various buyers**. ABN Amro also faced legal and regulatory issues, as well as market turmoil** due to the coronavirus pandemic, which forced it to **cut costs** and **exit some businesses.**

Name/Country/ Year	Brief History and Reasons for Collapse
Facebook-Cambridge Analytica UK/2010s	Personal data belonging to millions of Facebook users was collected through an app called "This is your Digital Life" without their consent by British consulting firm Cambridge Analytica, predominantly to be used for political advertising. The app harvested the data of up to 87 million Facebook profiles. Cambridge Analytica used the data to provide analytical assistance to the 2016 presidential campaigns of Ted Cruz and Donald Trump. Cambridge Analytica was also widely accused of interfering with the Brexit referendum. Information about the data misuse was disclosed in 2018 by a former Cambridge Analytica employee, in interviews with *The Guardian* and *The New York Times*. In response, Facebook apologized for their role in the data harvesting and their CEO Mark Zuckerberg testified in front of Congress. In July 2019, it was announced that Facebook was to be fined $5 billion by the Federal Trade Commission due to its privacy violations. In 2019, Facebook agreed to pay $5 billion to resolve a Federal Trade Commission probe into its privacy practices and $100 million to settle U.S. Securities and Exchange Commission claims that it misled investors about the misuse of users' data. In May 2018, Cambridge Analytica filed for Chapter 7 bankruptcy.

Name/Country/ Year	Brief History and Reasons for Collapse
Volkswagen's emissions scandal 2015	In September 2015, the EPA (Environmental Protection Agency) found out that Volkswagen had been cheating in emission tests by making its cars appear far less polluting than they are. The US Environmental Protection Agency discovered that 482,000 VW diesel cars on American roads were emitting up to 40 times more toxic fumes than permitted. Since, VW has admitted that the cheat affected 11 million cars worldwide. As a consequence, CEO Martin Winterkorn resigned. Volkswagen also had to recall 8.5 million cars in Europe and 500.000 in the US. And in April 2017, a US federal judge ordered Volkswagen "to pay a $2.8 billion criminal fine for rigging diesel-powered vehicles to cheat on government emissions tests."
. BP and the Deepwater Horizon oil spill/2010	On April 20, 2010, the oil drilling rig Deepwater Horizon, located in the Gulf of Mexico, exploded and sank resulting in the death of 11 workers. It's the largest oil spill in history, and it's also the biggest environmental disaster in the US. 4 million barrels of oil flowed from the damaged Macondo well over an 87-day period, before it was finally capped on July 15, 2010. In November 2012, BP and the United States Department of Justice settled federal criminal charges with BP pleading guilty to 11 counts of manslaughter, two misdemeanors, and a felony count of lying to Congress.

Name/Country/ Year	Brief History and Reasons for Collapse
The Deutsche Bank spying scandal	In 2006, Deutsche Bank were caught spying on their management members and also on the personal lives of some of their investors. The bank had a paranoia since someone from the board leaked information about their result to Reuters back in 2001. Therefore, the security department hired a detective agency to spy contacts between board members and media figure Leo Kirch. Due to this spying scandal, the government promised to have a new privacy-protection law for workers.
GE's corporate double-jet practice	In October 2017, it surfaced that former General Electric CEO Jeff Immelt for many years had an empty business jet follow his corporate plane on several trips around the world. The second plane was used as a backup, in case the one Immelt was flying in had "mechanical problems." GE no doubt knew this practice would be perceived as unethical and wasteful, and so flight crews for both planes were told not to talk about the unfilled jet. To make matters worse, the story of the empty jet surfaced a few months after new General Electric CEO John Flannery had to slash thousands of jobs to cut costs.
Northern Rock UK/2008	This was originally a building society. It demutualised and became Northern Rock bank in 1997, when it floated on the London Stock Exchange with the ticker symbol NRK.

Name/Country/ Year	Brief History and Reasons for Collapse
	During the early 2000s the company borrowed substantially to fund mortgages, with the aim of ambitious growth, and also donated large amounts to charitable purposes and communities directly and through sponsorships. The global banking crisis beginning around 2007–08 meant that it was **unable to produce income as expected from its loans, and was at risk of being unable to repay the amounts it had borrowed.** The news that the bank had approached the government for support with its liquidity led within 24 hours to a public lack of confidence and concerns that savings were at risk, and the bank failed following a **bank run** as people rushed to withdraw their savings. It was the first British bank in 150 years to fail due to a bank run. It was **taken into public ownership** in 2008, as an alternative to insolvency. By that point the government had extended liquidity support of tens of billions of pounds to Northern Rock. An inquiry concluded that the **board had failed to properly protect the bank from the risks inherent** in its strategy, or to restrain the executive directors where required, therefore although the bank had sufficient assets, it had become vulnerable. The branch operations were eventually returned to private ownership when the branches and other retail operations were acquired by Virgin Group in 2012, being rebranded as Virgin Money the same year.

Name/Country/ Year	**Brief History and Reasons for Collapse**
Bear Stearns USA/2008	Bear Stearns was a New York City-based global investment bank and financial company that was founded in 1923. It collapsed during the 2008 financial crisis. Prior to the financial collapse, Bear Stearns was one of the most well-regarded financial institutions. By 2008, the firm's flagship **hedge funds were over-exposed to mortgage-backed securities and other toxic assets,** which had been purchased with a high degree of leverage. The company was ultimately **sold to JPMorgan Chase for $10 a share, well below its value** before the crisis. The collapse of Bear Stearns precipitated a wider collapse in the investment banking industry, which also took down major players like Lehman Brothers.
Nortel Canada/2009	Canada's largest telecommunications company, failed because of a **culture of arrogance leading to poor financial discipline, a loss of key customers through lack of technological innovation and a harsh external business environment.** The researchers found the company had a structure that encouraged poor management decisions, was ill-equipped to adapt to the changing marketplace, consumer needs or the pace of technological advances

Name/Country/ Year	Brief History and Reasons for Collapse
Arcandor Germany/ 2009	Was a holding company located in Essen, Germany, that oversaw a number of companies operating in the businesses of mail order and internet shopping, department stores and tourism services. Arcandor, which has over 50,000 employees in Germany, requested financial assistance from the German government, which was rejected by the European Commission on 3 June 2009.It had asked for 437 million euros ($603 million) in emergency funding and state guarantees of 650 million euros to help the company obtain badly needed bank refinancing. On 6 June 2009, the company announced it was no longer able to pay rent for its department stores, which the company had previously sold and leased back. Three days later, the company filed for bankruptcy.

Name/Country/ Year	Brief History and Reasons for Collapse
Anglo Irish Bank Ireland/2009	This Irish bank was nationalized in 2009 after a scandal involving hidden loans. It merged with another bank in 2011 and formed a new company called the Irish Bank Resolution Corporation. Like the other major Irish banks, Anglo Irish was hard hit by the **downturn in the property market**. But the problems at Anglo Irish were much more complicated. From 2000 to 2008, Sean FitzPatrick, the **CEO, used Anglo Irish funds to make massive loans to himself. These personal loans were hidden from the public and from regulators by moving the loans temporarily to another bank to avoid an end of year audit**. After further investigation, it was revealed that although directors were recorded as having €41 million in personal loans from Anglo Irish, the true figure was €150 million. Legality of the actions of the CEO which were questioned included - fa*ilure to act in a* ***virtuous and ethical manner; failure to act virtuously;*** **Lack of Integrity; Breach of Trust; Unfairness towards Investors; Failure to exercise Self Control; Failure to act with Humility.**
Dynegy USA/2012	After a series of attempted takeover bids, and a finding of **fraud in a subsidiary's purchase of another subsidiary,** it filed for Chapter 11 bankruptcy. It emerged from bankruptcy on 2 October 2012.

Name/Country/ Year	Brief History and Reasons for Collapse
China Medical Technologies-CMED Cayman Islands/2012	In 2009, an anonymous letter alleging possible illegal and fraudulent activities by management since 2007 was sent to KPMG Hong Kong, then CMED's auditor, and investigated by law firm Paul Weiss Rifkind Wharton & Garrison. Since 27 July 2012, pursuant to an Order by the Grand Court of the Cayman Islands, CMED has been under the control of Joint Official Liquidators. Post-bankruptcy filing, CMED's liquidator found itself probing an alleged **$355 million insider fraud.** In March 2017, the U.S. Department of Justice **criminally indicted the CMED founder and CEO, as well as former Chief Financial Officer, charging them with securities fraud and wire fraud conspiracy for stealing more than $400 million** from investors as part of a seven-year scheme. In November 2017, **91 partners of the auditor KPMG faced contempt proceedings** in Hong Kong High Court, as CMED liquidators took action against KPMG with regard to its refusal honor a February 2016 court order to produce Chinese working papers, correspondence, and records to the liquidators. The **liquidators** are asking that 91 defendants be held in contempt of court, which could result in criminal penalties, or weekly fines.

Name/Country/ Year	**Brief History and Reasons for Collapse**
Banco Espinto Santo (BES) Portugal/2014	An audit performed in 2013, for a capital raise performed in May 2014, uncovered **severe financial irregularities and a precarious financial situation** of the bank. In July 2014, Salgado was replaced by economist Vítor Bento, who saw BES in an irrecoverable situation. Its good assets were bought by Novo Banco, a vehicle founded by Portugal's financial regulators for that purpose, on August 3, which hired Bento as CEO, while its toxic assets stayed in the "old" BES, which got its banking **license revoked** by Portugal's regulators.
Woolworths Group, PLC. UK/2016	**Woolworths Group** was a British company established in 1909 as a subsidiary of an American Company established in 1879. In UK it owned the high street retail chain. There are different reasons for Woolworths' failure depending on the country and the time period. For example, in the UK, Woolworths collapsed in 2008 due to **poor management, poor customer offering, a rapidly evolving retail world, technology, and the competition from discount pound stores**. In Australia, Woolworths had a massive ERP failure in 2016 that resulted in **massive losses, frustrated employees and a brand image setback**.

Name/Country/ Year	Brief History and Reasons for Collapse
Theranos Inc USA/2016	The founder Elizabeth Holmes was **criminally charged** in June 2018 with **defrauding investors** following the collapse of her blood-testing startup. The revolutionary technology she pitched proved irresistible: a machine that could run an array of tests run on a tiny amount of blood, doing away with frightening, inefficient and costly intravenous draws and vials. Investments from Silicon Valley's most prominent funds poured in, making Holmes the world's youngest female self-made billionaire. But it proved too good to be true. A 2015 Wall Street Journal expose revealed uncertainties about the accuracy and viability of Theranos' blood tests. By 2016, the company once valued at $9 billion was besieged by **investor lawsuits and government investigations.** It was sanctioned in July of that year after federal inspectors found **laboratory failures jeopardized patients' health.** Holmes settled a civil suit by the U.S. Securities and Exchange Commission in March 2018, while former Theranos President Ramesh "Sunny" Balwani, Holmes's onetime romantic partner, continues to fight the agency. After a three-month criminal trial in California, Holmes was found guilty of four counts of defrauding investors. The jury found her not guilty of four other counts and couldn't reach a verdict on three of the charges.

Name/Country/ Year	Brief History and Reasons for Collapse
Dick Smith Australia/2016	The Dick Smith group of companies collapsed in early January 2016 with debts of close to $400 million. Administrators took control of the group and subsequently appointed as receivers. In the much-anticipated report into the companies' collapse, Administrator said the total shortfall to creditors will be "in excess of $260 million", which is substantially different to the $170 million book value of the group's assets as of June 30, 2015. Receivers had attempted to sell Dick Smith's assets, including stock, throughout the receivership. The receivers successfully sold the group's online business and intellectual property to Kogan. com for $2.6 million but were unable to find a buyer for the chain's retail stores, all of which ceased trading by early May. Company's **expansions ate up** all its surplus earnings. **Huge borrowings** were required at the same time as **customer preferences** began to change and the retailer began to lose market share. Company carried **too much unsaleable overvalued stock** **Administrators** was appointed on 4 January 2016.

Name/Country/ Year	Brief History and Reasons for Collapse
Wirecard Germany 2020	The Company followed **corrupt business practices** and **fraudulent financial reporting** that led to its' insolvency. It was a payment processor and financial services provider. The company was part of the DAX index. They offered customers electronic payment transaction and risk management services, as well as the issuance and processing of physical cards. The subsidiary, Wirecard Bank AG, held a banking license and had contracts with multiple international financial services companies. Allegations of **accounting malpractices** have trailed the company since the early days of its incorporation, reaching a peak in 2019 after the Financial Times published a series of investigations along with whistleblower complaints and internal documents. On 25 June 2020, Wirecard filed for insolvency after revealing that **€1.9 billion was "missing"**, and the termination and arrest of its CEO Markus Braun. Questions have been raised about **regulatory failure** on the part of Federal Financial Supervisory Authority (BaFin), Germany's top financial watchdog, and possible **malpractice of Wirecard's long time auditor Ernst & Young.** €1.9 billion, which apparently never existed, were found missing in a special audit. The **CEO was arrested,** the board filed for **insolvency,** and a **warrant for the missing COO** was issued.

Name/Country/ Year	**Brief History and Reasons for Collapse**
Kmart Corporation, founded in 1899 as SS Kresge Company, USA/2022	This US No. 3 discount retailer and an American icon for 40 years, filed for bankruptcy protection under Chapter 11 on January 22, 2022. The decision followed the dizzying spiral of Kmart stock, which plunged from over $5 a share at the end of December to as low as 68 cents on January 21, after an unprecedented series of **downgrades by credit rating agencies** Standard & Poor's and Moody's Investors Service. The retailer operated 2,114 stores employing about 275,000 workers. Kmart declared bankruptcy due to **increasing competition with Walmart and other discount stores.** Walmart's new stores and lower prices made Kmart stores look shabby and more expensive[3]. Kmart was struggling to compete with Walmart's low prices and Target's trendier offerings. Kmart entered bankruptcy after a poor holiday selling season.

Name/Country/ Year	**Brief History and Reasons for Collapse**
FTX, Bahamas-Crypto Currency Exchange Bahamas/2022	FTX collapsed in early November 2022 following a report by CoinDesk highlighting potential **leverage and solvency concerns** involving **FTX-**affiliated trading firm Alameda Research. FTX's collapse shook the volatile crypto market, which lost billions at the time, falling below a $1 trillion valuation. FTX in November 2022 **faced a liquidity crisis and searched for bailout funds;** rival exchange Binance considered buying portions of the company but quickly backed out. By Nov. 11, 2022, FTX's **CEO stepped down and the company filed for bankruptcy.** In the hours following, FTX experienced a possible hack in which hundreds of millions worth of tokens were stolen. FTX founder and **ex-CEO Sam Bankman-Fried was arrested** in The Bahamas and extradited to the United States in late December. He pleaded innocent to all criminal charges on Jan. 3, 2023.

Name/Country/ Year	Brief History and Reasons for Collapse
Silicon Valley Bank (SVB) USA/2023	SVB—the 16th largest bank in the United States—was shut down by federal regulators on March 10, 2023. The bank's failure came as a result of several factors, including **its investments losing value and its depositors withdrawing large amounts of money.** According to report by the Federal Reserve, blame was ultimately attributed to the **bank's management, the regulator, and social media.** In the aftermath of the collapse, federal regulators promised to make all depositors whole, even for those funds that weren't protected by the Federal Deposit Insurance Corporation (FDIC). The Federal Reserve took steps following the collapse of SVB to improve confidence in the banking system and prevent future banking failures, including its Bank Term Funding Program. First Citizens Bank struck a deal with the FDIC to buy SVB's deposits and loans, in addition to certain other assets.

Name/Country/ Year	**Brief History and Reasons for Collapse**
Signature Bank USA/2023	The bank, in addition to banking products, provided services specific to industries such as commercial real estate, private equity, mortgage servicing and venture banking. The Bank was **shut down by federal regulators** in March 2023 due to the **concerns about depositors withdrawing large amounts of money** after the failure of Silicon Valley Bank (SVB) and the **fear of continued contagion.** Federal regulators said Signature Bank customers would get all deposits back, even amounts over $250,000 that are uninsured by the Federal Deposit Insurance Corp. (FDIC). An April 2023 FDIC report blamed Signature's failure on bank mismanagement, a lack of corporate governance, and failure to listen to and respond quickly to the FDIC's recommendations. Signature Bank's failure raised many policy questions around FDIC insurance, and bank and cryptocurrency oversight.
First Republic Bank USA/2023	Due to a global banking panic, mainly from the preceding collapses of Silicon Valley Bank and Signature Bank, a bank run forced the bank to be placed into receivership by the FDIC and then sold to JPMorgan Chase.

{Wikipedia Plus}

Chapter XII

Some of the Failed Start Ups in India

A. General

The Government of India defines a startup as an entity less than ten years old with an annual turnover under one billion Indian rupees and headquartered in India.

Propelled by government's support, access to capital, skilled workers, and a supportive business environment, the country has emerged as one of the leading startup ecosystems in the world.

The Startup India initiative helped build a positive, and effective ecosystem in the country, turning business ideas into a reality. States and union territories across the country introduced startup policies following the central government's initiative which helped incentivize startups through tax exemptions, funding, and support for incubators and accelerators.

The total number of recognised startups in India rose from 471 in 2016 to 99,371 startups (as on May 14, 2023).

According to Source: Venture Intelligence, India has 53 companies with Unicorns status as on August 2023. Unicorns are privately held, venture-capital backed startups that have reached a value of $1 billion. The valuation of unicorns is not expressly linked to their current financial performance, but largely based on their growth potential as perceived by investors and venture capitalists who have taken part in various funding rounds.

Survey by the Institute for Business Value and Oxford Economics reveals that 90 per cent of startups fails within the first 5 years. There are a number of reasons why Indian startups fail the most important of which is a lack of funding. Startups fail to attract funds for a number of reasons. The problem of lack of funds faced by Indian startups is often a result of their founders' inability to articulate their business model to the right audience.

India is the most populous country in the world and the fifth largest economy; however, most startups serve the fraction of Indians who live in urban India. The majority of Indians who live in rural areas and small towns remain untouched by most startups. Too many startups serving too few consumers are saturating the Indian market. In India, less than 20 online retailers are enough to serve the current market, but there are too many online retailers chasing too few consumers. Similarly, there are too many startups serving other crowded industries as well. The increasingly crowded startup ecosystem means there aren't enough funds to go around.

A study of the failed startups has any or all of the following commonalities:

i. Lack of capital or Inadequate Capital

ii. Failure to attract customers

iii. Failure to set realistic ad measurable marketing goals

iv. Failure to recognize strength of Competition

v. Failure to design own customer-oriented marketing plan after studying that of the competition.

vi. Failure to take decisions based on facts instead of gut feel.

vii. Create a marketing strategy with the customer in mind.

viii. Business with low-profit margins not avoided.

ix. Setting unrealistic goals

x. Not avoiding Technological failures

xi. Pre-empt Legal Issues by anticipation

xii. Failure to Conduct SWOT Analysis of the Company vis a vis competition

xiii. Absence of good Record-keeping and MIS

xiv. Inability for quick adaptation to the needs of customer

xv. Fail to hire Right People

xvi. Avoid trying to do too many things at once

xvii. Lack of Business acumen

xviii. Wrong Partners

xix. Lack of Vision, Strategic and Business Planning

xx. Inability raise capital after the first round.

xxi. Failure to do SWOT analysis before commencement.

xxii. Lack of Mentorship

xxiii. Failed leadership

xxiv. No self-evaluation or inability to earn from failure

xxv. Premature scaling of business

xxvi. Not choosing right location

xxvii. Losing sight of business profits and good financial management

xxviii. Good Inventory management

xxix. Losing focus on business

xxx. Mixing personal expenses with that of the business.

xxxi. Overexpansion

xxxii. Plan successor to run business

xxxiii. Ethics and Governance Policy

B. Recommended Foundation Framework for a Start Up

1. The Investors may prefer an organized set-up which has a long-term desire to stay in business. A set up as a One-man show may not be preferred. It is desirable to have a corporate governance structure with due identification of roles, authority, accountability and timing in key business decisions between shareholders, directors, and the management.

2. A typical startup board will have one or two founders, one or two investors, and rarely an independent director. Boards of private, venture capitalist-backed companies focus almost primarily on growth as a mission. In contrast, boards of mature public companies have more oversight and focus on regulatory and compliance duties.

3. Decide on the form of the Entity - One-Person Company, Partnership, LLP, Private or Public Company. Compliance requirements will be more in the case of public company.

4. Have a matured professional who has knowledge of the business as Mentor.

C. Importance of Corporate Governance for a Start-up

Corporate Governance is the soul of an organisation and must be adhered to while indulging in daily working of the organisation. It may be a system of creating Management accountable towards the stakeholders for effective management of the businesses. Corporate governance concerns with the morals, ethics, values, parameters, conduct and behaviour of the organisation and its people The underlying principles of corporate governance revolve around three basic interrelated segments. These are:

A. Integrity and Fairness

B. Transparency and Disclosures

C. Accountability and Responsibility.

D. Normal Challenges faced by start-ups

1. **Inception**

   At this stage, it's going to be enough to adopt a 'check the box' approach and just meet all mandatory legal, financial and accounting requirements. Avail of the services of external consultants who can handhold the start-up in compliances. and streamlining of business procedures.

2. **Initial Capital Infusion**

   investors like venture capital would expect to put in place strong corporate governance practices, to safeguard their investments and make sure that the business achieves its maximum potential. With the presence of nominees of investors, the board becomes stronger and more seasoned, which might monitor the actions of the management. All major decisions are often board-driven, with fair and adequate disclosures to the board including of any conflict of interest.

3. Follow-on Capital Infusion

For consolidation of business or for expansion one may have to approach the same investors or the new private equity players. They may like to see the development of the business since the first infusion of the capital and if the deployment were in line with the understanding with the capital provider. Valuation for new investment will also be based on future business plans. Corporate governance assumes utmost significance at this stage given the stakes involved. Institutional investors would have their own requirements including on being governed by, an approved business plan, and internal policies on prevention of cash laundering and corruption.

What the Indian Start up Did?

The Indian startup ecosystem showed the path to a promising future through innovation and digitization despite the effects of the coronavirus outbreak. 2022 saw the emergence of several new unicorns and a great deal of market activity, despite a minor decline in the quantity and value of funding deals.

But it is also true outside everything appears to be very simple. A 20-year-old entrepreneur who has access to venture capital money and trendy technology becomes a billionaire.

However, there is proof that the number of venture-backed startups failing is much higher than what the sector often claims. And, 9 out of 10 firms fail in the conventional startup ecosystem.

This is due to the founder's anguish of having to shut down their unsuccessful firm. Unfortunately, founders who choose to launch their businesses in India are continually disappointed.

Key Facts and Statistics of Startups in India

The ease of doing business study assigns economies a score between 1 and 190 depending on a number of criteria, with 1 being the best. The index score represents the proportion of the best outcome any nation can obtain. A high rating indicates that the regulatory climate is favourable for conducting business.

India has the youngest startup population in the world with 72% of its entrepreneurs being under the age of 35. The average tenure of startup founders is 28 years.

One in nine students from the 2013–2015 cohort chose to work for startups or e-commerce enterprises, up from one in 19 from the 2012–2014 batch, according to an ET study. Pay ranges between 10 and 18 lakhs are available in the startup and e-commerce sectors.

In 2014, there were 3100 startups in the nation, and by 2020, there were projected to be more than 11500. The startup ecosystem employed more than 65000 employees in 2014. In 2020, this number was anticipated to reach 250,000.

90% of startup activity in India appears to be concentrated in the top 6 cities: Bangalore (28%), Delhi-NCR (24%), Mumbai (15%), Hyderabad (8%) Pune (6%), and Chennai (6 percent).

As the upcoming emerging startup locations, Kolkata, Ahmedabad, Kochi, Jaipur, and Thiruvananthapuram are dominant.

In Bengaluru, 62% of startup founders had prior technical experience.

13% of the company's founders have zero professional experience.

$2.256 billion (Rs. 14,228 crores) in venture capital investments were made in Bengaluru last year, a 4X increase in funding. By virtue of this, Bengaluru is currently Asia's 7th-largest investment destination.

Facts Associated with Funding and Investors in India

Global validation of the skills and vision of Indian startups has occurred. Startups raised $131 billion in funding between 2014 and the first quarter of 2022.

With cumulative funding of over 892 million dollars as of June 2022, the Gurgaon-based FinTech start-up was the most promising firm for digital lending. Navi, a personal lending marketplace with headquarters in Bangalore and funding of $444 million USD, came in second. A significant online business lending company, Lendingkart, received 231 million dollars in investment.

Fintech and e-commerce had dominated the funding landscape for entrepreneurs in India. In terms of capital, edtech surpassed fintech in 2021. Direct-to-consumer, food tech, and e-commerce sectors have seen growth in recent years as a result of changes in Indians' consumption habits since the pandemic's early years.

In 2022, artificial intelligence and big data, which accounted for around one-fourth of all global acquisitions over the previous five years, was the most VC-funded startup industry.

Life sciences, fintech, sophisticated manufacturing, and robotics, on the other hand, each accounted for 10% of the agreements. With only 2%, agriculture, and new food was the smallest sector. However, during the last five years, the industry has seen a 64% growth in funding deals.

Sources: The Hindu, World Scientific, Livemint, Your Story

SOME FAILED START UPS IN INDIA

1. **Lido Learning {Founded in 2019}**

   Lido Learning is a Mumbai-based ed-tech startup that provides K12 education services to students.

   Raised 33.5 mn. USD in three rounds.

Lido Learning struggled to meet parents' refund requests, failing to deposit employees' provident fund (EPF) deductions, stalling full-and-final settlement for former employees, ignoring tutors' minimum guaranteed pay and delaying payments to vendors

Reason of Closure Failure in February 2022

1. Lack of Funding That too within six months of raising nearly $10 million of the third round of funding.
2. Over-ambitious plan to go global.
3. Losses.
4. Unhappy Customers.

Eventually, the startup declared bankruptcy.

2. Qin1 {Founded 2019}

In the first half of 2022, this ed-tech startup ceased its operations. The stated reasons for closure were stated as: inability to secure new round of funding; unfeasible acquisition opportunities.

3. Guruji.com {Founded in 2006}

The startup achieved early success in two funding rounds and secured $15 million from well-known investors.

Unfortunately, media reports suggest that the CEO of this distinctive Indian search engine, Anurag Dod faced legal trouble for copyright infringement.

Reason of Failure

The downfall of Guruji.com can be attributed to its music search feature, which allowed users to search for and access music from various websites, including those with copyrighted material that was not licensed for distribution.

This feature made it easy for users to find and download music without paying, which violated copyright laws and resulted in legal action against Guruji.com.

4. **ShopX {Founded in 2015}**

   This was a startup that provides a digital platform for small retailers to access a wide range of products and services.

The company leverages technology to enable small retailers to connect with suppliers and customers.

Reason of Failure

Due to insufficient cash flow and the inability to raise new capital by selling its stakes, had to close its operations and declare bankruptcy.

5. **GoNuts {Founded in 2019}**

   GoNuts is an online platform enabling users to book personalized video messages and shoutouts from their favorite celebrities and influencers.

Reason of Failure includes

Failure to secure funding and the lack of growth in the target audience over the past three years.

6. BabyBerry {Founded in 2014}

Objective was to simplify parenting for new parents by offering them an all-inclusive solution to meet all their childcare needs.

In 2016, BabyBerry secured $1 million in funding from an angel group to support growth and expansion plans.

Reason of Failure

The startup shut down its operations, and its reasons remain unclear.

TechCircle suggests that BabyBerry did not have a revenue model, which could have contributed to its shutdown.

7. RoomsTonite {2014}

RoomsTonite was an app that allowed travelers to book hotel rooms at the last minute when travelling to or within India. Its primary focus was displaying hotels with unoccupied rooms that could be reserved with short notice.

Reason of Failure

Despite the company's announcement of raising $1.5 million in funding, it faced severe financial difficulties, most likely due to a delay in receiving funds. *(Source: Failory)*. Closed 2017

8. Turant Delivery {Founded 2014-Closed 2016}

This B2B startup specialized in intra-city capital - intensive logistics services, setting itself apart from its competitors with an innovative algorithm that allowed them to offer its services at 15% lower prices than competitors' charges for the same trip.

Reason of Failure

Failure to raise sufficient funding.

9. Roder {Founded 2014} {Closed 2017}

Travelling expensive100km or more for various reasons, such as work location, meetings, or visiting friends, the startup designed to make intercity travel more accessible and affordable for everyone.

The platform quickly gained traction due to its affordability, dependability, and convenience.

Reason of Failure

Inability to effectively manage customer acquisition costs and retain customers led to its demise. Could not compete with companies like Ola and Uber.

10. Yumist {Founded 2014} {Closed 2017 }

Established to revolutionize India's food industry by catering daily meals.

Initially, the promoters secured about $3 million in seed funding through investment rounds.

Reason of Failure

Yumist had a high burn rate and needed substantial capital to expand could not be raised and defective business model.

11. **Udayy {Founded 2019} {Closed 2022}**

    Udayy was an ed-tech startup launched in Gurgaon. Forbes 30 Under 30 featured the startup and its founders for their Asia 2021 list. Apart from seed funding of $2.5 million to expand its operation, it also raised around $10 million in funding from US-based Norwest Venture Partners. However, the startup closed its operation and shut down in 2022.

Reason for Failure

Lack of user interest after schools opened post-pandemic.

As per the founder, "the company had enough capital in books, but the business no longer made sense in the offline world, customer acquisition cost became expensive." *(Source: Economic Times)*

12. **SuperLearn {Founded 2020} {Shut 2022}**

    SuperLearn, was an ed-tech startup that targeted kids aged 3-13 to offer curricular, co-curricular, and extra-curricular activities for learning.

    Based on its potential for growth, the startup had managed to secure $300,000 in pre-seed funding. But that was that for the startup!

Reason for Failure

Inability to raise funding owing to the dwindling interests of its targeted customers (kids aged 3-13) when the schools opened post-pandemic.

13. **Crejo.Fun {Founded 2020} {Shut 2022}**

    This Bangaluru-based startup was founded on the idea of providing extracurricular activities to children on an online platform.

    Despite hefty seed funding, acquiring more than 2000 customers, and employing more than 170 people, the startup shut down just like some other ed-tech startups in the country.

Reason for Failure

Unable to raise more funds to sustain their operations.

14. **Protonn {Founded 2020} {Shut 2021}**

    It provided a platform for independent professionals like lawyers, graphic designers and nutritionists to launch their businesses online.

    The company had secured $9 million in seed funding just six months before ceasing its operations.

Reason for Failure

The company, however, was unable to fit the right product-market fit.

The situation worsened when the founders could not agree on a pivot to save the business.

15. **Ola Cars - Used Car Division**

    Ola started as a ride-sharing app but has lately ventured into multiple avenues.

    The company has even spread its wings beyond India and operates in Australia, New Zealand, and the UK.

    After less than a year of starting the business, Ola Cars scaled down its operations and ultimately closed it down in May 2022, citing the repurposing of the brand.

Reason for Shutting Down Ola Cars

Ola has struggled to maintain operations with its Cars venture and has announced to "repurpose its infrastructure, technology, and capabilities towards growing its Ola Electric sales and service network." *(Source: Team-BHP, Economic Times)*

16. **Meesho Superstore {Established 2015} {Shut 2022}**

    Meesho is one of the largest online reseller platforms in India. It provides a platform for customers to launch their businesses via its online services.

    Meesho grew to be one of the largest networks of resellers, acquiring more than 2 million resellers, and 20,000 suppliers. *(Source: Startup Talky)*

Reason for Shutting Down {90% of stores except Nagpur & Mysuru}

The closure of Meesho Superstore was caused by "low revenue and high cash burn".

17. Shuttl {Founded 2015} {Shut}

Shuttl is a mobile app offering commute services to office goers via ride aggregation.

The service ran 1200 buses under its digital platform, fulfilling almost 60,000 rounds.

Shuttle had secured a total of $36 million in its funding rounds, the latest being in November 2019.

Reason for Failure

The pandemic directly impacted the Shuttl business model, and the company could not bear the sudden loss in its demand.

The company is currently looking for buyers to sell its business.

The path to growth was not going easy as the company was facing various regulatory issues with state governments.

The transport department of Delhi government impounded over 50 Shuttl buses for permit violations. Besides, the department also threatened the two co-founders of Shuttl for 'illegally' plying buses in the national capital.

18. **Mastree {Started 2016} {Closed 2021}**

Mastree promised an outcome-based ed-tech app to its customers.

The app promises live and personalized attention to each child.

The app focused on teaching application-driven English language courses to kids studying in grades 5-8.

In 2020, Unacademy acquired the business operations of Mastree.

But within one year of its acquisition and investing $5 million, Unacademy decided to shut down Mastree for unexplained reasons.

Reason for Failure

While openly announcing the shutting down of the company, Unacademy did not give any reasons for Mastree's closure.

But like with other ed-tech businesses shutting down this year, the downward trend in students' interest in online learning platforms might have been the cause behind the folding of this ed-tech startup.

19. **Drivezy {formerly Just Ride} {Start 2015} {End}**

Drivezy is an auto-tech firm launched in 2015 by the name of Justride.

The earlier version of the app served as a ride-aggregator.

Post-2017, the company pivoted towards two-wheelers as well as cars-rental services. It allowed people to rent their rides when idle.

The company had raised $30 million in funding and had 1600 cars and 800 two-wheelers on its platform in 6 cities across India. The company, since inception, had raised total funding of $49.45 million before closing the huge asset financing deal. In 2018, Drivezy secured $100 Mn in an asset financing deal with which the Drivezy team plans to induct close to 50,000 vehicles.

Drivezy has taken its investor Yamaha to court alleging that the Japanese vehicle manufacturer **stole its private intellectual property** after proposing a full buyout. Drivezy by approaching the Bengaluru Civil and Sessions Court in September 2022 alleging that Yamaha had proposed a cash infusion and a buyout at a valuation of $100 million but later refused to go ahead with the deal, *{Source: Financial Express}*

20. Hike Messenger {Launch 2012} {End 2021}

Hike Messenger, also known as Hike Sticker Chat, was an Indian freeware, cross-platform instant messaging service application.

It acquired US-based calling company Zip Phones in 2015 and started providing free voice calling over cellular networks and WiFi across the globe even before Whatsapp

On 6 January 2021, the company announced via a text message to its customers that it would no longer be effective post-14 January 2021.

Reason for Failure

The company's co-founder Mittal tweexed that global network effects were too strong for them to continue operating their messaging app. (Source: Economic Times)

21. Niki (Niki.ai) {Start 2015} {Closure: 2021}

Niki is an artificial intelligence company. The company acquired unknown seed funding from Ratan Tata in 2016. It later raised $2 million in a Series A round of funding from multiple international investors.

The app offered virtual assistant services in four languages: Hindi, Bengali, Tamil, and English.

Reason for Failure

The app has disappeared from the surface without offering any official explanation.

However, one source quotes that the reason for the discontinuation of the app lies in the lack of funds.

The company did explore acquisition opportunities but failed to reach any conclusive deal. *(Source: Entracker)*

22. SMAAASH {Launch 2012} {Close: 2019}

SMAAASH, was one of India's acclaimed gaming and entertainment centers with a perfect combination of sports, virtual reality, music, and dining into an advanced, collaborative, and revolutionary social experience for a range of users' categories. SMAAASH established itself in sports simulation technology and proprietary gamification technologies with enlisted unique twilight bowling zone, motor racing, and bike racing simulators, and the go-karting tracks.

SMAAASH at the time of closure was spread at 32 centers across 16 cities across India.

Reason for failure

The continued lockdown due to the non-improving Covid-19 spread.

Lack of Capital infusion.

23. Reid & Taylor {Start 1998} (Shut 2020}

Reid & Taylor, known for custom-made compelling first-class suits of top-quality exclusive materials, was a Scottish company that had set shop in India and had established a name for itself across the country in the last few years. The brand has been endorsed by India's notable film actor, Amitabh Bachchan.

In 2008, 24.5% stake of Reid & Taylor with a valuation of US$121 million was acquired by an affiliate of GIC Special Investments.

Reason for failure

the company did not have any working capital to keep the operations going, resulting in the factory's closure and relieved all its employees from services.

The company is liquidated under the National Company Law Tribunal (NCLT) for bearing high non-payment loans.

24. **Harley-Davidson India– HD: {Start 2011} {End 2020}**

    H-D, is an American motorcycle manufacturer making motorcycles. The company manufactures heavyweight motorcycles that are designed for cruising on the highway Harleys.

    The Indian subsidiary of H-D had 11 models during their early years sold across 29 dealership facilities across India.

Reason for failure

Harley-Davidson has put an end to operations in India as part of the 'Rewire' strategy.

The company reported its first quarterly loss to happen between April to June 2020 at the value of US$96 million.

Although the brand itself became a local trend, the company faced financial constraints for a certain period.

Thus, the motorcycle manufacturer implemented the 'Rewire' strategy to focus on profitable markets across North America, Europe, and selected parts of Asia by winding up operations from low profitability markets, including India.

25. HuffPost India {Start 2014}

HuffPost started in India in its 13th international edition in late 2014, under Times Group's management, which owns India's Times.

Three years later, in 2017, HuffPost India separated from the time's group and relaunched its operation as a separate entity.

The India team of HuffPost India has constituted 12 team members.

Reason for failure

The decision to end the website's operation was influenced by the new FDI policy that limited the foreign investment in news and media websites. HuffPost India was the first affected news website because of the further 'restriction.' Its shutdown was a strategic decision taken upon the BuzzFeed-HuffPost merger.

26. Vigo Video

Vigo Video (Formerly Hypstar) was a social network application using which short videos can be created.

The app inspired its users to capture their best moments daily, and share and discover more people with the same interests.

Vigo Video users had actively posted around 80 million posts in the app, channeling to more than 200,000 posts per day during its first year in India.

A few months after the app made itself available to download, Vigo Video topped the free app chart on Google Play India.

Reasons for failure

In June 2020, the Government of India suspended Vigo Video's operation alongside 58 other Chinese-based apps due to data and privacy issues. The border conflicts in 2020 between India and China may also influence the factor of the suspension.

27. Net4India {Start 1985} {Closed}

Net4 Network Services Limited was considered one of India's leading Web Services and Network Services Providers, prioritized providing services to the various scales of businesses and its offerings, including Enterprise Messaging & Hosting Solutions and Domain name registration.

At its peak, the company had 1000 SME customers for a wide range of Web Services and over 2000 Medium to Large businesses for Enterprise Services.

Net4 services were once considered the largest provider in the Asia Pacific region, offering mainly digital addresses such as hosted email, web hosting, and domain name registration.

The company received an investment of US$9 million in 2000, out of which US$2 million was spent to acquire firms with related business opportunities.

Reasons for failure

The downfall of Net4India started when the company failed to repay loans and the government's service tax. In 2013, the government arrested Net4Inda's promoter for not depositing service tax collected from their clients.

Many customers have filed their disputes with ICANN, Indian Corporation for Assigned Names and Numbers, the body responsible for I.P. and TLD, and top-level domain management. ICANN has said that it is currently in discussion with the government regarding transferring the responsibility of the domain and email registered on Net4India to any other potential company.

28. Jabong.com

Jabong.com was an Indian fashion and lifestyle e-commerce portal founded by Praveen Sinha, Lakshmi Potluri, Arun Chandra Mohan, and Manu Kumar Jain. Rocket Ventures, Germany, founded the company.

Instead of keeping the inventory sold by enlisted vendors, Jabong.com acts as an online mall where the customer can access products sold by all the partners.

ComScore reported Jabong.com had the second-highest traffic on its website within a few months of its launch. In March 2013, Jabong.com ranked 44th in India by Alexa Traffic and 10th in Google Zeitgeist India in 2012.

Jabong.com was glorified as the third-most visited digital shopping portal right after its rival-later-acquirer Myntra.com and Flipkart.com in India in less than 20 months.

In July 2016, Flipkart acquired Jabong through its unit Myntra for about US$70 million. In February 2020, Flipkart formally shut down Jabong to entirely focus on its premium clothing platform Myntra. The portal sold apparel, footwear, fashion accessories, beauty products, fragrances, home accessories, and other fashion and lifestyle products. The company headquarters was in Gurugram, NCR, India.

Reasons for failure

The decision from Walmart-owned Flipkart to formally shut down Jabong was taken to concentrate on its premium fashion marketplace, Myntra.

The move is a strategic move that will benefit Flipkart consolidating operations and making its marketing budget more efficient as the traffic to Jabong had been dropping over the years and the two brands, Myntra and Jabong, owned by the same parent company, Flipkart did not make any sense for the parent company.

29. VIU {Start 2015} {Shut}

Launched on 26 October 2015, Viu is a Hong Kong-based over-the-top (OTT) video streaming provider from PCCW Media, a subsidiary of PCCW.

Viu had reached 6 million monthly active users in March 2017 from 4 million monthly active users in November 2016.

Reasons for failure

The top-level exits, downsizing of the team, and rejection of new ideas or concepts were all hints at the shaky future of Viu India.

There was no way they were to compete with giants like Netflix and Amazon Prime.

30. Doodhwala {Start 2015} {Shut 2019}

The hyperlocal delivery platform, Doodhwala, worked on a subscription model to deliver milk and groceries directly to your doorsteps.

The company offered a wide range of products ranging from milk to fruits and delivered the products before 7 AM daily.

The company believed that its unit economics were robust.

By lowering their delivery cost to Rs.3, Doodhwala positioned itself uniquely in a very competitive market where other players were struggling.

The company failed even after raising a recent seed investment of $2.2 million from Omnivore, a venture capitalist firm, in a minority stake in the company.

Reasons for failure

Doodhwala failed to raise subsequent financing.

One of the biggest challenges was prominent players like BigBasket, who were absorbing smaller players in the given segment.

The competition forced Doodhwala to shut shop.

31. Russsh {Start 2012} {Closed}

Russsh was an on-demand delivery service offering first mile and last mile solutions to individuals and businesses.

Reasons for failure

Self-funded Russsh lacked the capital to take on bigger competitors in the space.

Since it lacked the capital, it couldn't offer great discounts like other emergent players—a prerequisite to succeed in the discount-driven Indian Market.

32. Koinex {Start 2017} {Shut 2018}

Koinex quickly established a name for itself as India's largest cryptocurrency exchange company that maintained a high standard of service in trading digital assets.

As per Koinex's site, over a million registered users, over 3 Billion Dollars of Trade volume, and over 20 million orders were executed before closing.

Reasons for failure

On April 6th, 2018, the Reserve Bank of India issued a statement where it said that all government-regulated exchange platforms had to stop trading with and exit relationships with any individual or organization that dealt with cryptocurrency transactions and block such transactions from taking place.

Koinex took the case to court and, to this very day, has a writ pending in the Supreme Court of India, but things move slow and there hasn't been any progress in the case so far.

33. Doctalk {Start 2016} {Shut 2018}

Doctalk was an app for Doctors with patients.

Through Doctalk, messages could be sent to doctors, store medical files, get detailed prescriptions, save your medications, etc.

It built an electronic medical record (EMR) solution, which helped doctors write prescriptions digitally and provide customized prescription templates.

Doctalk had raised roughly $5 million from Matrix Partners and Khosla Ventures and was also backed by Y Combinator, Vy Capital, Liquid2Ventures, Venture Highway, Altair Capital, and some angel investors.

Reasons for failure

- Inability to pivot.
- No plan B if its initial business model failed.
- No acceleration for transition into the electronic medical record solution (EMR) business.

34. Loanmeet {Start: 2015} {Shut}

Loanmeet {Start: 2015} {Shut: Company was founded after realizing that a large section of borrowers could not get personal and business loans from banks and other financial institutions due to lack of credit history, insufficient documentation, or other reasons.

When capital is to be deployed by financial institutions, the firm's size plays a considerable role. In such a scenario, Loanmeet attempted to revolutionize banking at the grass-root level.

LoanMeet financed working capital requirement, B2B marketplace financing, cash credit line, and channel financing in the range of Rs 5,000 to 5 lakh for short term period ranging from 15 days to 9 months.

It raised an undisclosed amount of seed funding from Chinese investors and entrepreneurs Cao Yibin and Huang Wei, and Madhusudan, CEO of KrazyBee.

Until Jan 2017, Loanmeet was growing well at about 50% month over month.

Reasons for failure

The lending market was an overcrowded market dominated by established players, and Loanmeet couldn't sustain the competition.

As a result, it failed to raise further investment.

35. eBay-India {Start 2005} {Close:2018}

It was more of an acquisition and then shut down for business strategy reasons. The US-based company sold its India business to Flipkart in 2017 for a cost of $211 million. Not to be left behind in the race to be a part of one of the fastest-growing eCommerce markets globally, eBay invested $514 million in Flipkart to get a 5.4% stake in the home-grown online marketplace.

And they intend to profit from their investment in the future by selling their stake for a whopping 1.1 billion dollars.

Reason for shutdown or exiting the Indian market

eBay forayed into the Indian market by acquiring Baazee.com for $50 million to get their foot in the door. But, they lost business to their native competitors, including – Flipkart, Snapdeal, and ShopClues.

Their auction business model's failure to attract Indian customers led to the company after the tried and tested eCommerce model and competing with existing competitors leading to investment in Flipkart.

36. Zebpay India {Start 2015} {Close 2018}

Zebpay, was a cryptocurrency startup helping users in cryptocurrency trading.

It was a popular platform for buying and selling cryptocurrencies, including Bitcoin Cash, Ripple, Ethereum, and Litecoin. It also sold airtime and gift cards.

Zebpay was forced to shut down when it had over 3 million users due to RBI's financial policy to prevent cryptocurrency from entering the market.

37. MonkeyBox {Start 2015} (Close 2018}

The consumer service company started by offering Recommended Dietary Allowance (RDA) approved vegetarian meals to school.

Starting with a few schools, it soon added 85 schools to its service list. In July 2017, Monkeybox provided meals for over 1,500 kids of age group 3-18 per/day.

After adding 2K subscribers to its website, it acquired food businesses – 75 In A Box and RawKing.

Reasons for closure

For its closure, the company only mentioned its services temporarily because it failed to meet its targets.

As per an official statement from the company "Unfortunately we are at a point where we will not be able to fulfill our promise of delivering healthy and nutritious meal to the kids going forward due to constraints on our end and don't want to falter on the quality of our services.

38. Just Buy Live {Start 2015} {Shut 2018}

A meaningful platform for retailers to buy directly from brands.

They also offered unsecured credit lending and working capital to small retailers to buy branded products.

In August 2017, a Dubai based investment group, Ali Cloud Investments, invested a massive $100 million (INR 699.25 crore) Series B funding in Just Buy Live. Yet the funding proved insufficient.

Reasons for failure:

The company failed because it had an Unscalable business model and a negative cash flow.

Other than the negative cash flow, a faulty business model too was attributed to the company's failure

The founders are hopeful of the revival of the brand with the help of fresh funding.

39. MrNeeds {Started 20} {Shut: 20}

Grocery on-line business catering to the NCR Region.

MrNeeds closed its operations despite the overwhelming response they received to their services.

Reasons for failure

According to its owners, the company was doing reasonably well. And yet closed business abruptly without providing any specific reasons for its closure.

It is speculated that the failure of MrNeeds was because of the stiff competition offered by BigBasket and DailyNinja.

40. Tazzo {Started 2014} {Shut: 2016}

In 2014, Bengaluru saw a fleet of bikes running on its roads. Tazzo, the new kid in the startup world, offered point-to-point commuting on bikes at INR 5 per/km.

This easy, quick, convenient, and affordable commuting options – soon became the talk of the town.

They had a mobile application integrated with GPS technology for real-time tracking of their fleet.

Reasons for closure

Non-profitable nature Is reported as the biggest reason for its failure.

The project was capital intensive, but there was no profit model for the business.

41. Shotang {Started 2013} {Shut: 2018}

Started as B2B platform for manufacturers, distributors, and retailers.

The idea was to offer an online trading platform and to earn a commission in financial transactions. They primarily worked for the mobile and apparel market.

According to VCCircle, Shotang was heavily funded by V.C.s. They received $5 million by Exfinity Venture Partners in December 2015 and $864 thousand (by Patamar Capital in February 2018.

Just before the venture plummeted, its market valuation was $40 million (INR 279.7 crore).

Launched in 2013, it shut shop in 2018 under colossal pressure from competitors.

Reasons for failure

Shotang tried its best but failed miserably due to rising debts and a funds crunch. According to Techcircle, they did the last fundraising to pay off debts - creditors, employees, and partners.

The real reason for the failure of shotang was - fierce competition from Flipkart, Amazon, and Paytm Mall, who, with their deep pockets, were Fastly wiping off competition.

As per CEO Dinesh Agarwal, "the decrease in sales and the effect of demonetization on the company are some of the reasons for the company's shutdown.

42. Stayzilla {Started 2006} {Shut: 2017}

Stayzilla ventured into the profitable segment of hotel rentals, establishing a niche for itself. The company raised USD 33.5 million. After the funding, it became the largest homestay network in India.

Stayzilla's closure was a big shock for the startup community.

Reasons for failure

StayZilla's massive marketing spend.

Not Focusing on Retention

Bungled Finances

To survive all the legal troubles and pay off the past debts, the company filed for insolvency. Unfortunately, the insolvency proceedings were dismissed by Supreme Court.

43. Overcart {Established 2012} {Shut: 2017}

Overcart started as an online marketplace of pre-owned, refurbished, and unboxed goods. The company started on a promising note, receiving USD 3 million capital funding.

Unluckily, the company could not build upon the initial hype.

A company that dealt in all kinds of orders turned into a company that only started accepting bulk orders.

One of the prominent reasons attributed to the failure of Overcart was the inability to grow their demand and supply, business model. A typical complex business model is adopted by all marketplaces.

Other factors contributing to the failure were business model issues like maintaining the quality of pre-owned goods and finding standard pricing for refurbished products.

The business's complexity and inability to raise further funds ultimately led to its closure of a business.

44. Kaaryah {Established 2014} {Shut: 2017}

Kaaryah was backed by none other than Ratan Tata. It also received funding from Infosys Mohandas Pai and The Saha Fund in 2015.

As per the founder of Kaaryah, the company had plans to touch a 100-crore turnover within five years.

The promising startup had to close in 2017 due to a lack of funds to grow further.

As per Nidhi, "It was not sudden. We have been trying to raise funds for the last 18 months. We had broken even twice in 30 months."

Kaaryah Lifestyle Solutions Pvt. Ltd. reported a loss of Rs. 4 crores in 2015-16. The company waited for another 18 months to raise more funds before laying off all 60 employees and announcing the business's shutdown in 2017.

45. Finomena {Established 2015} {Shut: 2017}

Finomena offered quick loans to people who lacked access to traditional loans.

The company worked on a unique algorithm backed system that checked the creditworthiness of buyers.

Finomena received USD 1.7 million in funding.

Unluckily, the company lost all its steam within a few years. High Cash burn left them with little money to survive, and no investor invested money in them at a later stage.

The attempts to sell the company went futile because of the higher cost of acquisition.

46. Dial A Celeb {Established 2016} {Shut within one year}

Dial A Celeb was a short-lived but exciting business idea.

Dial A Celeb offered video chats with celebrities, booking celebs for events like weddings, and anniversaries.

The company also gave fans opportunities to have birthdays and celebrity signed products like teddy bears and diaries.

Not much information is available about Dial A Celeb as it closed operations within a year of starting.

Today DialACeleb.com is available for sale. The website is inactive, and the last update on the Facebook page was made on 1 May 2017.

The reason for the closure of the service is changing trends in celebrity service.

The celebrities in India started making their apps, which put a huge dent in its revenue model.

47. Tiny owl {Established 2014} {Shut 2017}

TinyOwl develops location-based mobile application for ordering food. The company provides an Android application that enables users to find restaurants and order food. Its application can detect the user location and show restaurants in their vicinity.

Reasons for Tiny owl's failure were:

(a) The uncoördinated hiring, and later retrenchment.

(b) Fewer orders and not giving discounts.

(c) No artificial intelligence was used. There was no data analytics when ordering from the app.

(d) Astronomical salaries paid to employees:

48. Pepper Tap {Established 2014} {Shut 2016}

It was built to deliver groceries from local stores to neighborhood customers within two hours.

The main **reasons for pepper tap's failure were**:

(a) Lacking technological resources

(b) Too many stores opened online far too quickly.

(c) Customers were unable to view all items for sale.

(d) Unable to conserve funds to keep the company financially solvent.

49. AskMe Bazaar {Established 2012} {Shut 2016}

AskMe, a Gurugram-based e-commerce company, decided to shut show. The move left about 4000 of its employees jobless.

AskMe's principal investor Astro Holding said it would appoint a forensic auditor to check the books of the startup's parent firm Getit.

The **reasons for AskmeBazaar's failure** were:

(a) Non-payment issue from Astro.

(b) Owing to mismanagement and lack of corporate governance.

(c) Considerable Investments in celebrities to endorse the brand.

(d) AskMe also saw resignations from more than 650 of its employees.

50. FranklyMe {Established 2014} {Shut 2016}

FranklyMe was a video micro-blogging website with the premise of letting people express themselves through videos.

Reasons for Franklyme's failure:

(a) Not able to meet sustainable product-market fit.

(b) They tried to solve a lot of use cases at the same time.

(c) Shortage or Non-availability of funds.

51. Nivio

California and Gurugram-based cloud desktop startup Nivio was founded by Sachin Dev Duggal and Saurabh Pradeep Dhoot in 2004. Nivio's flagship product was a Windows-based online desktop that enabled users to access a personal virtual desktop from any device connected to the internet.

Nivio's innovative service offerings accorded it with a lot of success and it managed to partner with Microsoft and Bharti Airtel to expand its services in India. The startup was also termed as a technology pioneer at the World Economic Forum in 2008.

In 2012, Nivio had raised $21 million from Videocon and AEC Partners. Yet, the startup was closed in 2013 without any news or updates.

52. Wishberg {2014}

Mumbai-based social wishlist platform Wishberg was founded by Pravin Jadhav and Kulin Shah in 2011. Wishberg inspired its users to pursue their dreams by enabling them to share their wishes on its platform and connect with the people with similar wishes. Prior to being rebranded as Wishberg in 2012, the startup was known as Tyche'd.

The startup had managed to raise $150,000 in seed funding from Paytm's Vijay Shekhar Sharma, India Quotient and Uday Sodhi in October 2013. Flush with funding, the startup decided to shut shop in the middle of 2014.

Wishberg announced its shut down through a blog post.

53. Etable

Bengaluru-based foodtech startup Etable was founded by Maninder Singh, Bharath Belur, Rohit Iyer and Madiman in 2012. Etable was established as an online community of foodies where the users connected with other foodies and had conversations about food which included reviews, check-ins and recommendations.

Etable managed to raise a total of $200,000 from undisclosed investors across two funding rounds in 2012 and 2013. Post fundraising in 2013, the startup claimed to have over 1,600 restaurants and more than 3,000 registered users.

However, the online food social networking startup failed and was closed in 2014.

54. Zoogaad

Jodhpur-based AI-powered news provider Zoogaad was founded in 2014. The startup offered customized news stories to the people using its AI-powered platform.

Before shutting down in the same year for unknown reasons, the startup had managed to raise $500,000 in funding, according to CrunchBase.

55. SpoonJoy {2015}

Bengaluru-based foodtech startup SpoonJoy was founded by Manish Jethani in 2013. SpoonJoy worked on a subscription-based model along with the on-demand lunch and dinner model with the goal of becoming a pan-India internet first restaurant.

The startup started operations in 2014 with a funding from notable angel investors like Flipkart co-founder Sachin Bansal, Tracxn's founder Abhishek Goyal, Delhivery's founder and CEO Sahil Barua and Mekin Maheshwari.

Like most online food delivery startups, SpoonJoy was burning through its cash reserves and not even a $1 million funding from SAIF Partners in 2014 could save it from shutting down.

56. Dazo {2015}

Bengaluru-based foodtech startup Dazo was founded by Shashank Shekhar Singhal and Monica Rastogi in 2014. Dazo, formerly known as Tapcibo, was India's first curated meal platform which enabled the customers to get fresh meals from its partner restaurants on-demand.

While investors were pouring in money into foodtech startups, Dazo was facing fierce competition from other foodtech startups in the space like Zomato and Swiggy. Amidst fierce competition, Dazo had to burn through its cash reserves in order to expand quickly and gain customers which lead its downfall.

In 2015, Dazo had managed to raise more than $235,000 from prominent angel investors like Sequoia Capital' Rajan Anandan, TaxiForSure's Aprameya Radhakrishna, Unacademy's Gaurav Munjal, among others.

57. Eatlo

Bengaluru-based foodtech startup Eatlo was founded by Rahul Harisanka and Sai Priya Mahajan in 2014. Eatlo delivered handpicked meals from the best chefs to the customers. According to media reports, the startup claimed to be delivering over 1,200 orders a day.

However, just like numerous other online food delivery startups in Bengaluru, Eatlo couldn't manage to keep up with its competition and had to shut down in 2015.

Before shutting down, Eatlo had managed to raise nearly $160,000 from marquee investors.

58. PepperTap (2016)

Gurugram-based hyperlocal grocery delivery startup PepperTap was founded by Milind Sharma and Navneet Singh in 2014. PepperTap was one of the early and successful grocery delivery startups in India at the time with more than 20,000 daily orders across 17 cities.

Operating on a 100% inventory-less model, PepperTap was seeing success among both customers and the local stores because of deep discounts and enhanced sales. However, operating in tier 2 and tier 3 cities, PepperTap found it extremely challenging to keep up with discounts and address the logistics issues at the same time.

This model was eating away at PepperTap's cash reserves at accelerated rates. The startup was only able to ride through the cash burn in 2015 with massive funding to the tune of $51 million from investors like Sequoia Capital, SAIF Partners, Snapddeal and InnoVen Capital.

59. LocalBanya (2016)

Mumbai-based online supermarket LocalBanya was founded by Amit Naik, Karan Mehrotra and Rashi Choudhary in 2012. The startup offered a range of products across categories including fruits, vegetables, personal care and kitchenware.

The startup had managed to raise more than $5 million across various funding rounds from investors like Karmvir Avant Group, Oliphans Capital and Brand Capital.

While the reasons for the shutting down of the startup were not confirmed, numerous reports cited lack of funds as a possible reason. Considering the competitive nature and low operating margins of the online grocery delivery business, LocalBanya couldn't manage to sustain its business despite raising a large amount of funds.

60. Frankly.me

Noida-based video microblogging platform Frankly.me was founded by Nikunj Jain and Abhishek Gupta in 2014. Frankly.me became a hit in the Indian market which enabled the users to connect and have live conversations with Indian celebrities and public figures.

In 2015, Frankly.me raised $600,000 in funding from Matrix Partners. According to Nikunj Jain's post in Inc42, the startup had raised additional undisclosed funding from new and existing investors in 2016.

However, the founders decided to shut down the popular platform weeks after their last funding round. Explaining the reasons, Nikunj Jain said that despite the early success of the platform, Frankly.me had failed to achieve sustainable market fit.

Flush with funds, the startup tried to scale prematurely and tried to solve a lot of use cases too early leading to unsustainable growth. It was the reason the founders decided to pull the plug on their startup after a short but enlightening journey.

61. Taskbob {2017}

Mumbai-based home services startup Taskbob was founded by Aseem Khare, Abhiroop Medhekar, Ajay Bhatt and Amit Chahalia in 2015. Taskbob facilitated high-quality professional services including drivers, electricians, plumbers, carpenters and maids on demand.

The startup had managed to serve over 1.5 lakh orders during the two years of its operation before it shut down in 2017.

Taskbob had racked in nearly $6 million across all funding rounds from marquee investors including Orios Venture Partners, IvyCap Ventures, Mayfield Fund and Google Launchpad Accelerator. The startup had also managed to acquire its Bengaluru-based rival in 2015.

The reasons for shut down as claimed by media reports included the inability of the startup to scale profitably due to tough competition and low margins.

62. PropheSee (2017)

Delhi-based data analytics startup PropheSee was founded by Harshil Gurha, Ishaan Sethi and Jitesh Luthra in 2014. The startup enabled brands to discover and analyze data from across different social media platforms in order to create effective strategies through its SaaS-based platform.

The SaaS startup had raised a total of $500,000 in funding from a number of investors from the Indian Angel Network. However, the reason for the startup's shut down remains unknown.

63. Shopo (2017)

Chennai-based Shopo was founded by Theyagarajan S and Krithika Nelson in 2011. Shopo started as an online marketplace for traditional Indian hand-made products by Indian designers. It was acquired by Snapdeal in 2013 and relaunched as a zero-commission marketplace which enabled small and medium-sized businesses to chat, buy and sell.

In 2017 as Snapdeal was fighting for survival in the Indian ecommerce market, it had to shut down Shopo in a bid to cut costs and reduce losses.

Shopo's innovative model enabled it to raise funds from prominent investors including Sequoia Capital and SRI Capital's Sashi Reddi.

64. BabyBerry

Bengaluru-based online parenting startup BabyBerry was founded by Bala Venkatachalam, Dev Vig and Subhashini Subramaniam in 2014. BabyBerry offered an online platform for new parents that provided holistic child growth and development through various features like digital vaccination chart, health records management and doctor discovery.

While the reasons for BabyBerry shutting down remain unclear, a report by TechCircle suggests that BabyBerry did not have a revenue model to it. Before shutting down, the startup had raised $1 million in funding from a group of angel investors led by Nitin Bagmane in 2016.

2019

65. Buttercups

Bengaluru-based online lingerie brand Buttercups was founded by Arpita Ganesh in 2014. The startup provided exclusive lingerie buying experience to its customers through its online platform.

Buttercups was backed by some of the prominent angel investors in India including Sequoia Capital's Rajan Anandan, Fireside Ventures' Kanwaljit Singh, Anand Chandrasekaran, among others. The online lingerie brand had managed to raise $1 million in funding before it shut down.

While Arpita Ganesh announced the shutdown of Buttercups on her LinkedIn page, she did not disclose the reasons behind her decision.

Chapter XIII

A True Case on Paradox of Powers

The case discussed in this chapter highlights the extent of damage that can be caused by unethical acts of humans who have in themselves in abundance non-divine attributes or demonic attributes (Chapter II}.

This is the case of handful of vindictive and powerful Officers of a reputed Financial Institution who consciously caused financial and reputational losses not only to their own employer Institution and their dozen fellow institutions but also deprived thousands of households essential product of the borrower company and snatched away employment rights of innocent employees of the Borrower. Collective losses suffered is many thousand crores of rupees. No action was taken on perpetuators of such crimes which but for them would have been termed as "fraud."

This is also the story of how, even after being snubbed by the Courts for their misdeeds including mismanagement and illegal actions which resulted in irretrievable all - round financial losses, the very same officers were allowed to walk out on superannuation merrily to enjoy their princely retired lives while their employers lost thousands of crores of loans disbursed to the borrower mis-applied by these officers due to their series of ultra vires acts.

One has come across cases of corporate collapses where persons at the helm of affairs diverting funds provided by lenders for non-sanctioned purposes and thereby causing losses to the lenders. But this case is totally unique wherein the lenders forcibly stepped into the shoes of an entrepreneur with the sole objective of finishing him and the company promoted by him notwithstanding that in the process several lending institutions, public at large and most importantly the employees who were on the rolls of the borrower company were also be uprooted without any livelihood and unpaid salaries and benefits.

This case bears testimony to the realty that the privileged and unethically powerful persons can escape punishment for their open heinous acts for years without being branded as financial criminals even after the courts pulled up such erroneous persons in unambiguous manner!

I. Main Players

(a) Lead Lender of more than a dozen other lenders.

The lead lender called P-1 is an awardee of treasured "crown" among Institutions by the Government.

(b) Promoter P-2. A financially weak party. His strong connections ensured that P3 project remained with him even when he failed to make his share of contributions.

(c) **Borrower - P3.** A closely held Company of P2. It had a highly attractive, prestigious but capital - intensive project of national importance. It had over 200 employees on roll. P3 has been in existence for many decades with a single languishing project.

II. Background of the Case

P3 is an SPV which was promoted by P2.

P3 was recognized as a project of great importance. P2 managed to get the project allotted to him despite weak financial strength to build this capital-intensive project.

After the first financial closure, P2 could not infuse further capital into P3 to enable the lenders to disburse the balance of sanctioned loans.

The duration of suspended activity continued for half a decade.

With the interventions of the Governments, P2 ensured P1 and co-lenders sanctioned funds for the revival of the project but on the renewed terms and conditions insisted by P1.

Officials of P1 had strained relationship with P2 for years. With the passage of time, it only worsened. Though P1 could not take harsh actions against P2 earlier, they considered the government's intervention as an opportunity to deceive the desperate P2 and sabotage completion of the project of great importance.

III. Dubious Terms put forth for Rescuing P3 by P1 and accepted by all:

(a) Strip P2, of all his powers and rights over P3. He shall be only an NED with no more board representation from his side.

(b) Board of P3 shall consist of certain number of employees of selected lenders and directors appointed by P3 only with exclusive approvals by P1.

(c) Several one-sided and *ultra vires* agreements were forced on P2 and P3. AOA of P3 was altered to reflect, inter alia, surrender of voting rights by P2 in favor of P1; Quorum for board meetings; continuation of pledge of shares {including new once, if applicable and personal/ corporate guarantees}. In consideration, P1 agreed to fund the project fully and complete it in four years. It was specifically agreed that P2 need not bring any more funds.

(d) P1, refused admit that by virtue of such arrangements P3 had become: a Deemed: Subsidiary; Associate; Company under same management; Related Party of P1 or even a Government Company. In fact, P1 was guilty of failings related in their governance standards by not making the mandatory statutory disclosures in their Annual Reports.

IV. The Hidden Agenda of P1:

(a) The intention of the handful of officers of P1 who called shots in P1, was never to complete the project to be ultimately handed over to P2 after full recovery of the lenders' loans, because the attractive benefits and upsides of the project will be enjoyed by P2 for generations.

(b) Hence, they designed following illegal scheme to the detriment of P2 in clandestine manner:

- ✓ P1 constituted a committee of its senior employees to act as de facto supervisory board of P3. For most part of the decade during which management control vested with P1, an employee of P1 who was also member of this committee, chaired every board meeting of P3. The same person was member of audit committee always along with two other lenders' employees.

- ✓ The committee made the board of P3 redundant by controlling every material aspect of its functioning such as: release of funds to the TRA; timing of drawl of funds; purpose of usage of funds; extending dates for commissioning the project; revised means of financing the cost escalations and so on. Thus, there was no independent decision-making powers of the BOD of P3 and it served subservient to P1.

- ✓ As the intention of P1 was never to complete the project of P3 and to torpedo the project by making it unviable, quite contrary to the agreements, P3 was compelled to make payments to selected lenders in priority to that for the project construction. What is noteworthy is that P3 would have remained a "standard" account in the books of every lender for at least five years from the date of assumption of management control by P1. The committed construction period was only four years. There was no need for P1 to have starved the project of funds as P3 would have remained a standard account from lenders perspective under the RBI's dispensation on classification norms even without such diversions.

- ✓ P1, contrary to agreements for take-over of control of P3, started harassing P3 for infusion of additional equity and arrange debts to bridge cost over-runs. P1 even wanted P3 to sell the project to another promoter of their choice. Every board meeting of P3 was converted into an extension of hostile lenders' meetings.

- ✓ Aggrieved by such harassments, P2 complained at higher levels in the governments. But it did not yield any result.

- ✓ P1 and the board of P3 were in gross violation of several provisions of Companies Act, 2013 especially on matters related to board constitution; appointment of independent directors; appointment of woman director; constitution of audit committee; participation of directors on board proceedings etc. When such matters were drawn to the knowledge of P1 and the board of P3 by the compliance officer in writing, he was abruptly removed from P3 without any notice; without clearance of massive arrears of salary and without appointing anyone to take charge from him. Simultaneously P1 without notice, closed the corporate office of P3 without paying employees and making arrangements for assuming charge from them.

- ✓ P1 chose to declare P3 as "NPA" followed by other lenders; recalled the loans extended to P3; appointed its own persons again as Managing Director and Director Finance of P3 and made them sign letters endorsing the charges levied against P3 invoked personal and corporate guarantees of P2; Revoked pledge agreement and in improper manner transferred substantial portion of the pledged shares in favor of P1 and selected lenders at zero value and reduced P2 to status of a minority shareholder.

- ✓ In hurried manner, P1 appointed persons of their choice as Independent directors and Woman Director. The IDs and Woman director resigned within months once they got wind of the serious lapses in management of P3.
- ✓ P1 even disbursed loans to this NPA company (P3) after appointment of new KMPs, just to pay their salaries and expenses and more importantly to recover interest dues.

V. The Aftermath

(a) A Whistle-blower, complained to the Registrar of Companies on all the misdeeds of P1 vis a vis P3 and sought their intervention as a valuable project in which thousands of crores of public money was invested is being wasted with vengeance. The complaint also covered the innumerable gross contraventions of Companies Act, 2013 mostly concerning *ultra vires* alterations to the Articles of Association of P3; the board structure; appointment of Independent Director, appointment of Woman director; conflict of interests; non-validity of board resolutions; P3 having become a subsidiary of P1; abrupt closure of office and removal of employees without taking charge and settling arrears of dues etc..

(b) P2 approached the MCA with his complaints against P1 on grounds of mismanagement of affairs of P3 leading to non-commissioning of the project even after more than a decade's control by P1; loss of thousands of crores of public funds invested; illegal acts of transfer of pledged shares; invocation of guarantees etc., seeking their intervention.

(c) The Registrar marked P3 as "Management Disputed" disabling filing of any Return relating to P3 by anyone.

(d) The Registrar issued notice seeking information u/s 206 of the Companies Act, 2013 to P1, P2 and P3 to commence inquiry.

(e) Officers of P1 unsuccessfully adopted coercive efforts on the Registrar not to intervene on the matter. Thereafter, overcome by nervousness, P1 petitioned in hurry the NCLT u/s 241/242 of the Companies Act, 2013 citing oppression and mismanagement of P1 and lenders by P2. P1 also levied number charges of financial irregularities in P3 by P2 and the whistle-blower employee.

(f) After series of hearings, NCLT rejected P1's Petition as malicious, unwarranted and not maintainable under the law.

(g) P1 appealed to NCLAT criticizing NCLT, P2 and Whistleblower for causing damage to P1 and other lenders.

(h) NCLAT dismissed the appeal reprimanding P1 for irresponsible, illegal and malicious acts. The agencies of the Governments were also criticized for not taking proactive measures to save the important project and protect public funds. Every act of P1, including take -over of management control, transfer of shares, alterations to AOA of P3 etc., were declared invalid.

(i) P1 appealed to the Supreme Court only to meet the same humiliation.

(j) The courts directed concerned Governments to take pro-active measures to ensure rectification of the defects in the arrangements and to ensure that the project of national importance is commissioned fast and public funds are not lost.

(k) Years have rolled by after the Court Order. Yet the project is shut without any management. Theft is a reported regular feature due to no security and no employee on rolls. There is no Board of Directors for the Company.

(l) P1 filed petition before NCLT under IBC.

(m) P2 filed petition u/s 241/242 of Companies Act, 2013 before NCLT for oppression and mismanagement by P3; another petition against P3 for award of damages extending to thousands of crores.

(n) The Annual Reports of P1 never disclosed any of the contentious facts related to P3 or the adverse reports of the Registrar or Courts or claims of damages filed in court against them; or illegal transfer of shares and their reversals due to court order.

(o) When the lapses of P1 were brought to the attention of their independent auditor and independent directors by the whistle-blower, both parties openly expressed that they do not wish to risk losing their attractive offices!

(p) Ironically, even the market regulator informed the whistleblower that they cannot rake up a matter involving a "crown" company, notwithstanding adverse orders by the courts.

(q) The only gainers were the unscrupulous handful officers of P1, who walked out with all their hefty retirements benefits after destroying P2, P3 and corporate governance framework of P1 etc.

(r) The main loss was thousands of crores of public money deployed in the project of P3 which was destroyed intentionally by P1.

Conclusion

The reputation of an institution is built or marred by actions of set of individuals who are powerful at a given point in time. Human nature is such that one can never predict when the demonic traits will rule minds of individuals to attain their immoral goals.

www.ingramcontent.com/pod-product-compliance
Lightning Source LLC
LaVergne TN
LVHW091247150826
845673LV00006B/1341

9798891336933